ESSENTIAL
Psychic Healing

OTHER BOOKS BY DIANE STEIN

A Woman's I Ching
Diane Stein's Guide to Goddess Craft
The Woman's Book of Healing
All Women Are Psychics
All Women Are Healers
Prophetic Visions of the Future
Natural Healing for Dogs and Cats
Essential Reiki
On Grief and Dying
Gemstones A to Z
Healing Herbs A to Z
Essential Energy Balancing
Essential Energy Balancing II
Essential Energy Balancing III
Reliance on the Light
Pendulums and the Light
Essential Reiki Teaching Manual

Diane Stein on Video

Diane Stein's Essential Reiki Workshop
The Lords of Karma and Energy Balancing: A Workshop with Diane Stein

Visit Diane Stein's website at www.dianestein.net for books, jewelry, workshops, and more.

ESSENTIAL
Psychic Healing

A COMPLETE GUIDE TO HEALING YOURSELF, HEALING OTHERS, AND HEALING THE EARTH

DIANE STEIN

CROSSING PRESS
Berkeley

Published in the United States by Crossing Press, an imprint of the
Crown Publishing Group, a division of Random House,Inc., New York.
www.crownpublishing.com
www.tenspeed.com

Crossing Press and the Crossing Press colophon are
registered trademarks of Random House, Inc.

Library of Congress Cataloging-in-Publication Data
on file with the publisher.

ISBN: 978-1-58091-173-3

Cover and interior design by Lisa Buckley Design
Front cover photographs by Getty Images
Interior illustrations by Ian Everad

First Revised Edition

CONTENTS

Preface viii

Introduction: Healing with the Goddess 1

CHAPTER ONE :: Meditation 12

CHAPTER TWO :: Visualization 23

CHAPTER THREE :: The Chakras and the Aura 36

CHAPTER FOUR :: Energy 53

CHAPTER FIVE :: Spirit Guides 66

CHAPTER SIX :: Hands on Healing 79

CHAPTER SEVEN :: Emotional Release 97

CHAPTER EIGHT :: Crystal Healing 109

CHAPTER NINE :: Distance Healing 122

CHAPTER TEN :: Karma 135

CHAPTER ELEVEN :: Soul Retrieval 146

CHAPTER TWELVE :: Spirit Attachments 158

CHAPTER THIRTEEN :: Death 171

Bibliography 184

Index 186

ILLUSTRATIONS

Diagram 1   Soul Structure I 38

Diagram 2   Soul Structure II 41

Diagram 3   Soul Structure III 42

Diagram 4   The Kundalini Line—Central and Auxiliary Channels 42

Diagram 5   The Kundalini Channels and the Chakras 43

Diagram 6   The Etheric Double Chakras—The Kundalini Line 44

Diagram 7   Twelve Strand DNA—The Twelve Chakras
             of Barbara Marciniak 47

Diagram 8   The Hara Line 50

Diagram 9   The Microcosmic Orbit—Small Heavenly Cycle 61

Diagram 10   Circuit of Ki in the Body 62

Diagram 11   Reiki I Hand Positions—Self Healing 84–88

Diagram 12   Reiki I Hand Positions—Healing Others 89–94

Diagram 13   The Aura Body Levels 124

Diagram 14   Reincarnations 139

The Divine Mother's magic
is ancient as life itself.
She existed before gods and mortals,
and she will still exist even after the great
 dissolution.
Mother is pure energy in subtle form,
but in times of need
or just out of a desire to play, she manifests.

ELIZABETH U. HARDING,
Kali: The Black Goddess of Dakshineswar

The more compassion you have for others,
the quicker mass consciousness will change.
We are asking all of you to play this heart game
much more than just when you have spare time.
Make a commitment to have your heart open,
and see that it stays open and that you will use
the heart energy of the Mother Goddess. This
will make all the difference, because it is not just
your heart that is involved—it is the heart of the
Goddess. However, the Goddess needs your heart
open to have her energy move through you.

BARBARA MARCINIAK,
Earth: Pleiadian Keys to the Living Library

For if, each day, you make one movement in
thought and one movement in deed that emanates
from you, it is like a wave that may cover Planet
Earth to great benefit. In the same manner, if you
do one thought or one deed of negativity, it helps
bring destruction.

PHYLLIS V. SCHLEMMER AND PALDEN JENKINS,
The Only Planet of Choice: Essential Briefings

From this moment we ask you to remove your
doubts. You have the power and love and strength
to prevent chaos, tragedy, and loss of life upon
your planet.

PHYLLIS V. SCHLEMMER AND PALDEN JENKINS,
The Only Planet of Choice: Essential Briefings

I see these things not with my external eyes, nor
do I hear them with my external ears. I see them
rather only in my soul with my bodily eyes wide
open, so that I am never overcome by ecstatic
consciousness, but see these things when I am
awake during the day and during the night. The
light that I see is not confined to space. . . . I am
told it is the shadow of the living light . . . . When
and how long I can see it I cannot say. But as long
as I see it, all sadness and all fear are taken from
me, so that I feel like a simple young girl and not
like an old woman.

HILDEGARD OF BINGEN (1098–1179),
IN WIGHARD STREHLOW AND GOTTFRIED HERTZKA, MD,
Hildegard of Bingen's Medicine

There should be no suffering by any creature
except what they accept for themselves.

MARLO MORGAN, *Mutant Message Down Under*

PREFACE

Essential Psychic Healing presents the 10th anniversary edition of *Psychic Healing with Spirit Guides and Angels*. Though written ten years ago, the information in this book is as current today as it was in 1996, maybe more so. Where the material seemed quite radical at the time of the book's first release, it seems much less so by today's healing standards. The book presents a complete course for learning to do psychic healing. It starts with beginning skills and proceeds to advanced psychic healing work. I have long felt that while there is a great deal of beginner's metaphysical information available, there is little to interest and help advanced healers. This book tries to cover both, by proceeding from beginning material through intermediate and advanced information.

Yet, what would have been considered advanced ten years ago may only be intermediate now. To go beyond *Essential Psychic Healing*, the next step is the karmic release and ascension information of *We Are the Angels*, followed by the *Essential Energy Balancing* series. These books are available from The Crossing Press. To do the work that precedes *Essential Psychic Healing*, I recommend taking Reiki (all three degrees) and learning the work of *Essential Reiki*. These books, and the book in your hands, provide a full course of training for anyone who has the dedication, discipline, and desire to learn to become a psychic healer.

Essential Psychic Healing contains chapters for getting started—information on meditation, visualization, the chakras and aura, and running energy. It contains the intermediate skills of working with spirit guides, hands on and distance healing, emotional release and crystal work. More advanced skills include beginning karmic release, soul retrieval, removing spirit attachments, and aiding in the death process. While the information is accurate and comprehensive, whole books can be written (and certainly have been written) about each skill. If you are especially interested in any of the topics of this book, you will want to look further.

No matter how many books you read, however, the only thing that will teach you psychic healing is to do it. Like most skills, this one can only be partly learned by reading about it. To learn it, you must do it. Use the information and the methods of this book in frequent healing and you will become a healer. If you don't do the work, don't do the healing, you will not. I wish you well in your work and explorations with *Essential Psychic Healing*.

January 30, 2005
Third Quarter Moon in Libra

Healing with the Goddess

The healing that I do for others has always been based upon my own healing journey. What works for me in my own growth I develop into techniques to use in healing sessions and ultimately to

teach other healers. The techniques that prove successful continue, and by using them in varied situations they evolve into healing tools with basically predictable results. Techniques developed by others or learned from reading about them take on new form and I adapt them for best results, often changing others' methods drastically. I combine methods and frequently use more than one technique at a time, sometimes several in one healing session as I work very selectively.

My own healing process began in 1983 and is ongoing today. I started it by dedicating myself to the Goddess at Candlemas and choosing Wicca and Goddess Spirituality as my life path. I opened to the Goddess for the first time as a religion and lifestyle, replacing the intellectualism I had viewed it with for the previous five years. When I finally made the connection between Wicca, healing, and psychic ability, my life changed in ways I could not have dreamed of. I accepted my growing psychic awareness as part of the package and welcomed it as part of my life. I frantically sought information on what it meant and how to use it. I began to explore and study Wicca.

For the first time, I started to meditate, to learn visualization and ritual, work with crystals, and to study the folk remedies that I was beginning to be aware of.

In June 1983, a Tree of Life meditation from Starhawk's *The Spiral Dance* (Harper and Row, 1979) became a kundalini opening experience, my first. I saw and felt myself as the living, growing tree and the colors of the chakras rushed through me from roots to leaves. The same day I received laying on of hands energy briefly for the first time from a woman friend. I felt it move through me in the same way as the colors had and with intense heat. The energy on my hand and arm completely and immediately healed a painful hairline fracture in my palm, and as soon as I felt it I knew I had to learn to do it, that healing from that moment on would be my life.

That day was preparing me for what I afterwards termed a walk-in, though I had no name for it at the time. In bed in the middle of the night a few weeks later, in a state somewhere between sleep and waking but very alert, I felt and watched vivid green and red ocean waves move through my body. They were beautifully formed, like the ocean breakers in a Japanese painting, and intensely hot like the energy that had healed my hand. I perceived them as stunningly beautiful and was not afraid. Then I felt and saw myself hovering above my body, detached from it while being in it at the same time. An aura of bright white mist enveloped that hovering self, took her completely away, and a different "me" returned and settled into my body on the bed. There was a discussion with someone I couldn't see about just how to enter and several readjustments before it was done. From that time of soul exchange, I felt that I was someone else, and my former self, though present, seemed moved to the background, watching but no longer active. All my perceptions were greatly different in every disconcerting way.

Every aspect of my life immediately and often frighteningly changed. I had difficulty functioning in my body for the next few weeks, had trouble remaining upright to walk at first and difficulty in remembering how to do many formerly automatic actions. I couldn't remember the route driving to work that I had taken every day for the past three years or how to fit the key into the car ignition. Those first few days of driving were definitely scary, too. What made it more difficult was that I didn't understand why I was having so much trouble doing these things, or why I was even doing most of them. I quickly became a strict vegetarian, eating rice and fresh vegetables, and drinking herb teas. I who had always kept a complete diet of meat and donuts. I left my high stress, emotionally destructive office job within days, after being caught meditating on working time, and started my first published book, *The Kwan Yin Book of Changes* (retitled *A Woman's I Ching*, The Crossing Press, 1985), two days later. I broke contact with my even more destructive parents and family within the next few months.

That August I went to my first Michigan Women's Music Festival, though I had been out as a lesbian for many years. Abandoned at the gate by the women I had traveled with, I was there all alone, with little in the way of warm clothing or camping equipment. I had never been camping before; it was cold and raining, and there was no indoor shelter. Unable to manage my dyslexia and agoraphobia in that situation, yet thrilled by the festival itself, I ended up camping at the DART (Differently Abled Resource Team) community sleeping tent. There I received a thorough education in disability awareness and positive self-image from the women, and I began to know my own abilities and disabilities.

I attended my first workshops on women's healing—on herbs and meditation, Goddess ritual, and crystal healing. I discovered women's music and crafts, women's culture, and knew I belonged. There was no turning back. In just a few weeks I had become someone very different from who I had thought I was. The old self and old life were irrevocably gone, and the new life, totally unknown, was just beginning. When I returned from the festival, my apartment of twelve years no longer felt like I lived there, and my agoraphobia was gone.

The following summer, having completed *Kwan Yin* and looking for a publisher, I moved. I took a job out of state that proved too exploitative to tolerate, and I returned home destitute, my savings gone. I was all but homeless for three months and on welfare. I experienced extreme poverty and solitude for the next several years. Refusing to return to office work where the new computers gave me chronic migraines and seizures, I waitressed but made little money at it. I was on Food Stamps for several years, while sometimes also working two jobs for fourteen hours a day. When the survival issues eased and books became my source of money, the next steps in healing began.

I had to come to terms with my physical limits first, to understand and validate myself within those limits and then to overcome and heal them. I was in chronic neck and back pain with a curvature of the spine, and frustrated by dyslexia—neurological disabilities that manifested as a lack of directional sense, with poor spatial ability, poor physical balance, clumsiness, and a confused sense that things were never in the same place twice. I lived in a state of chronic stress, hyper-nervousness, anxiety and fear, poor self-image, close to the surface rage, and frequent debilitating panic. I was chronically exhausted for no obvious reason. I had devastating migraines during which I thought I was dying and wished to die. I began to lose my reading ability, as my vision focusing muscles failed, and I began to realize that I had been severely battered and emotionally abused by both parents and my sister as a child and into adulthood. Emotional abuse along with sexual harassment had continued with many male bosses.

When an attempt at a much wanted relationship failed miserably, I knew that I needed healing that was not available from any doctor. I had to find it for myself. I began with herbs, crystals, and Reiki I. I started receiving monthly massages, and finally was able to have optometric vision therapy, which corrects reading disabilities, balance, and short-term memory. A friend learned neurolinguistic programming (NLP) and wanted someone to practice on. I volunteered and experienced extensive NLP sessions twice weekly for a year, opening up all the buried issues of my miserable childhood. I examined every incident of battering all the way back to diapers and even in the womb. I then entered two years of bartered nontraditional Gestalt therapy with a woman who was also a psychic healer.

I moved from Pittsburgh to Florida. On my own again and very alone in a new place, I worked at healing depression and rage. I gained my Reiki II and III degrees, and learned to work with spirit guides and spirit guide teams from the Earth and other planets. After a few weeks of using Machaelle Small Wright's MAP (from the book, *MAP: The Co-Creative White Brotherhood Medical Assistance Program*, Perelandra Publications, 1990), my curved back began to straighten. It normalized completely and dramatically over a period of a few months. I learned deeper meditation that led to chakra healing, inner child work, past life regression and release, uncording, soul retrieval, karmic release, and the ongoing art of emotional healing. I received help from others I felt drawn to as often as possible, but did much more of the process alone. Every forgotten and half-forgotten episode of emotional and physical pain in my life surfaced again and again to be viewed and then relinquished, and the process seemed to go on forever. Then the past lives started. I learned to feel emotions fully instead of denying them until they exploded into rage.

I completely healed my spinal curvature and greatly relieved a newer, lower back injury, healed many of the neurological problems, the adrenal exhaustion, and all of the migraines and seizures, plus an infected uterus and large fibroid tumors. I combined the psychic techniques with massage, herbs, homeopathy, crystals and gemstones, flower essences, and Reiki. The years of poverty dissolved as well. I no longer live in pain, fear, misery or anger, and I want to be here—a very new feeling.

Along the way I learned what worked and what didn't, and began using the things that helped me to help others. I participated in two-and-a-half years of healing work with AIDS patients, a year with a woman who had breast cancer, many sessions with incest and multiple personality disorder survivors, as well as healings with women for countless other emotional and physical dis-eases. The techniques in this book (and my previous books) come directly from that learning.

The strongest thread through the whole process was Reiki. While the techniques in this book do not require Reiki training, I recommend it strongly for all healers. The 1995 release of my book, *Essential Reiki* (The Crossing Press), has gone a long way toward making this healing system available to all who choose to learn it. When I train a psychic healer I begin by giving her Reiki training, as it is a basic framework for all psychic healing and laying on of hands touch healing methods. The attunements also open the receiver to her psychic abilities and connect her with her spirit guides and healing guides. By the time a healer has received the Reiki Third Degree, most of the methods in this book have been opened to her, if she frequently uses the healing for herself or others. Without Reiki, women's psychic abilities open, too, but not so quickly, naturally, or easily.

After Reiki training, healing ability develops the most fully by experience. No matter how much information a woman receives, it is doing the healing sessions that make the healer. There is no substitute for doing the work, and every healing is a learning session for both parties. Once I give a student Reiki, I ask her to do healing on others, coaching her through the sessions as she needs it and helping her to define what she perceives. Within a few healings, she has learned how to access her spirit guides and how to gain nonphysical level healing information. After many healing sessions the information comes easily and is easily understandable.

Connection with healing guides and the ability to work with them is the central skill new healers must learn. Reiki opens this connection quickly and reliably, though it is not the only way to develop it. I sincerely recommend Reiki training, all three degrees if possible, to every serious psychic healer.

Psychic healing is not medicine nor is it in any way accepted by the standard medical system, yet it offers profound answers in the quest for wellness and the healing of dis-eases both physical and emotional/mental/spiritual. The modern medical system focuses its "cures" on the dense physical body only, while psychic healing looks to nonphysical levels for the sources of dis-ease. Medicine cures by suppressing symptoms while healing works by addressing and releasing the non-body causes of illness. In finding the emotional, mental, and spiritual sources of dis-ease and thus healing the whole person, illness is finally released from the physical body. Symptoms disappear and the dis-ease is healed, but healed on more than dense body levels.

Medicine has until very recently denied the existence of anything but the body. It is now slowly opening to the idea that mind and body are connected, but only very slowly. When patriarchal medicine stole its basis from witches, midwives, healers, and shamans of the pre-Inquisition, pre-Christian female past, it turned its back on the nonphysical totally and irrevocably. Women's healing—state of the art medicine in every culture before the male takeover—has always honored the body's nonphysi-

cal levels. Medicine without the feminine psychic has become a cold and mechanical bodyshop of isolated human parts. Drugs with dangerous, noxious side-effects and too many unnecessary surgeries and amputations are modern medicine's invasive and mechanical answers to pain and illness.

Such cures are more painful and debilitating than the original dis-ease; they have crippled the patients rather than cured them. Medicine's technological horrors and soul-raping excesses have resulted in a reawakening of older and gentler methods, less invasive and more holistic ways to heal. Women as the most frequent victims of medical excess are also the more frequent seekers of alternatives to it.

The awakening is growing by leaps and bounds and a variety of methods have proved useful. The methods run the gamut from the strictly physical to the totally nonphysical. Herbal healing (a gentler drug pharmacopoeia), vitamins and minerals, optimal nutrition with awareness of toxins, naturopathy, massage, chiropractic, and many other natural methods work primarily as drugless therapies on the physical body. Many holistic methods reach beyond the physical level, or beyond what can be explained by scientific proof. These bridging methods between the dense physical and nonphysical levels include homeopathy, acupuncture and acupressure, flower essences, gemstones and crystals, biofeedback, and hypnosis. They are often referred to as vibrational healing. Methods that affect the physical body by going completely beyond it include meditation and visualization, emotional release, inner child work, Reiki, and every form of psychic healing.

Statistics are available supporting the recent popular growth of holistic and vibrational healing. In the United States in 1990, Americans spent nearly as much on alternative health care as they did on standard medicine—$10.3 billion for alternative care and $12.8 billion for hospitalization. In a 1985 Associated Press survey of 1,500 adults, over half said they would prefer "unsanctioned" treatment to standard medical procedure. A 1992 survey reported that one-third of all Americans had tried—and now preferred—alternatives to conventional therapies.

Holistic remedies are estimated as a $27 billion a year industry and growing.[1]

Increasingly today, people are rejecting technological horrors and body-only "cures." They are refusing slash and burn medical quick fixes, choosing instead healing that goes deeper than the skin. Holistic healing that honors the integrity of the physical body is the first step. Vibrational healing that goes beyond the physical into the mental-emotional levels to heal dis-ease is next. The new quasi-medical field of psychoneuroimmunology (PNI) is included here. Psychic healing goes further yet, reaching beyond the dense physical into emotional, mental, and spiritual levels for the complete changing of the dis-ease energy template into total wellness of the whole Be-ing/individual. This wellness means bodily comfort and freedom from dis-ease, but it also means emotional health, peace of mind, and spiritual joy. This ultimate form of healing is a return to the psychic feminine, a re-membering of the past to birth the future.

Psychic healing does not preclude physical or vibrational methods; they all work together. Psychic healing can be used along with standard medical treatment, as well as with natural remedies, acupuncture, bodywork, emotional therapy, flower essences, etc. As a healer, I usually work eclectically, combining nutrition, detoxification, homeopathy, and herbs with nonphysical methods. The goal is to heal on all four levels—physical, emotional, mental, and spiritual—in the quickest and most effective ways possible. It is against healing ethics to advise anyone to reject medicine, and in most Western countries against the law to do so. I have occasionally asked a woman to go to the medical system because I felt such care was needed. I have also worked with women who reject medicine completely. Psychic healing works beautifully with holistic health care as well, and I personally find holistic care more positive in most cases.

Although I write of levels, human Be-ing is not divided into parts. The physical body is not well or ill in isolation. Where there is physical pain, there is almost always emotional and mental or spiritual pain. Where there is spiritual (or mental or emotional) dis-ease, there is rarely a healthy physical body—the illness will surface somewhere. We are not parts but whole entities, and wellness means health at all levels. Holistic healing derives from the world "wholeness." It also derives from "holy"; people are spiritual Be-ings. A denial of spirituality is a denial of selfhood and one's place in the universe (you are Goddess) that inevitably leads to dis-ease. Likewise, a woman spiritually well is usually well also in body, mind, and emotions, or easily healed into that wellness.

Psychic healing, unlike the medical model, means healing oneself, others, and the planet. A healer does not do healing *to* the receiver but *with* her. All healing is a three-way, active and cooperative agreement between the healer, the receiver of the healing, and the Goddess (or however else you care to designate Source energy or divinity). No one heals another person, she can only heal herself, and the healer's role is facilitator or channeler of the process. I like to give a simple example. If a child falls and skins her knee, her mother can kiss it and her sister can put a bandaid on it, but only her own body can form a scab and make it go away.

We all heal ourselves, and the role of psychic healer is to find the best methods to encourage the deepest (all levels) healing possible. The healer might boost the child's healing energy to speed the process. But the child with the cut knee if not healed even though new skin has formed, is still afraid to go outside again. Emotional healing is needed along with physical healing here—the work is not complete. Her own body (with the Goddess' help) heals the physical dis-ease, but she may need more help to heal it emotionally.

This is where most healing begins. It helps to release the fear by finding and reassuring it at the source in childhood or in a past life. The healer facilitates the child in overcoming her fear and returning to normal activity. The fear may not originate in the recent fall but could have originated from something that happened in the recent or distant past, or even in a past life. Healing insights come to the healer and receiver from the Goddess, and healer, Goddess, and child are all involved. This is a much simplified basic example of the healing process that extends to far more complicated issues and dis-eases.

In much of psychic healing, the healer and receiver are the same person. Few women needing and wanting psychic healing today have access to it from others, though this is changing. It is too new a field with too few practitioners, and most of those doing it must work underground. The healers themselves also are too often isolated from others. They need this work as much as anyone else. Whereas in the patriarchal medical system, only a doctor can "cure" (and anyone else can be jailed for "practicing medicine without a license"), in nonphysical healing we are all healers. Women can use the same methods for self-healing as they use in working with others.

Probably most psychic healing is done as self-healing, and though it is often easier and more effective for a healer and receiver to work together, healing alone is done every day. Being one's own facilitator takes skill and objectivity, but sometimes only an honest desire for change and trust in the process and Goddess are required. Working with spirit guides can fill the gap, but healing alone is often a slower process. I recommend healing with trusted other people wherever possible, along with positive self-help. If no other healer is available, do what you can alone and you will learn a great deal. The methods in this book work both in self-healing and with a facilitating healer.

Women heal themselves and each other, as well as children, trees and plants, animals, men, governments, and the planet. No one is here in isolation from the whole, and no one can be fully healthy until we have a healthy society and Earth. Many healing and self-healing methods can be adapted to healing the planet. Look to distance healing to encompass the Earth or any part of Her. Every healing is in effect a planetary one, as every person, animal, or plant is a part of the Earth. Gaia is the Goddess Earth and we are all a part of Her living Be-ing.

Each healing for oneself or someone else, for any, domestic animal, bird, wild creature or rose bush is an Earth healing. Each activist statement— peace march; protest against racism, sexism, homophobia, or poverty; vote for honest life-affirming government; letter to a Congress person; or freeing of real truth and information anywhere—is a planetary healing. Every bottle, can and newspaper recycled helps, every tree planted, every healing for any living Be-ing helps everyone and the Earth. Every statement against violence heals every one of us, as does every meal offered to someone hungry.

The Earth and all nations and people are in the process of a major healing and cleansing, known to New Age metaphysics as the Earth changes. Though some people refuse to believe in the concept and its prophecies, which were first popularly introduced by Edgar Cayce before 1945, the daily news reflects the increasingly happening fact. My 1991 book *Dreaming the Past, Dreaming the Future* (retitled *Prophetic Visions of the Future*, The Crossing Press) presented an overview of Earth change theory and some then-current predictions. The events were beginning at that time and have intensified considerably. They will continue for the next several years, offering an opportunity for evolving positive change in individuals and the planet. Whatever has not worked in the life and organization of nations and people is being cleared to make room for what works effectively and humanely. The result of the chaos is ultimate good.

Says Barbara Marciniak in *Earth: Pleiadian Keys to the Living Library:*

> Earth is going to go through tumultuous changes. . . . We see this probability as being inevitable because of the extensive polarity on your planet. Rest assured that the more you pollute and destroy Earth, the more energy will go into shifting and shaking to clean things up.
>
> Between the years 1994 and 1999, you will move into peak chaos.
>
> This present-day epoch involves the fall of global civilization and a reawakening of a brand new form of consciousness.[2]

The predictions and prophecies are unfolding globally. Since the writing of *Dreaming the Past, Dreaming the Future (Prophetic Visions of the Future)*, the world map has changed. The Soviet Union has broken into numerous smaller countries, the Berlin Wall has fallen, unifying East and West Germany, and the European Economic Union has erased the borders and boundaries in a continent. Apartheid is gone in South Africa, fascism in Haiti, and there are peace efforts in divided Ireland and between Israel and the Arab states. More negatively, genocidal wars in Bosnia, Rwanda, and Burundi, and famine in Somalia and Ethiopia also are rewriting the maps, killing millions of people, and horrifying the world. AIDS is sweeping the globe and depopulating several African countries.

Changes in the surface of the Earth are also happening daily, some in devastating ways. The January 1994 Northridge earthquake in Los Angeles killed sixty people, left thousands homeless, and cost billions in property damage. A year to the day later (January 17, 1995), the earthquake in Kobe, Japan, left 5,100 dead and 300,000 people homeless. Earthquakes in Sumatra, South America, India, Iran, Mexico, China, the Philippines, Japan, the United States, and other places have caused damage and deaths while thousands of smaller tremors and aftershocks continue. The magnitude of these earthquakes is increasing alarmingly.

Hurricanes have created similar havoc in Florida, the Carolinas, Hawaii, Japan, the Philippines, and St. Croix, including 1992's Hurricane Andrew. Severe storms, tornadoes, and freak weather patterns are occurring planetwide since 1993, with Europe, the United States and Africa hard hit. Tornadoes in Florida, the South, the Midwest, the March 1993 East Coast Superstorm, rainstorm damage with flooding and mudslides in California and throughout Europe have disrupted and taken many human lives.

Flooding along the Mississippi River and in Georgia in 1993, and along the Rhine River and in Holland in Europe in 1994–95 caused many thousands to leave their homes. River patterns and land have been permanently changed in many places. In California, Colorado, and the Pacific Northwest, uncontrollable forest fires burned countless acres of living trees and many homes, in Laguna Beach and Malibu. Many of the natural disasters are a direct result of land mismanagement—building on flood planes and in fire areas, for example, and rerouting rivers for human convenience. Extremes of heat, cold, wind, rain (or lack of it), and snow are evident nationally and internationally.

Despite societal and natural disruption and human bad attitudes, there is on the positive side a new awakening of spirituality and human freedom. To counteract Christian and Islamic fundamentalism there is also Goddess and New Age spirituality, interest in Eastern philosophies, and anti-racism and feminism. Despite random violence, drug abuse, repression, homelessness, and abuse of women, children, and minorities there is also a growing comprehension of the oneness of all life and an intolerance of oppression. Where there are plane crashes, earthquakes, floods, fires, and massive fatalities, there is also a mobilization of people taking care of others. Along with new virulent dis-eases like AIDS and the Haitian virus, and the return of old ones like tuberculosis and cholera, there is a new and increasing focus on healing and compassion. Coexisting with the lack of health care for too many people is a new and increasing return to safer natural ways.

Though change is not always comfortable, it is the first law of energy and life. Where change has been resisted strongly it manifests strongly. As the nonfunctioning old world collapses, the new one begins to return to positive living. Barbara Marciniak describes the Earth changes as an initiation in which the test is to face and overcome fear:

> If you find yourself immersed in what you fear, hold the image of who you are as a whole and happy being and transmute the energy of fear by learning about yourself. . . . . When your energy field no longer holds the fear, what you fear no longer has the life to destroy you.[3]

The tests and challenges result in empowerment and growth, a healing process that the Earth Mother is leading her inhabitants through. The healing of the planet/Goddess is reflected in the healing and empowerment of women. Each living Be-ing on the planet is the Earth.

Women's internal changes may be as difficult as earthquakes, and some who cannot change will die, but there are positive results for those who go through the initiation process. Empowerment and personal growth manifest as emotional opening, and shifts in spiritual life manifest in women's outlook and consciousness. Women are becoming more psychic, more aware of having a life purpose and of being a part of the oneness of all life on Earth. Rigid patriarchal religions are giving way slowly to Eastern, Native American, and Earth-based philosophies, and a return in many cases to divinity as female. Spirituality for many women is becoming more central than religion, and more focused on giving, opening, and love. There is a return to the once universal concept of reincarnation and life beyond death.

The Earth changes also mean a focus on healing from within, and it is this form of healing that prompted this book. Both women and men are learning that healing their bodies means healing their emotions, minds, and spirits from the traumas and abuses caused by the patriarchy and their own past history. Healing the trauma of both this life and past lives is the way to face and overcome fear, and to move forward and grow beyond all previous limits. By returning to past pain—of former incest, abuse, rejection, and other hurts—the pain is acknowledged, felt, healed, and released. Past life traumas will surface in the healing and be settled to prevent them from returning again.

Facing personal herstory and emotion brings collective healing and the healing of the Goddess Earth. A woman who has experienced incest or abuse and heals the pain in herself goes on to help heal the pain in others and to raise awareness of the pain of the planet and heal it as well. One who regains her sense of Goddess self after being abused by racism, homophobia, misogyny, random violence, or religious discrimination goes on to help erase these wrongs from society. Those who have experienced war will help the planet become peaceful, those who have been poor or homeless learn prosperity and help others gain it, and so on. With the release of fear comes health, abundance, peace, and the ability to love oneself, others, and the planet into healing and a new age. As individuals' auras change, so does the aura of the Earth.

When these healings happen, lives change. Many people are changing their jobs and careers, risking security for livelihoods more fitted to their real liking and emotional needs. Some are choosing careers of service to others. Many are becoming self-employed. Many women are leaving long-term homes or the place where they were born to move to other parts of the country or even other countries, and some move several times. Others change their long-term mates, and some who have previously been alone find partners. A few choose to live communally for the first time. The changes can be scary and chaotic for a while, but lead to peace of mind and wholeness. There have been many deaths—from AIDS, cancer, plane crashes, car accidents, natural disasters, etc.—and there will be many more. Those who cannot change or face their fear may die. Those who do change may find themselves experiencing never before known joy.

What needs to be healed in most people and nations is the idea of separateness. Separation and aloneness are only false, surface perceptions, fostered by patriarchal jealousy and greed. At the root and source of life we are all one and all a part of the Goddess who is the Earth we live on. We are all alike in essence and what hurts one of us hurts everyone. Earth, the Goddess, and Her people share a karma of oppression and abuse that is healed by awareness of the oneness of all life. If there is any definition of psychic healing or of any healing, it is a process of returning the individual to oneness with other Be-ings and the Goddess.

Recognition of that oneness leads to the understanding that the chaos makes sense, and each of us is healed of the fear of being alone. As each woman learns to love herself, she learns to love all others and the Earth. As she learns to trust the Earth/Goddess, she learns to trust others and herself and to find that trust honored and returned. Separation melts by trust and love; no one is separate from the whole.

When separation is healed and people gain self-love, each person sees the other as herself. In this frame of mind, war, oppression, violence, and abuse become intolerable. Since no one would do these things to a well-loved and properly respected self, they become impossible to do to others. The end of separation is also the end of poverty and racism, planetary pollution, cruelty to animals and children, incest, battering, ableism, and ageism. Experiencing herself with love and as one with all life, the individual is whole and complete, lacking nothing, and able to give and receive wisdom, blessings, and compassion. Such oneness partakes of Goddess in the fullest sense.

Illness in people reflects the illness of the planet, and overcoming it is a process of conscious growth. Overcoming illness indicates healing and continuing, but it may also lead to acceptance of what is, and the healing process may end in death, as well. Death is not defeat or the triumph of evil or dis-ease. It is another rite of passage and an avenue to a healthier rebirth. Everyone who has been born eventually dies. A woman who dies after confronting and releasing the traumas and karma of her past dies peacefully. Her comprehension and understanding bring her to new wholeness, and her work for this incarnation is completed. Her next lifetime will reflect her growth and bring her new learning, free from the limits of the present. Likewise, the woman who comes to terms with her dis-ease, and learns to love herself living with it, has made a breakthrough into health. By healing herself on the nonphysical levels she attains wholeness and inner peace, with or without her physical dis-ease.

The concept of self-love is perhaps the central issue and the heart issue of women's healing. Patriarchal society operates on and fosters the illusion of separateness and the notion that anyone who is not a white, Anglo-Saxon, wealthy, or male is inferior. This is the mindset that is bringing Earth to the deterioration she is now experiencing and the reason for the need of the Earth changes. The fact is that women are the spiritual heart and salvation of this planetary culture and are the only hope of saving it. Women remember the Goddess and are made in her image as living examples of the creative life force. Without us no one can be born on this planet, and it is only by returning to women's Goddess-based values that humanity can survive. Women's focus on relationships, compassion, creativity, ethics, civilization, and nonmaterialism is the root of the New Age now being born. The violence of our present culture is rarely being perpetrated by women.

Women are the Goddess and are the Earth. We birth and raise the children, make the homes, and create cooperative civilizations and communities. When men make war, women make peace; when men make technology, women make humanity; when men make chaos, women make compassion, sense, and order. It is only by women's awareness that men can change and patriarchy end. The patriarchal system does not want women to know how consequential our acts and Be-ing are. By recognizing our real influence, women learn how crucial we are to the survival of Earth, and that loving ourselves is only our due respect to life and the Goddess. All healing for women, therefore, means healing women's sense of self-respect, self-image, and self-love.

Reciting the Wiccan Self-Blessing nightly is a good start for healing every woman's dis-ease. Stand skyclad (naked) in front of a mirror by candlelight. Take a drop of essential oil (rose or jasmine are lovely), red wine, menstrual blood, salt water, or pure water on your index finger. Touch each chakra in turn while saying the following aloud.

While touching your crown (top of head), say:
"Bless me Mother for I am your child."

While touching your third eye (between your eyes), say:

"Bless my sight that I may see clearly and see you in my life."

While touching your throat, say:

"Bless my speech that I may speak truly and speak of you."

While touching your heart chakra (between your breasts), say:

"Bless my heart that it be open and filled with love for all."

While touching your solar plexus (body center at the lowest ribs), say:

"Bless my life energy that comes from you."

While touching your belly chakra (below the navel), say:

"Bless my ovaries and uterus for sacred, loving sex."

While touching your root chakra (vagina), say:

"Bless my vagina, the gateway of life and death."

While touching the bottoms of both feet, say:

"Bless my feet that they may follow your path and my life's own."

While touching the palms of both hands, say:

"Bless my hands that do your work, which is my work in this world."

While touching your crown again, say:

"Bless me Mother for I am your child and I am part of you."

Miracles come from this healing and open the way for all the healings that follow. The methods in this book begin with opening women's oneness with Goddess and all life through meditation, and continuing that opening for communication with the Goddess-self through visualization. Next are chapters on the nonphysical anatomy of the chakras,

Hara Line, soul body, and aura levels and then basic energy cleansing, enhancement, and protection techniques. These are the primary tools of psychic healing. Learning to work with spirit guides follows as another essential tool for nonphysical healing work.

Using these techniques leads to information on emotional release and healing the past in this life, laying on of hands, distance healing, and working with gemstones and crystals for laying on of stones. The last chapters include more advanced psychic healing methods and information—karmic healing and release work, soul retrieval, and releasing attachments and entities from the aura bodies. These may originate from the present or past lifetimes, from the Earth or other planets, and may involve the help of alien allies. The book's final chapter is on healing and the death process, and the possibilities of healing into future lifetimes.

The material begins with basic techniques and continues to advanced ones, with the focus primarily beyond the elementary. There are many books available on beginning healing skills, but little presently in print to teach advanced techniques. Women who have completed Reiki II and III, and those without Reiki who have practiced psychic healing over time and are experienced with it, need further guidance. Until now, most of us have been working alone, attempting to make sense of what we see and learning to implement that perception by trial and error. The methods presented in this book represent what I have seen and how I have learned to understand it through trials and errors of my own.

No two healers work in exactly the same ways and those reading my methods may choose to use them differently. You have my blessings on this, as long as the methods are used for healing and good, not to harm or manipulate. Each healer becoming experienced in a method will go beyond it, and has my blessings in this as well. It is what I wish to be. The point of psychic ability is to use it for the good of people, animals, and the planet. With that as a focus, healing is highly guided by the Goddess and her spirit guides for the good of all life.

Healers are priestesses and midwives, helping the Earth and women to enter the New Age and create a gentle and positive new world. Remember that what you send out returns to you, and that healing others results in healing and many blessings for oneself. The best advice I can give to any healer is to let go of ego (which is separateness), have compassion, and allow the Goddess to work through your hands. All healing is a three-way agreement between the healer, the receiver, and the Goddess Earth and only good and love can come from such a partnership. An attitude of spiritual respect in healing changes lives and leads to the wholeness of individuals, the Goddess, and the world.

January 20, 1995
Third Quarter Moon in Virgo

Notes

1 Mark Ian Barasch, *The Healing Path: A Soul Approach to Illness* (New York, NY, Arkana Books, 1993), pp. 218–219.

2 Barbara Marciniak, *Earth: Pleiadian Keys to the Living Library* (Santa Fe, NM, Bear and Co., 1995), pp. 220–221.

3 *Ibid.*, p. 219.

CHAPTER ONE

Meditation

Health and healing begin with good physical habits: eating uncontaminated whole foods, taking vitamins, drinking pure water, and consuming as little as possible of sugar, fat, alcohol, drugs (including prescription drugs), tobacco, chemicals, pesticides, and additives. Health and healing mean cleanliness and restful sleep, sunlight and exercise, pleasant surroundings, and living in physical safety. Being surrounded by beauty keeps women healthy. Health also means good mental and emotional habits: time alone and time shared with trusted others, calm relationships, many hugs, reasonably fulfilling work and play, creative outlets, companionship with children and animals, and keeping interested in one's activities with as little worry, rush, and stress as possible.

Stress is the direct cause of 85% of human disease, and 85% is only a conservative, medically accepted estimate. Stress is defined loosely as strain upon the systems of the organism. A certain amount of strain is necessary to promote function, but too much "juice through the circuits" is negative and harmful. This negative overload results in a breakdown of optimal physical and mental/emotional function, and eventually the breakdown of organs and body systems. Individuals vary in their tolerance and definition of stress, and the overload can come as much from positive events as from traumatic ones.

Symptoms of emotional stress include irritability and feeling close to tears; restlessness and restless habits; inability to concentrate or make decisions; lack of joy; insomnia; nervous smoking, alcohol intake, or eating habits (or the inability to eat); chronic tiredness; lack of interest in sex; and an inability to cope.[1] Each individual has a tolerance level for handling stressful emotions and situations. When that level is exceeded, symptoms begin to develop. When stress exceeding the boundary becomes chronic, disease begins and can lead to increasingly serious illness, immune dysfunction, chronic dis-eases, and even eventually to death. Each person has a final limit to the amount of stress she can withstand.

The symptoms of stress are also the symptoms of spiritual separation, the separation of body from mind, emotions, and spirit that is so endemic in modern society. They are the symptoms and results of not knowing you are Goddess. Stress is not only a result of separation from the Goddess, but also may be a factor in the impulse to change. We live in a too rapidly changing world that shows no signs of slowing down. The discomfort of stress can be a pressure that forces the individual to change the things that aren't working in her life, pushing her toward healing and growth. This is positive ultimately, but may not seem to be so at the time, and is typical of what's happening to women in these Earth change days. Stress symptoms can be a simple warning to slow down and smell the roses (reconnect with Goddess), and return to a simpler, more spiritually oriented life. Returning to the knowledge that you are Goddess defuses the stress and eases the rapidity of change.

The human immune system is directly affected by stress and is the very real link between the body and the nonphysical levels. Negative emotions arising from stress cause the formation of chemicals in the brain that travel to flood the body, reaching the thymus via the vagus nerve.[2] The chemicals are the result of unreleased fight or flight syndrome hormone production that becomes chronic and unrelieved with frequent or chronic stress. The vagus nerve, seat of the autonomic nervous system, controls the heart and respiratory systems and in metaphysical terms connects the emotions to the higher mind. Negative emotions are usually defined as anger, fear, bitterness, denial, greed, guilt, blame, hate, jealousy, resentment, anxiety, rage, frustration, depression, etc.

The thymus is the physical center of immune system function, and the thymus chakra on the Hara line (see Chapter 3) is also the psychic link between the body and emotions, the dense physical and nonphysical, emotional aura levels. It connects the etheric double (physical level aura) to the emotional body, and emotions to physical function. The vagus nerve takes the connection a step further, from emotional body to the mental. Thus the physical body, etheric double, emotional and mental bodies are all tied together. Dis-ease in the dense body results from this change of events: stress–>negative (painful) emotions –> negative chemicals in the brains –> vagus nerve –> depressed thymus function –> depleted immunity –> physical dis-eases from colds to cancer.

Stress-related dis-ease (most, if not all, dis-ease) is therefore a need to return to oneness within, to reconnect self with Goddess Source. It is a warning to transcend the strains of physical living by returning to the stillness of the spiritual levels, where we are Goddess (Goddess-within). Dis-ease is also a symptom of resistance to change in one's life, emotions, or thinking. When a way of living (job, relationship, addiction, emotional state, habit) is not positive and the individual refuses to change it, the resulting stress leads first to emotional discomfort, then to mental and spiritual unease, and finally to pain or dis-ease in the body. The answer again is to return to Goddess, to spiritual values, to trust and allow the change, and let go. The most significant change is in turning negative thoughts and emotions into positive ones. This spiritual rebalancing moves through the levels and reverses the dis-ease process.

The progression looks like this: negative life function –> stress –> resistance to change –> emotional discomfort –> mental discomfort –> spiritual pain –> physical dis-ease. Reversal goes this way: physical dis-ease –> change and letting go –> emotional release –> mental (often karmic) release –> spiritual reconnection –> healing the body. This is the process of psychic healing that the healer leads the receiver through. To be an effective healer and to heal oneself requires access to the above reversal process of dis-ease.

The secret of this access, the way to effect the healing process, is the meditative state. Every spiritual training and every psychic healing technique in every culture and religion planetwide begins with this skill. Self-healing begins with meditation as well. It is the optimal way to transcend the physical, emotional, and mental body levels to reach the spiritual and connect with Goddess. At the Goddess Source spiritual level, all negativity (pain on all levels), stress, resistance, and fear are let go, filling the self with calm, security, peace, love, acceptance, oneness, and healing. Healing is a return to oneness—with the spiritual self, the Earth, and all that lives—and that oneness is reached through meditation.

Deepak Chopra describes how both physicist Albert Einstein in the 1920s and the ancient Hindu rishis sought an underlying source for the transformation of space and time, mass, and energy. It is interesting how modern physics is only beginning to understand the basis of healing (and still does not understand it) that ancient civilizations' women healers have always know. Einstein wanted to find a "unified field theory," a single source state that explains change or the transformation of matter. In ancient terms, what he sought was the source of creation and healing that could only be defined as the transformation of consciousness.

The rishis identified three states of reality or consciousness: waking, sleeping, and dreaming, as compared to Einstein's space and time, mass and energy. They defined Einstein's unified field as the fourth state, which they termed *turiya* (the Buddhist samadhi). The rishis explained turiya as another state of awareness beyond the first three, but hidden by the first three states. They said that turiya or samadhi could be experienced by transcending the normal activity of the senses, by going beyond the three states of waking, sleeping, and dreaming into the source of all consciousness, the Void. That source (Goddess) or transcendent state (Goddess-within, spiritual level) of awareness is the place beyond Einstein's definition of space and time, mass and energy, where life is created and matter can be transformed.[3]

"Unified" in "unified field theory" of course means oneness, and that place of oneness as Goddess and Goddess-within is reached and healing is achieved in the turiya (samadhi) of the meditative state. The place to go to connect with Goddess or Goddess-within is known in Buddhism as the Void. The other three levels are the Nonvoid. The Void is the nonphysical place of creation, the template from which matter is made, the spiritual, Goddess level of Be-ing. The Nonvoid is the created world or physical body, the endless potential of the physical, emotional, and mental states.

All reality, including the dense human body, is created through the Nonvoid from the Void. The Void or Goddess level is reached by disconnecting the distractions of the senses and going into the place or source of transformation, consciousness, creation, and life. It is a place of silence, emptiness, nothingness, and completion, beyond which is total joy and liberation (nirvana).[4] To reach the Void, one must let go of ego (separation) and enter oneness— turiya, samadhi, the transformative meditative state, Goddess/Goddess-within, or the unified field.

Mahayana Buddhism describes this state of bliss or completion, the Void, as the inner nature of everyone and all that lives. I equate the Buddhist term "Buddha-nature" below with the Wiccan "Goddess-within."

> Our original Buddha-nature is, in all truth, nothing which can be apprehended. It is void, omnipresent, silent, pure; it is glorious and mysterious peacefulness, and that is all which can be said. You yourself must awake to it, fathoming its depths. That which is before you is it in all its entirety and with nothing whatsoever lacking.[5]

In seeking the Goddess-Void, one finds in oneself the source of all creation, love and healing.

Physics has also discovered that solid matter is not very solid at all. Even in the most dense of objects, there is much more open space than there is atomic volume. The potential for transformation is not in the atoms and molecules but in the arrangement and rearrangement of their intervening spaces. Likewise, body cells contains much more of this intervening space than they do of solid matter. They are surrounded by electrical fields, and the entire human body is surrounded by layers of electrical fields (the layers of the aura, as well as the fields surrounding cells and organs). Solid matter is sparse and the space is vast—these spaces between atoms, physical/electrical emptiness, is also the Void. The electricity in the nonmatter spaces is the Nonvoid, the potential from which transformation and healing emerge.

All healing begins from this place of emptiness reached through meditation. At this spiritual level of electrical space between atoms and cells, stress is left behind as well as its negative effects. The Earthplane but not the astral senses, the ego, and the body are left behind and so is dis-ease. In the perfection of the Void only wellness can exist, the perfect template of wholeness and primal Goddess creation. By accessing this state, the progression of dis-ease is reversed and perfection is brought back through the Nonvoid. From this change comes physical healing. By the action of mind on the Void (visualization, described in the next chapter) in the meditative state, transformation and healing occur. The changes move through the levels, from the spiritual through the mental and emotional bodies to the dense physical. With the physical changes come the release of stress, calm emotions, and a peaceful, often blissful, state of mind and body.

Meditation is a skill that anyone can learn; children learn it more easily than adults. It results in a process of growth, and the process itself is more important than any goal or result. To be optimally effective, it must become a way of life, something done every day at a set time like brushing your teeth. Once you are experienced with meditation, with how it feels to be in the meditative state of concentration and one-pointed focus, it is easy to enter the state at any time. This movement in and out of light meditation at will constitutes the healing state, the basis for all psychic healing.

The process of learning the skill, of doing a daily or twice daily half-hour period of meditation, also has profound self-healing results for the woman who practices it. Transcending the senses, the ego, and the physical Earthplane level clears and brightens the energy of the nonphysical bodies (the electrical field between atoms), and is a healing in itself. Stress and its negative effects are greatly reduced and dis-ease is lessened or prevented in the physical body. The woman experiences growing peace in her life, and a calm ability to cope. Her mind is clear and her skill in freeing herself from others' influences and designing her own life increases. Even addictions may be healed. And though Eastern theory attempts to suppress this knowledge, psychic opening occurs and with it comes an increase in the psychic senses and healing abilities for oneself and others.

The term *meditation* usually connotes "trance," a word that can be misunderstood. Trance suggests a lack of control or consciousness, which is just the opposite of its true meaning. Rather meditation and trance consist of a state of quiet, aware concentration and one-pointedness—a deep, undistracted, fully calm focusing of mind. A trance, as I define it, is a process of going within, focusing on one's inner self by reducing the distractions of the outer, daily world. It is not an attempt to make the mind a total blank—this is probably impossible even in the East and definitely so in Western culture. Meditation does not hypnotize; you must choose to be hypnotized, and hypnosis (see the next chapter) is a different process.

The average human uses only 5% to 10% of her total brain capacity, and meditation is a systemic mental training that helps to increase the use of brain potential. Meditation trains the mind in focusing attention and increasing one's use of free will. It is a way of gaining access to deeper levels of awareness and the subconscious, of connecting and cleansing the energy layers and levels. It slows body functions and stills the mind to one thought at a time. In meditation, the woman goes within herself to find Goddess. The process releases the illusions of the senses and the physical world, including the illusion that we are our bodies. We are not our bodies, or even our minds or emotions, but something far greater that includes them. Meditation makes us more aware of who we really are as spiritual Be-ings.

The effects of the meditative state are measurable medically as "deep relaxation coupled with a highly alert mental state."[6] Metabolism slows, along with heart and respiration rates (vagus nerve), and less consumption of oxygen. Blood lactate levels decrease, a physiologic measure of decreased anxiety and tension (stress). Skin resistance increases, another indicator of decreased stress. Brain wave electroencephalogram (EEG) patterns slow from the more rapid, daily beta waves to the slower alpha (right to thirteen cycles per second). In the deepest states of an experienced meditator or healer, brain waves may drop even to the higher ranges of the very slow theta level.[7] The meditative state is one of neither waking, sleeping, nor dreaming, and is the rishis' and Einstein's creative fourth state of the unified field or transformation of consciousness and matter. It accesses the spaces between atoms and molecules, the Void.

Anyone can learn to meditate, simply by practicing it. The ego and conscious mind, however, resist letting go. Expertise in meditation only comes with time, repetition, and consistent practice. Despite this resistance, it does not take long to experience the very pleasant shift from outward to inward focus, from daily activity to the calm healing of the light trance (early alpha) state. To experience this immediately, as an introduction to the greater focus of meditation, try the following exercise.

———————— : : ————————

In a quiet, comfortable place where you will not be interrupted, sit on the floor in the tailor position. Do not try the Eastern half-lotus, legs crossed, and one foot on top of the opposite knee, unless it is easy for you. Relax your body and with back straight and hands open on top of thighs, take a few slow, deep breaths. Lean your weight to the left slowly, then return to center. Lean to the right, then return to the center. Lean forward, then rock back to the centered position again. Then, holding still, relaxed and centered, take more slow breaths and pay attention to them.

Note how you feel. Your weight is balanced, so much so that you may not feel your body, and your mind is calm and still. Continue the slow, deep breaths, focusing on the breathing. Slow your thoughts to one at a time and pay attention to them. This process, called grounding and centering, is the beginning of meditation and may be used daily to start it, but the mind will not stay still long unless you give it more to do.

Meditation that trains the mind and transcends the physical state must be done for a period of twenty minutes to half an hour once or twice a day. Do not exceed this timespan until you are more experienced, and able to handle the rise of Kundalini energy it may cause. Meditate at the same time every day. Upon waking or just before bedtime are considered to be the most effective times. Sit on the floor like a tailor or in the half-lotus position or sit on a straight-backed chair with armrests. Do not meditate lying down as you may fall asleep. Close your eyes during meditation but remain alert and awake. Removing eyeglasses or contact lenses makes a softer focus.

The place and setting of a meditative space are highly important. Use the same room and place in the room every day. The space needs to be as quiet and free of distractions as possible. Close the door and unplug the telephone. Some women meditate using music as a background, but I prefer not to. If music is used, it needs to be nonvocal and nondistracting classical or New Age music kept at very low volume. If you find yourself focusing on the music and not the meditation, shut it off. Allow no one to disturb you; this half hour daily is yours alone. It is fine to meditate with other people. Children can learn to meditate easily, but for shorter periods of time. Pets in the house may join in; allow them to do so if they are quiet.

A room used for daily meditation develops its own aura of spirituality. When I meditate I like to sit on the rug in front of the Goddess altar on my bedroom dresser. I meditate before going to bed. The energy greatly aids my sleep afterwards and the room feels like an ancient temple. The lit candles on the altar were an important focus when I first learned meditation. I don't always light them now. Candles and/or incense set the mood and create a focus or habit, becoming signals for shifting to the meditative state if they are always used.

The grounding and centering exercise is a good beginning. From that point there are a variety of meditation methods. Choose the one that interests you. Once you have chosen one method, however, stay with it daily for at least a month before trying something else. If you choose to continue using that method, fine. All of the methods lead to the same place: a stilled mind, calm emotional state, and relaxed body. Getting there is more important than how it is accomplished.

For beginning meditators who may have never experienced a relaxed body, full body relaxation exercises are a good place to start. Sitting in position in your meditation space, do the grounding exercise first. Then, starting with the toes and moving upward to the top of the head, clench tight and release each muscle group and body part in turn. Do this slowly and thoroughly. The muscle clenching makes you aware of each part and its tightness, intensifying and increasing the releases by contrast. Pay particular attention to the muscles of the back, neck, jaw and face, as these are places that hold tension for most people. Everyone has some muscle group that reflects stress.

After completing the exercise, notice how it feels. Direct your breath into any area that may still feel tight. Repeat the relaxation process again. Then sitting quietly, breathe slowly and notice the thoughts that pass through your mind. Slow the thoughts down and follow each one until it passes by and disappears. Allow only one thought at a time, but give it full attention as it passes. Then let it go; don't hold onto it or add to it.

A variant of this method is to memorize the following (or similar) phrases. In your meditative space and with eyes closed repeat each phrase in your mind slowly twelve to fifteen times.

My arms and legs are heavy and warm.

My heartbeat is calm and regular.

My breathing is free and easy.

My abdomen is warm.

My forehead is cool.

My mind is quiet and still.[8]

———— : : ————

Full body relaxation is the first step to emotional and mental relaxation and is the beginning of the healing state. Dr. Norm Shealy and Caroline Myss in *The Creation of Health* (Stillpoint Publishing, 1988, 1993), write that at least 80% of all dis-eases response positively to daily meditation or full body relaxation alone. The method above becomes a daily habit and eventually sitting down to meditate becomes an automatic cue for the body to relax. Each step in the meditation process leads further into the consciousness shift and deeper toward reaching turiya, samadhi, and the healing Goddess-Void. Some of the many methods of meditation to choose from come next.

My own beginning exercise after grounding and relaxation techniques was the Wiccan Tree of Life meditation that is also a beginning technique in Tantric Buddhism. The Tantric Buddhist methods are likely the root of most Wiccan practice, healing techniques, and rituals. This meditation combines visualization (next chapter) with Kundalini energy raising. The Tree of Life is a Goddess metaphor for the Kundalini channel itself and for the nonphysical energy/electrical structure of the body.

———— : : ————

Begin with the grounding and centering exercise and full body relaxation. Then imagine yourself an ancient spreading tree and feel roots emerge from the bottoms of your feet, growing into the ground. The roots move deeper into the Earth until they reach the golden core of the planet. Draw in this golden Earth energy through your roots and into your feet, through your legs, upward through the channel of your spine. Imagine your spine as the trunk of this tall and wise tree, and bring the energy through every part of your body. Draw the golden Earth energy ever upward through your neck and head, out your crown, and beyond your physical body.

Then feel branches begin, spreading like arms up and outward from your trunk, dividing into smaller and smaller branches and twigs. The twigs unfurl green leaves and golden, soft-petaled flowers. Feel the flowers first as buds, then opening wider and fuller until the over-full petals fall from the branches to the ground. Follow the rain of golden petals back to the Earth, where their essence sinks through the surface to the planet's core. They become one again with the golden center and then are drawn back up your roots. Always end the meditation back at the center of the Earth.[9] return to the present slowly. Stretch and move a bit; be fully present before getting up.

———— : : ————

The Tree of Life is traditional in both Buddhist and Wiccan meditation. There are many variations. In Tibet, instead of becoming a great tree, one may meditate on a yak or some other natural Be-ing in the environment until she feels herself become that Be-ing. The student may also focus on an object—a clay disc, a bowl of water, the glowing tip of an incense stick, or a fireplace in which a round hole is cut in the dark firescreen to expose a circle of glowing light.[10] (More on this type of meditation later in the chapter.) The goal is to make the image appear as real in the mind when the eyes are closed as it appeared when looking at it. In these simple exercises the images increase in complexity until intricate mandalas become as real in the meditation as they are on actual paintings, and then more real. The Goddesses in the mandalas become alive and will act as spiritual guides for the seeker. In Tantric Buddhism, this is called Yidam meditation.

Such work, the first stage in Buddhist meditation, develops the skills of concentration, visualization, and one-pointed focus. Identifying with the tree or yak until one becomes it is called displacing or transferring consciousness. If you are a woman and a tree or yak at once, you are also every other living thing. The exercise demonstrates the oneness of all life. As you merge with the Earth in the Tree of Life meditation, you are both nurtured by the Earth and become Her. This is the first step on the Path to Enlightenment represented in Reiki II as the Cho-Ku-Rei symbol.

Says Alexandra David-Neel about this form of meditation:

> People who habitually practice methodical contemplation often experience . . . the sensation of putting down a load or taking off a heavy garment and entering a silent, delightfully calm region. It is the impression of deliverance and serenity which Tibetan mystics call *niampar jagpa*, "to make equal," "to level"—meaning calming down all causes of agitation that roll their "waves" through the mind.[11]

Another form of meditation is to memorize an inspirational written passage and say it slowly over and over again in your mind. Use the same passage every day for a period of time. Get the most out of its meaning but don't let it become stale. Focus on each word of the passage slowly one by one to the exclusion of all other thoughts. This is done for half an hour once or twice a day seated in the meditative position in a quiet room with eyes closed and body fully relaxed. If your mind starts to wander from the passage and other thoughts intrude, start over, no matter how many times you may need to do so in the session. The mind does not discipline easily; it will

challenge you again and again. Starting over brings it back to work, and the resistance will eventually decrease.

Choose only passages that truly reflect what you want to model your life upon. These are available in the mystical writings of every religion including Wicca. Avoid passages that conflict with your beliefs, those that are harsh and judgmental, and those that disparage life on Earth, women, any minority, or the human body. Simple poetry is not enough, the passage must be more than beautiful—it must reflect a transcendence into one's higher, ideal self. It is fine to contemplate the meaning of the passage but do this outside of the meditative sessions, or in sessions set aside for just this purpose. In the passage meditation, simply repeat the words and focus on them to the exclusion of other thoughts and sensations.[12]

This form of meditation disciplines by filling, not stilling, the mind and teaching concentration and one-pointed focusing. The passage becomes imprinted on the meditator's consciousness, and with focused attention, the meditator becomes its principles. If you meditate on the oneness of all life, you open yourself to it. If you meditate on love and trust, goodness, or healing, you open yourself to these things also. The passage is a more developed form of affirmation, a phrase that states as present truth what one wishes to become. (Examples of affirmation include: "I am feeling better and better every day." "I am beautiful and I am loved." "I am filled with peace.") Use images of what you wish to become and avoid any that miss the mark.

Here are some possible and typical examples of passages to memorize. I have substituted "Goddess" and "She" for "Thy" and "He" forms below:

> Teach me to feel that it is Her smile manifesting in the dawn, on the lips of roses, and on the faces of . . . women.
>
> With the deepening of inner and outer silence, the Goddess' peace comes to me. I will try always to hear the echo of her footsteps.

> In the sound of the viol, the flue, and
> the deep-toned organ I hear the Goddess'
> voice.[13]

Quotes by Hildegard of Bingen, Mary Daily, or Theresa of Avila are positive as well, or from any great woman healer or mystic. My own favorite mediation passages, however, come from the traditional Wiccan "Charge of the Goddess." The excerpts below are from the version printed in *Casting the Circle: A Women's Book of Ritual* (Diane Stein, The Crossing Press, 1990), p. 54.

> Sing, feast, dance, make music and love,
> all in my presence, for mine is the ecstasy
> of the spirit and joy on Earth. My only
> law is love unto all.
>
> Mine is the secret that opens on the
> door of birth, and mine is the mystery of
> life that is the Cauldron of Hecate, the
> womb of immortality. I give knowledge of
> the all creative spirit, and beyond death
> I give peace and reunion with those gone
> before.
>
> I who am the beauty of the green Earth
> and the white moon among the stars and
> the mysteries of the waters. I call upon
> your soul to arise and come unto me. For
> I am the soul of nature that gives life to
> the universe.
>
> I have been with you from the begin-
> ning and I am that which is attained at
> the end of desire.

Any line or passage from the "Charge" can be used as a meditative passage. A suggestion would be to start with the first line, use it while meditating until you feel done with it, then go to the next line. (The full text is in *Casting the Circle* and a variety of other Wiccan books.) Do this until the full "Charge of the Goddess" has been meditated upon thoroughly over several months, repeated again and again in your mind and fully contemplated. (Such contemplation is another form of meditation practice.) I promise that stress will drop away, emotional and physical pain fade, and your life will change positively and profoundly.

———————— : : ————————

Yet another technique for meditating is focusing upon the breath, and this is also both Western and Eastern. Start by taking the meditative position, grounding and centering, and going through the full body relaxation process. Next, begin the breathing exercise. Exhale first, then close the right nostril with your right thumb. Inhale through the left nostril slowly to the count of four. Now close the left nostril with your right index finger, and hold your breath counting to sixteen. Lift your thumb from your right nostril and exhale to the count of eight. Repeat by leaving your index finger on the left nostril and inhaling through the right side to begin again. This is one full exercise, called the Purifying Breath. Do not repeat it more than four times at the same session.[14]

If the breathe-and-hold count of four-sixteen-eight feels uncomfortable or forced, try two-eight-four to keep the breathing pattern as normal as possible. Do not try to take in abnormal amounts of air or hold your breath for unusually long periods. Keep the breathing as comfortable as possible within the exercise. Focus on counting with the breaths, and if your mind strays to other things, bring it back to the counting. After completing the sequence four times return to normal slow breaths. Be inwardly as still as possible, paying attention to the thoughts that pass through your mind. Notice them and let them go.

———————— : : ————————

If you have a problem, this is a good time to inwardly pose the question, then be still and listen for an answer. Major insights can come in this way. By this time in working with meditation you have become still enough to hear (or otherwise perceive) them. The above process, as in other forms of meditation, calms, reduces stress, aids sleep, and helps to balance hormones—those brain chemicals that so greatly effect the immune system and health.

Using a mantra (or mantram), a Goddess-connecting phrase repeated inwardly over and over, is another meditative form. It is used differently from standard meditation formats. The mantra is repeated during meditation, but also in daily waking life. It may be used anytime. There is nothing else your mind needs to be doing. If you are waiting in line, washing dishes, taking a shower, lying down ready to fall asleep, or going for a walk, repeat the mantra over and over, focusing on the words and sound. Do not use it while driving, talking, reading, or at any other time that full attention is needed on the Earthplane.

Repeat the mantra at every opportunity, using it to fill any scrap of idle time. Or do it in meditation sessions for ten to fifteen minutes, then stop, and notice your feelings and thoughts afterward. Say the words slowly and with concentration, bringing your thoughts back to the mantra if they stray. Use it at times of fear, anger, or other intense emotions to calm, release, and transform them in positive ways. It is a purifier of emotions and mind that leads to healing in the body.

The mantra operates on the dual principles of words of power and repetition. Words have consequence and effect on human life, especially those reinforced by hearing them again and again. Negative thoughts and words create negative effects and ill health; positive ones cleanse and heal. This form of meditation has all the healing effects of the other methods but in a concentrated way. Despite its simplicity, it requires a surprising amount of mental discipline. While the mantra is not used during actual psychic healing work when the mind needs to be quiet and listen, it greatly helps in self-healing and to prepare the mind for healing states. I use it as an auxiliary to other meditative methods, but not as a substitute for them.

The phrase chosen as a mantra is a specific type. It must be short and positive, must connect the user to her concept of divinity, and must usually contain a holy or sacred name. Once a phrase is chosen it should not be changed during your lifetime, so choose carefully. While some meditation schools tell students to keep their mantra secret, the phrase loses no power if it is made public. Its power is in the repetition of the words themselves. The "Hail Mary" is a Christian mantra, developed from the mala

mantras of India. Buddhism's "Om Mani Padmi Hum" (the jewel in the lotus of the heart) is probably the best known mantra example. The Om's vibration and sound is considered to be the sound that created the universe, bringing matters into existence from the Void.

Wiccan mantras are easy to find. Any Goddess name chanted slowly is a mantra: Isis (Is-is, Is-is, Is-is), Kwan Yin, Kali Ma. Say each syllable slowly and rhythmically over and over. Also try slightly longer phrases or Goddess chants; most mantras are more than simple names. Try "Goddess Bless," "Blessed Be," "Mother Goddess, Mother Goddess," or "Yemaya, my Mother, Yemaya." Slightly longer chants like "I am Maat, Maat is me, We are one" is a good choice. My own mantra is "Brede is here"; she is the Celtic Goddess of inspiration, poetry, and healing, also called Brigit. Repeating her mantra fills me with calm, even at the most distressing times.

Eventually, with long use, the mantra begins to sing through your mind whenever you are not engaged in other things. This is considered a direct link to Goddess and is highly positive. It is said by Buddhists that if a person dies with the mantra in her mind, her soul goes immediately to Goddess (Buddha). She will then be reborn in a Pure Land, a place where all karma can be released and Enlightenment come in that lifetime.

———————— : : ————————

Contemplation is yet another meditation method, probably the one most used in the West, and the one most useful for healers. Start with grounding, centering, and full body relaxation. Then focus upon a simple object you have chosen before beginning. The object can be set in front of you or held in your hand. When I first started this method my objects included a pink carnation in a clear vase, a seashell, a crystal, a pine cone, and the flame of a lit candle on my altar. Use only one object per meditation session.

Place full attention on that item, excluding all else. Look at it for a while, then close your eyes and hold it in your mind. Be aware of the object in every way except words: examine it by its shape, color, fragrance, texture, size, and sound. Examine it with all your senses. If you are holding a seashell, be aware of the sea and the beach, the element of water, the life that was once in the shell. If using a candle, connect with the element of fire in both positive and destructive forms, and perhaps with a fire Goddess (Pele, Oya). If meditating on a flower, watch it grow from seed to plant, bloom, and seed again. When meditating on a crystal or gemstone, watch it forming in the Earth.

Try connecting with the Goddesses of each Be-ing or the devas of natural objects. If your mind wanders at any time from the focus-object, bring it back. You will need to do this many times. Start with ten minute sessions, then increase the time. Try some sessions focusing only on the object itself, without its associations. The ability to concentrate and keep the mind focused is essential in healing.

Once you have gained reasonable mind discipline (there is no such thing as perfect), try focusing on your own body. Meditate on your reproductive system, menstrual cycle, heart, muscles, bones, respiration, blood circulation, digestive, and eliminative systems in the same way as you did the flower or seashell. Examine how your body works and what it is. Do this without using words. In another session try focusing on only one organ or body system. Contemplate the system or organ itself first, then take your awareness inside it. If emotions come up, pay attention to them, letting them move through you. You may be surprised at some of the attitudes you have about your body. If a positive emotion comes through, praise it, and let it pass. If a negative one, ask where the attitude came from, then ask to release it. Feel it briefly moving through.

If the organ or system feels empty when the emotion has left it, fill it with light in the color that seems right, or fill it with praise. Give it a positive new attitude. Before stopping the session, ask for a message from the system or organ. You may hear it in words, see it in colors, feel it in sensations, or smell it as a fragrance. You will know what it means. If there is dis-ease in the area, ask it what it needs to heal and follow the instructions. You have just done both visualization and a psychic healing. End the session by doing a Self-Blessing.

——————— : : ———————

For women who are mind and mentally oriented and need words, try the Meditation of the Thousand Petaled Lotus.[15] This is a contemplation form similar to the one above but uses words instead of images. Know, however, that the ability to work with non-verbal forms is extremely important in healing and needs to be practiced, too. The Thousand Petaled Lotus in Buddhism is a symbol of the crown chakra and the oneness of all life. The center of this meditative lotus is a word you choose, and the word's connection to everything else is the lotus' many petals. Try the following for ten minutes at a time at first, increasing gradually to half an hour.

——————— : : ———————

Start by choosing a word that is positive and also has positive connotations for you. Words that are negative or have negative personal feelings can leave you depressed or anxious at the end of the meditation and possibly for days after. Nature words are good to start with, things like seashell, crystal, pine tree, a color, etc. Become experienced with the process before going to cosmic words like universe, galaxy, the Earth, the Void, or Goddess.

Choose a word and contemplate upon it, holding it in your mind. This is the center of the lotus. Soon another word appears, an association to the first, a petal of the lotus. Contemplate both words for three or four seconds, then let the association go, whether you understand the connection or not. Repeat the center word again, and wait for the next association/petal. Examine it and let it go as well, returning to the center. Continue in this way for the time of the session. Always return to the beginning word, and if your mind wanders, bring it back and start again.

——————— : : ———————

The associations can lead to inner awareness and self-awareness. Once you are experienced, the center word can be chosen in such a way as to use it for problem solving. For example, if the question is about a relationship, put the other person's name in the center and see what associations arise in the meditation. If the question is about what you need for healing a particular emotion or dis-ease, put those words one at a time in the center and be open to the associations and responses.

By the time you have become proficient in all the meditations in this chapter, you will have become familiar with the central skill needed for healing and self-healing. The shift from the daily mind that hops from one thought and subject to another to the alpha meditative state that is focused and still is the change from dis-ease to healing. It is the ability to make this shift that creates a healer, and the ability comes automatically by practicing meditation every day.

A controlled, quiet mind does not develop immediately. Any skill takes time and practice, but in meditation the practice is the goal itself. The peace that comes from it makes the daily exercise pleasant and worthwhile. Meditation is a positive, lifelong habit. Just doing it to reduce stress is a healing, and becoming skilled at it works seeming miracles. When visualization is added to the meditative state, profound changes result, coming powerfully and rapidly on every level.

Notes

1 Michael Van Straten, ND, DO, *The Complete Natural Health Consultant* (New York, NY, Prentice Hall Press, 1987), p. 43.

2 Deepak Chopra, MD, *Quantum Healing: Exploring the Frontiers of Mind/Body Medicine* (New York, NY, Bantam Books, 1989), p. 157, and Marc Ian Barasch, *The Healing Path*, p. 264.

3 *Ibid.*, pp. 176–180.

4 John Blofeld, *The Tantric Mysticism of Tibet: A Practical Guide to Theory, Purpose and Techniques of Tantric Meditation* (New York, NY, Arkana Books, 1970), pp. 61–62.

5 E. A. Burtt, *The Teachings of the Compassionate Buddha* (New York, NY, Mentor Books, 1955), p. 197.

6 Lawrence LeShan, Ph.D., *How to Meditate: A Guide to Self-Discovery* (New York, NY, Bantam Books, 1974), p. 29.

7 *Ibid.*, pp. 29–31.

8 C. Norman Shealy, MD, Ph.D. and Carolyn M. Myss, M.A., *The Creation of Health: The Emotional, Psychological and Spiritual Responses that Promote Health and Healing* (Walpole, NH, Stillpoint Publishing, 1988, 1993), p. 358.

9 Traditional. Adapted from Starhawk, *The Spiral Dance: A Rebirth of the Ancient Religion of the Great Goddess* (San Francisco, CA, Harper and Row Publishers, 1979), p. 44. Also Alma Daniel, Timothy Wyllie and Andrew Ramer, *Ask Your Angels* (New York, NY, Ballantine Books, 1992), pp. 109–111.

10 Alexandra David-Neel, *Magic and Mystery in Tibet* (New York, NY, Dover Publications, 1932, 1971), pp. 272–276.

11 *Ibid.*, p. 276.

12 Eknath Easwaran, *Meditation: A Simple Eight-Point Program for Translating Spiritual Ideals into Daily Life* (Tomales, CA, Nilgiri Press, 1991), pp. 38–40.

13 Paramahansa Yogananda, *Metaphysical Meditations* (Los Angeles, CA, Self-Realization Fellowship, 1964, 1989), pp. 54–57.

14 Earlyne C. Chaney and Robert R. Chaney, *Astara's Book of Life: The Holy Breath in Man*, Second Degree, Lesson Four (Upland, CA, Astara, 1966), pp. 23–24.

15 Lawrence LeShan, *How to Meditate*, pp. 63–66.

CHAPTER TWO

Visualization

Buddhist philosophy—Buddhism is much more a philosophy than an actual religion—states that all reality is a creation of Mind from the Void. Matter is then manifested by Mind through the Nonvoid of limitless possibility. Mind is the ultimate reality. Enlightenment (Liberation, freedom from rebirth) comes from within oneself through the human mind touching the Universal Mind. This is the only way to reach or achieve it. All things are Mind and the Mind is knowable. The Universal Mind is the combination of all individual minds, and the Buddha-Mind or Buddha-nature (Goddess-within in Wiccan terms), is present in all Be-ings and partakes of its reality. All Be-ings and states of Be-ing are created from it. Mind in its pure state is the perfection of the Buddha (Goddess) proceeding from the emptiness of the Void. It is the oneness of all life and Be-ing, the first Source.

The individual human mind is separated from the perfection of Mind and the Void by the ego that creates the illusion of separation. The ego sees a separate, isolated self rather than universal oneness, and its resulting miscomprehension of reality creates all the dis-ease and suffering in its lifetime and in the world. The ego in its quest for a reality it cannot comprehend creates and holds onto desires, greed, longings, attachments, and painful emotions.

These in turn "cloud the mirror" and prevent the person's full understanding and return to oneness. The illusions of an ego-clouded mind build during a lifetime and those that are unresolved at death become the soul's karma, to be resolved or built upon further in future incarnations.

Though the "mirror" may be clouded, Mind beyond it remains pure. When the seeker begins to understand that the ego is illusory, she begins to comprehend reality and to understand her own mind and the universal Source. In the quote from John Blofeld below, I have changed "he" to "she."

> Now looking deeply into her mind,
> the adept perceives that all appearances
> are her own preconceived concepts, and
> this knowledge makes them vanish like
> clouds. . . . She becomes aware that the
> mind shines neither internally or exter-
> nally, being omnipresent.
> The adept is then taught to perceive
> that her own mind and the minds of all
> sentient beings are inseparably one.[1]

What does this mean in Goddess and healing terms? It means that the mind is the operating force of all creation. The individual's mind creates the individual's lifetime, and the Goddess Mind creates the universe. Yet the Goddess Mind is a combination of all the individual minds. Reality is created in the mind as oneness. When incarnated into bodies, the desires (fear of separation from Goddess) of the individual mind cloud our understanding of oneness and the process of creation. Because we forget the oneness of all life and forget that we are Goddess, Earthplane illusions (the ego) mar the perfection of our Be-ings.

These illusions, basically negative thoughts and emotions that "cloud the mirror" and distort our perceptions of reality, cause dis-ease in individuals as well as collectively on the planet. By understanding that our minds create our realities and by choosing positive creations from the attitude of oneness and Goddess-within, we heal ourselves and the Earth. Women are only limited by our abilities to do this. And any ability can be learned and trained.

This is not to discount the effects of society on individual lives. Women and a variety of others on Earth—minority races and religions, poor people, gay men and lesbians, children, elders, the disabled, animals—are clearly and undeniably oppressed. Poverty is a primary source of stress and of other conditions leading to dis-ease. Yet the ability of the mind to create its own conditions and realities has great positive effect despite the errors of the prevailing society.

The development of lesbian culture, for example, has greatly lightened lesbians' perceptions of being alone in a hostile world. It has raised the quality of lesbian lives and lessened all women's oppression. Such changes of mind also ultimately affect and change the societal mind. The negative stresses of oppression have less damaging results on women who have the courage and support to refuse them and create a more positive reality.

Nor does the concept of mind creating reality mean that women cause or choose their own diseases. I hope no healer I ever train takes this view of blaming anyone for her illness or her pain. If she does this, she didn't learn it from me. The conditions of one's life or one's pain (one's painful emotions) may be the source (or one source) of illness, but no one chooses pain or dis-ease consciously or deliberately. Where the mind can be trained, however, to heal those conditions or pain, much dis-ease may also be healed.

The errors (fears) of one's mind in past lifetimes can also be a source of dis-ease in this life, and this is called negative karma. Again, there is no point in blaming someone for events of another lifetime, when she may have been the same soul but was literally a different person. If there is consciousness of that past life in this life, it is probably only rudimentary. Karma is simply life lessons, things to achieve and learn this time around, opportunities for growth and things to heal. That learning is why we are here for another lifetime. The ability of the mind to choose and create a new reality heals karma, allowing the women to heal old fears, change old patterns, resolve unfinished conflicts and relationships, and return to a positive balance that prevents more negative karma from accruing. Each success in this is to be applauded but there is to be no blame. Each soul has her own life path and curriculum.

We are who we think we are, so the first step in using the mind, instead of letting it use us, is to stop it from filling us with negative thoughts. When these are repeated they become negative beliefs. Women are generally taught to believe they are "not good enough," when in truth we are too good, too powerful a threat to patriarchal control. When any thoughts coming from a negative place surface, change the belief by changing the thought form immediately. Do this as often as necessary until the negative thought stops. Replace it with a better self-image. Women's self-image is the central challenge to our healing and this is a way to positive change.

For example, a woman spills something and she thinks, "Oh, I did it again. I always spill things. I'm no good." Stop the thought immediately, say "no" or "cancel that" or imagine painting a red X over it. Replace it with something supportive: "I don't spill things anymore. I'm getting better and better." This gives the woman something more healthy upon which to base her self-esteem. A positive self-image (unafraid ego) improves health on all levels.

Thought forms both positive and negative appear visually in the aura to those psychics with the skill to see them. They are quick-moving projectiles of color and light that burst through the emotional body aura. Prevalent thought forms, habitual thoughts, affect the aura in a permanent way, or permanent until the woman makes an effort to change them. Thoughts lead to feelings (and sometimes the opposite) and repeated thoughts register in the makeup of the emotional body that directly affects emotional and physical health. Negative thoughts –> negative emotions –> dis-ease in the physical. By learning to control and refuse unhealthy (negative, harmful, self-deprecating) thoughts, women learn to create good mental, emotional, and physical health.

Visualization is a way to train the mind into positive thought forms, changing damaging creations of reality to positive and loving ones. It heals the illusions (fear and pain) of the Earth-based ego into joining with and partaking of spiritual oneness. It unclouds the mirror. The mind creates human reality, and visualization is the tool for choosing what is created, as well as the skill of choosing positively in an effective way. It is an extension of meditation because it is in the meditative state that the fears and negative beliefs of the ego can be transcended and the Goddess-within Void reached. Woman as Goddess creates herself with her thoughts.

> . . . visualization is a yoga of the mind.
> It produces quick results for utilizing
> forces familiar to wo/man only at the
> deeper levels of consciousness. These
> are the forces wherewith the mind
> creates the universe.[2]

———————— : : ————————

Thought is energy, an energy than can be made visible to anyone, whether she has the skill of seeing thought forms or not. A beginning psychic development game is to light a candle, to sit facing the flame at eye level, and then go into the meditative state. Focus your mind on the candle flame, and when you feel fully focused and centered upon it, concentrate on the flame bending to the left. Imagine it bending in that way. If you have been able to merge your awareness with the candle, as you did with the Tree of Life in the last chapter, the flame will easily and slowly bend.

Play with the flame, move it to the left and right, forward and back. Stop before getting tired—this is surprisingly tiring to do. The same thing can be done with moving a bead suspended directly in front of you on a thin string or thread. Fasten it overhead to hang straight at eye level. Make it a game; working too hard prevents it from happening. Anyone who uses a pendulum is familiar with the phenomenon.

———————— : : ————————

If thoughts are energy forms, then all life is created from energy. Energy is the electrical makeup of the nonphysical aura levels and is the cosmic glue that holds atoms to molecules and molecules to cells. The spaces between atoms and molecules, the universal Void in microcosm, are composed of emptiness held together by energy. So is the human body at all its levels. The physicist's unified field and the Buddhist Void and Nonvoid are energy as well. The physicists say energy is eternal; it can be neither created (it is creation) nor destroyed. Life is energy itself and thoughts are energy.

Here it is in scientific terms:

> Thought is a form of energy; it has universal "field" properties which, like gravitational and magnetic fields and the L-fields of all living things, are amenable to scientific research.
> Thought fields . . . can interact, traverse space and penetrate matter more or less simultaneously, instantly, and with little or no attenuation.
> Thought fields of one person can intermingle with the thought fields (or energy systems) of another person . . . with physical results in the physical body(ies).[3]

Visualization in the meditative state is the way to influence change in the body's field of energy. Such changes can and do transform these energy fields and can be used to influence physical health. They bring a new version of creation from the Void and are the Nonvoid raw material of physical matter. Thought forms drawn from spiritual Goddess awareness and oneness first effect change on the mental and higher mental levels. They then move into the emotional body, healing emotions and releasing stress, and from there they reprogram the physical.

Deepak Chopra describes this medically, as "the reality you accept in the waking state is known to you only from the impulses firing in your brain."[4] I prefer more philosophical ways of putting it, but the fact is that all perception of the mind is interpreted in the brain. The human senses are women's connection between mind and the universe (Mind), and the senses are controlled by the brain. The brain is not the mind, but the mind's access to the physical. It is the brain's response to stress in the mind and emotions that creates negative chemicals which then affect the immune system and lead to dis-ease. The brain, too, is influenced by thought form energy, the transporting and creating vehicle of the mind.

Traditional Buddhist and Wiccan visualization work begins with the senses (and the brain), then goes beyond them. I have emphasized Buddhist philosophy in this book because virtually all the practices of modern witches is derived from Tantric Buddhist training in visualization, meditation, symbolism, and ritual and then Westernized. Tantric philosophy is highly developed; it fully explains what women do, often more completely than women have yet begun to analyze. Training in this skill starts simply and grows increasingly complex.

The seeker who has learned concentration is given a mandala with a Goddess image (perhaps Tara) in the center of its intricate design. She meditates on the mandala until the image is as real-appearing inwardly as it is in physical form. The Goddess inside it becomes real enough to come alive. She speaks to the meditator and becomes her teacher from that point on. The seeker knows that she has created her Goddess/Teacher from the Void with the action of her own mind, and that this Goddess is fully real.

This is a possibility for women who choose to try it in meditation. In healing, however, visualization has a slightly different goal. It teaches the student to reach beyond her physical senses to receive nonphysical information from the energy field of someone she is healing (or herself in self-healing). It also opens nonphysical anatomy to her perception, and connects her to the energy fields of Be-ings that are not in physical bodies, such as spirit guides. This information shows or tells the healer where mind energy (controlled thought) is needed to change dis-ease to health and how to do so. The healing changes work their way through the nonphysical aura levels to the physical body. Any nonphysical level can be healed in this way, and also karma can be healed and released.

——————— : : ———————

Begin with something simple. All visualization is imagination done in the meditative state, so enter meditation first, ground and center, and do full body relaxation. With time and experience most healers learn to shift into this state instantly at will, sometimes by a mind-shift, sometimes by the cue of a few deep breaths. The trance level for beginning healing is very light and will deepen automatically if the healer remains focused. This is the reason for all of the concentration and focusing exercises of the last chapter. The more experienced the healer, the deeper the trance states she learns to move into and the more profound the results.

In the meditative state think of a rose or some other flower. You may place a real one in front of you if you wish. With eyes closed, examine the rose in your mind. What color is it? How does it smell? Is it open or a bud? Does it have leaves? Thorns? Imagine what it would feel like if you touched its petals; stroke it in your mind. If it had sound, what would it sound like? Contemplate the rose for a few moments. Then change the image. If the rose was open, fold it into a bud; if it was a bud, open it. If the rose was pink, change it to red, then white, then yellow, then back to pink again.

Can you imagine a blue rose? If there were thorns, take them off, or put them on if there were none before. Put a drop of water on the flower. Make it smell like a gardenia, and change its sound. Bring in a butterfly and see it flying around the rose, settling on it. Hear the butterfly's wings. Return the rose to its original form, dissolve it and make it reappear.

Experience each change in as many of your senses as possible. Some women are visually oriented, others derive their psychic impressions primarily from sound or touch. Some healers (most experienced ones) use a combination of senses with one sense dominant. My own psychic dominance is in sound—I hear information sooner than seeing it. Touch is second and visual imagery is only third in line for me. Sometimes I receive information visually, but usually receive much more by being told it by my guides. Everyone perceives in her own way and no one way is either better or incorrect. What matters is that you receive the information, not how it comes.

Repeat the exercise above with other objects. Use other flowers; grow a tree from an acorn into oak and back to an acorn again. Visualize yourself putting on and taking off clothing one item or layer at a time. (I won't go into the other possibilities of this, you'll figure them out! Be aware of ethics when you do.) Along with training your ability to visualize (imagine, create), these exercises train your psychic senses and being to show which are your dominant psychic sense abilities. It is more ideal to train all of the senses rather than only the dominant ones. The senses that seem easier to access are dominant for now, but with training different ones may surpass them. The more psychic senses a healer can operate with, the more information that is available to her in healings.

———————— : : ————————

Now go to more complex visualizations. Seated in meditation with your eyes closed, visualize your living room in as clear detail as possible. This sounds easy but at first it isn't. Westerners are not taught to pay attention. Don't change anything yet, but visualize what is there. Remember to include all the senses again. After the meditation go and look at the room and see how close your memory has come to physical truth. When you are able to visualize the room with accuracy, begin in meditation to remove objects one at a time until the room is empty. Then put them all back again. Then try rearranging the furniture, and put it all back again. Try these exercises with a different room.

———————— : : ————————

In another session look inside your body. Do not contemplate it as in the last chapter, just look at it, engaging as many of the psychic senses as you can. Start at your head and look inside. If your knowledge of anatomy is faulty don't worry about it at this time, just pay attention to what you perceive. I recommend that every healer develop a basic knowledge of human anatomy. Get a health book or *The Anatomy Coloring Book,* and at least learn the shapes and placements of the major organs. There is no need to memorize the names of bones, muscles, or nerves. Move through your body from head to feet, just paying attention.

You may see or otherwise sense organs, or more likely the energy forms that will be discussed in the next chapter. Some women perceive bones and skeletal structure, or you may view the muscles and fascia under the skin. Are there sounds, symbols, sense impressions, feelings, fragrances? How is this image of your body different from the last chapter's contemplation exercise? Draw love through all your organs as rose-colored light before stopping.

———————— : : ————————

Any direction to "see" in this book includes all of the other senses you can access. *Visualization* is likewise a word indicating vision, but it means much more. With this in mind, now look at your body as an energy field. You may see/perceive chakras, aura layers, energy flows, or only a shadowy outline. Whatever you perceive is fine. Remember to bring in the other senses. Imagine a ball of silver light above your head. Bring it into your head, then down through your body, through neck, chest, torso, abdomen, legs, and out your feet. Bring it back up from feet to head and out again, then let it go or dissolve. Imagine the ball as gold, copper, blue, green, any other color, or a rainbow. Imagine it is various sounds moving through your body—violin, electric guitar, flute, piano. Imagine it as various fragrances—lilac, rose, jasmine, gardenia—moving through your body from head to feet and feet to head. Notice how each color, sound or fragrance makes you feel as you play with the ball.

———————— : : ————————

These meditations are deeper than those of Chapter 1. When ending them, make very sure you are fully returned to the present before getting up and going back to Earthplane life. Stretch your legs and arms. If you still feel floaty or spacy, wash your face or drink a glass of water. Some women feel hungry after deep concentration or healing work. The craving is for sugar but what your body really needs is protein; keep cottage cheese on hand. You may think you have been meditating for ten minutes but it's been much longer, an hour may have passed. This type of meditation is better done at bedtime than before starting the day, and working with it before sleep may bring vivid dreams. Some women, however, feel energized by it rather than relaxed.

Begin using visualization for healing. When you drew silver light (or sound or fragrance) into your body, did the energy seem to get stuck somewhere as it moved through? Whether the "stuck" place seemed to be in an organ, chakra, or flow line, it represents a blockage of the free movement of life force energy. There may be several of these, with the light, fragrance, or sound stopping and starting its flow. Fill the stuck area with a concentration of silver light, violin sound, or lilac until it moves through and past the area. The blockage is cleared. Do this again if the energy meets another obstruction.

After the session notice any difference in how you feel. The stuck places often occur where there is physical pain or at the site of an old injury. Though medically "cured," the nonphysical energy of the injury may not yet be healed. Try this exercise again the next night and see what energy imbalances may still remain. Are they in the same areas? Are they the same size? Try it using different colors from those of the night before and compare; try visualizing with different sounds and perfumes. If you have been working with light and color, try different sensory images for the movement of healing energy. Where only light was comfortable to use before, other senses may feel easier to work with now.

——————— : : ———————

In another exercise of this type, in the meditative state with closed eyes, focus again on your inner body. Do not use the ball of light, sound, or fragrance. Instead, ask to feel, see, or otherwise be made aware of any energy constrictions or blockages. Focus on the first of these. Say in your mind to the stuck area, "I love you," and send love to the area. Perceive love with any or all of the senses—is it the color

pink or blue, the sound of violin or oboe, the touch of velvet or cat fur, the fragrance of roses or lily of the valley? Send love without determining what it is and notice what comes through. Be aware of what happens to the blockage as the love energy reaches it. Do this, moving from head to feet at each stuck area you may find. End the session with the Self-Blessing and notice how you feel afterwards.

——————— : : ———————

To do the next visualization, ground and center, do full body relaxation, then fill yourself with Earth or Goddess energy drawn into your feet or crown. This exercise differs from the Tibetan mandala meditation in that the meditator here creates her own image of Goddess instead of focusing on a picture. Imagine what the Goddess looks like and create that image as you did the rose above. You may already have an image or Goddess in mind, or can create Her spontaneously. Is She short or tall, large and big breasted, or small and petite? What color is Her skin? Is she Kwan Yin or Kali, Brede, Oshun, or you? How is She dressed, if She is dressed at all? Create Her clothing in detail and don't forget Her shoes. What is Her hair like in color, length, and style? Is She holding anything in Her hands? Does the Mother appear alone or with other people, animals, or flowers? Does She come with a fragrance or a sound?

Ask the Goddess if She has a message for you, and listen for it. Accept from Her a gift, then give Her a rose and a hug. Imagine Her getting smaller and smaller until She is standing on the palm of your hand. Place Her into your heart, and watch her turn into a pink rose that becomes your heart itself. See the rose fade within you, and its light and warmth fill every part of your body, mind, emotions, and spirit. Thank the Goddess and come back to now, knowing She is there within you. You can reach Her anytime you ask for Her presence, Her healing, or Her advice. Notice how you feel in your heart both immediately and in the days ahead.

——————— : : ———————

In another visualization, return to the ball of silver light exercise. This time, however, give the silver ball, the sound or fragrance the name of a positive quality you wish to bring into your life. Some suggestions of these might be love, wisdom, abundance, joy, patience, or healing. They can also be more concrete things like a new job, new home, or a new lover (name and face unspecified). As the ball enters your body at the top of your head, ask it to become the most effective image for the quality it carries. As the energy moves through, feel the quality you have chosen (the sound, color, fragrance, etc.) filling you inside. If the energy flow stops or slows, ask what the thought or emotion might be that is blocking the quality from your life. Meditate on the obstructing thought or emotion. I suggest using contemplation or the Thousand Petaled Lotus method to do this.

If you choose to let go of that blocking energy form, say so in your mind. Release it by breathing it out or filling it with the color, light, or other image to dissolve it. Do this again if there are other blocks. If you do not choose to release it, meditate on why not. What is the emotion or thought giving you that you wish to keep? If you choose to hold onto the obstructing energy for now, move past the stuck place and go on. When it is time for you to let go of the obstruction, do the exercise again and release it. Sometimes we learn as much from understanding our blocks and obstructions as from healing them. Sometimes (often) understanding becomes the healing or leads to it.

LaUna Huffines in her book, *Bridge of Light* (Fireside Books, 1989), carries this meditation further. Bring the ball of light with its positive quality (joy, in her example) into your heart where it expands and opens:

Next, imagine that you are spinning strands of light from your heart center . . .

> Focus completely on the strands of light as you spin them one by one until they form a bridge. Add more strands until you feel the connection getting solid and strong. Now open to receive the energy of joy as it flows to you across your Bridge of Light. Breathe deeply in order to draw this energy into your whole being. Notice the images that come to you, the thoughts and feelings of what joy is at its source.
> Now anchor your bridge (in your Temple of Light/meditation space) and walk across it to the very center of joy.[5]

Accept the joy energy as it fills you in every part of your Being. To end the meditation when full, return from the bridge and draw its fibers of light (or color, sound, fragrance) back into your heart. Repeat the exercise any time you wish with any positive quality you wish to invoke. The quality can be that of healing. LaUna Huffines uses the Bridge of Light as a tool for helping and resolving a wide variety of situations and conflicts. It begins at a very basic level that leads to advanced work, and I recommend her book highly.

———————— : : ————————

Visualization presents almost endless possibilities. It is the basis for psychic healing and all distance healing techniques (there is more information on these in later chapters). Why not visualize world peace, an end to rape, hunger, poverty, and violence, the regrowth of the rain forests? Meditations of this type are extremely powerful. They heal the Goddess and the Earth. Always visualize in the present tense, as if the image is an already attained fact. Only visualize what is positive, what you wish to create or invoke. Visualization is primarily controlled imagination in the meditative state. Thoughts are energy and they can be used carefully to transform negative energy to positive with profound results. Even the standard medical system is beginning to discover this.

Probably the first of the medically recognized visualization tools is biofeedback, though none of the following tools and methods are universally accepted in medicine. Biofeedback, developed in the 1960s, is based on three ideas. (1) Any physiological function that can be electrically monitored and amplified and then returned to the person through any of her senses can be regulated by the person. (2) Every physiological change is accompanied by a mental-emotional state change. And (3) the meditative state and visualization can be used to teach the patient to voluntarily control the physiological function.[6]

In biofeedback, the receiver is hooked to a monitoring machine that measures a biological function, heart rate, for example. The machine may show an electrocardiogram (EKG) pattern or beep at the heart rate speed. Then the woman is shown how to slow the heart and watches the monitor reflect the change. Simply by changing her breathing pattern or physical position, her heart rate drops. Imagining a pleasant, relaxed scene or willing a sense of warm heaviness to the heart area also decreases the rate, while unpleasant scenes or feelings of constriction or discomfort raise it again. The woman learns to lower her heart rate by using the monitor but may become dependent upon it. She is then encouraged to take up meditation, perhaps the guided visualization type that journeys to pleasant and relaxing scenes, for more permanent ongoing change.

This method of visualization is used to lower blood pressure, slow brain waves, reduce muscle tension, and lower body temperature. It is used to reduce all the symptoms of stress. Biofeedback can decrease stomach acidity for ulcer patients, reduce seizures in epileptics, alleviate chronic pain, and raise white blood cell levels and immune function for AIDS and cancer patients. People with migraines, most of whom are women, are taught to make their hands hot at the start of the migraine syndrome. This interrupts the blood vessel dilation in the head, aborting the disease process. Biofeedback is a visualization technique that probably could be utilized more effectively by including the meditation methods that medicine shuns.

Another method, this time using visualization more optimally, is hypnosis. This is a form of guided imagery based upon deep relaxation in which the receiver is led on a pleasant or strange journey invoking all of the senses. The relaxation level is deeper than in most meditation and the receiver follows the therapist's story line of sensory impressions without spiritual content. Behavior modification is the most frequent goal. The methods and focus are very different from meditation but the profound relaxation state is similar to a deep meditative (theta level) trance.

Though the receiver does not create the visualization herself, she is nonetheless in control of what happens. If an image is not acceptable she can refuse it easily, and leave the trance state at any time simply by sitting up. (Hypnosis, unlike meditation, is usually done lying down.) She practices the procedure at home by playing the therapist's tape instead of creating her own images and journeys. The images are positive and in the present tense, and the receiver participates in the scene; these concepts are followed in every effective visualization form.

Primarily practiced by psychotherapists, hypnosis is used as direct treatment for a variety of diseases, unlike meditation which is a spiritual tool and path. It is considered to be more effective than biofeedback as there are no machines, visualization itself is used more optimally, and the deep relaxation state is more successful in bypassing the resistance put up by the emotions and the conscious mind. Hypnosis creates a sense of wellness and sensory expansion, greater energy, stress reduction, and improved sexual response. It can have permanent positive results in a series of sessions, and is used for the same things biofeedback is used for, plus much more.

Hypnosis is highly effective for many dis-eases that medicine can't "cure," including phobias and stage fright, anorexia and obesity, smoking, and other addictions including alcohol and drugs. It can be used to enhance athletic and creative abilities, heal chronic pain, and stop migraines, insomnia, and depression. Hypnosis is also used to help balance immune function in arthritis, lupus, cancer, and AIDS, and to slow degeneration in dis-eases like multiple sclerosis. The deep relaxation is credited for these successes.

Some of the techniques used in this form of visualization are summarized below, from William Fezler's book, *Imagery for Healing, Knowledge and Power* (Fireside Books, 1990). First is *relaxation*, the state upon which all hypnosis is based. This is induced by the full body technique used in the last chapter, by counting down (induction), and then by creating a totally pleasant scene with imagery in all five senses for the receiver to place herself in and experience. The scene can be fanciful or real.

Next is pain relief, called *anesthesia* or *heat transfer*. In anesthesia, the receiver is given a snow scene (or some other cold image) and visualizes putting her hand in the snow until it becomes cold and numb. When she experiences this in her body, she is told to place her hand on the painful area and transfer the sensation to that place. Heat transfer uses heat instead of cold in the same way. In a state of deep relaxation, this process works and with practice it can carry over to daily life. The method can be highly effective.

Time distortion is another hypnosis technique. Speeding time by compressing a day, month or years into a five-minute visualization, or slowing it down in the image, distorts the mind's sense of it. Time is only an Earthplane construct; it is not real in the universe. Stress comes partly from trying to do too much in too short an amount of time, and distorting time relaxes and reduces the sense of hurry. This creates results like greater calm, lower blood pressure, and fewer migraines, and paradoxically more quality work gets done in less time.

The hypnosis method of inducing *dissociation* is basically going out of body (astral projection), something psychics and meditators do frequently. This is a state of euphoria that can be used to heal phobias: just don't be there, go somewhere else while facing the difficult situation. However, some women have a harder time staying in the body than going out of it, particularly women who have been sexually abused. The method can be used to help women become comfortable being in their bodies as well. The *sex energy* techniques (all energy is sex/Kundalini energy) are used to enhance sexual response, as well as overall energy levels in daily life. They invoke heat transfers to the genitals and use a positive post-erotic image to make an arousing "movie" of sexual success and self-confidence. These techniques are as important and useful for women as for men.

Age regression in hypnosis is also familiar to psychic healing. This visualization takes the woman to a time before a particular negative event or trauma happened and reprograms it, bringing the changes into the present. It can be used for everything from stopping a smoking addiction to healing past incest. There will be more on this technique later in this book; I have also discussed it in *Essential Reiki* (The Crossing Press, 1995). I use it for this life, past life, and karmic healing, though with different visualizations than most hypnotists would use.

One further hypnosis method is called *negative hallucination*. This does not mean creating a negative or unhealthy image but deleting something unwanted from the visualized scene. If the traffic on your street all night keeps you awake, use negative hallucina-tion to delete the sound from your awareness. Soon you won't notice the noise any longer. Deleting any of the senses deliberately also heightens the other senses that remain. For example, if the image involves eating an orange and the scene invokes sound, texture, wetness, color, and fragrance to the orange, but not taste, the other senses expand and the expansion continues in daily life. A variety of scenes are used, adding and deleting each sense. All five senses are always used in hypnosis imagery and these negative hallucination scenes seem very odd and fanciful.[7]

These methods are optimal Earthplane uses for visualization in the meditative state. They differ from visualization in psychic healing in several ways. First of all, healing has a spiritual intent that effects changes in all the nonphysical levels for a physical end result. Much in women's lives changes with it, far beyond the intent of healing a particular dis-ease or symptom. Biofeedback, however, is totally physical, targeting a specific nonvoluntary body function that can be machine monitored. Hypnosis is totally mental in its reach; it focuses upon a specific behavioral change made by mental reprogramming. Hypnosis creates a scene (often a fantasy) with Earthplane or physical connotations; biofeedback creates only rudimentary pleasant scenes. The imagery in healing comes from within the receiver, rather than from without, and psychic healing looks for the source of the dis-ease to heal it on emotional, mental, and spiritual levels.

Both biofeedback and hypnosis depend upon a therapist or technician, whereas in psychic healing a healer and receiver work together or the receiver creates her images alone in self-healing. In psychic healing, information and images may come from the healer, receiver, spiritual training methods, or nonphysical guidance rather than from technology, science, or psychotherapy protocols. These medical methods can be cold, mechanical and manipulative, rigid to the point where they miss the receiver's needs entirely. Yet healing can, and often does, use these techniques or adaptations of them from time to time, and uses them effectively.

One last visualization technique is the utilization of imagery to shrink tumors and enhance immune function, particularly in cancer. The methods are a bridge or synthesis between spirituality's forms of meditation and visualization and the medical system's visualization. It was developed by Stephanie and Carl Simonton, MD, in the early 1970s, popularized by Dr. Bernie Siegel (*Love, Medicine and Miracles*, Harper and Row, 1986), and is being used increasingly today. The medical system is divided about it, as it is about any form of mind-body connection work.

Science wants to know what makes healing with this method successful, but refuses to accept as explanation that the mind, emotions, and body are one unit. Medicine and science also deny the existence and effects of the spiritual completely. Even standard psychotherapy, which works so fully with the mind and emotions, refuses to accept—and actually considers pathological—spirituality and religion as real or useful in healing. Unable to accept why the visualization works, medicine tries to deny that it works at all.

Perhaps the Simontons' central discovery was the idea that patients' participation can create health. Though an ancient idea, this concept is still foreign to standard medical practice today where patients are expected to be passive and take orders without question. The Simontons' practice took the form of several daily fifteen-minute relaxation/meditation sessions. The patient was asked to visualize her disease, see the medical treatment she was receiving destroy it without harm to her, and her own body's defenses stimulating recovery.

The results of the first Simonton program with terminal cancer patients were dramatic. In those who died, the life expectancy average almost doubled from 12 to 20.3 months. In those who survived the three years of the first study (63 of 159), 22.2% (14) completely healed their terminal cancers, 19.1% (12) found their tumors regressing, 27.1% (17) were medically stable, and 31.8% (20) had new tumor growth; 75% of the people were as active at the end of the study as they had been prior to the diagnosis of terminal dis-ease with only a year to live.[8] This was in only the first study and success rates have increased.

The Simontons recognized that the success or failure of the method is in the individual's choice of imagery. They designated an image that is used today more creatively and effectively because it is then individualized by the patient herself. The program also included the receiver's medical treatment in the image, usually chemotherapy and radiation, though the program also works when no medical methods are being employed, or when the methods are holistic or spiritually based. The Simontons' work was primarily with cancer patients, but the imagery is effective and adaptable to any dis-ease, terminal or not.

In the typical Simonton visualization for cancer or AIDS, weak and confused cancer cells or HIV viruses are pictured as rotten hamburger, a grey blob or some other soft, decayed material. The treatment (holistic, medical, or spiritual) is viewed as something that pours over the dis-ease, breaking it down or making it shrink, but not harming healthy cells. An army of white blood cells, many more and stronger than the cancer or HIV cells and more aggressive, overwhelms the weak dis-ease. The dead dis-ease cells are flushed out of the body naturally. The meditator then sees herself as fully healthy and vital, dis-ease free, and fulfilling her life and goals with joy.[9]

This basic visualization in the meditative state is now adapted in a variety of individual ways—images appealing to the user are more effective in their results. One woman might see her dis-ease as fish or reptile food and her rescuing white cells as alligators, sharks, or fish. She might see her dis-ease as an ice cube and her white cells as heat blasters melting it, or her dis-ease as dirt and her white cells as an efficient vacuum cleaner. A child might imagine video game rockets shooting at a wad of tired bubble gum. Some women, disliking the assault and attack model, could see the white cells gently carrying the dis-ease out of the body, peeing it out perhaps, instead of shooting and blasting it. Another alternative is sending the dis-ease cells pink light and watching them absorb love and become healthy.

In a society as troubled by violence as ours is, this more peaceful viewpoint feels highly positive.

A patient once pointed out, "As my immune system became more ferocious and I saw it attacking the tumors, it only seem to intensify the tightness in my gut. And my stomach cancer became more of a problem. Rather than using aggression to encourage the immune system, visualizing white alligators (lymphocytes) ravaging rotten hamburger (cancer tumors), I began instead to imagine sending love. What a relief not to stimulate hate anymore in my gut, not to fear myself there anymore."[10]

When some teachers of this method ask their students to choose their images, they also ask them to draw them. The stronger the white cells/rescuer image and the weaker the dis-ease cell, the more effective the healing results. Jeanne Achterberg studied what kinds of images work best:

> Visualizations of archetypal figures who fight for God and country to protect their people presaged good clinical outcomes. Those patients whose disease-fighters were animals with killer instincts—sharks, bears, vicious dogs—fared slightly less well. . . . Weak or amorphous symbols had poor responses, and those with the worst prognoses could "see" their cancer but could not visualize their immune systems at all.[11]

Some effective visualizations for white cell rescuers might be Joan of Arc, the Angel of Healing, the destroyer Goddesses Kali or Oya, or gentle Kwan Yin. Positive medicine flooding the body could be golden light (or the color of your choice), love, a green disinfectant, or sweet music. Try sending "a group of loving troubadours to 'caress and massage and tickle' (the dis-ease) away."[12] The weak dis-ease cells could be herded out of the body like sheep or totally transformed, changing sides to become healed, healthy cells and positive helpers. One gay man with AIDS visualized his healing image as pink love-essence coating his body inside, healing and soothing every cell and organ. He then talked to the virus, telling it, "You're in a body that loves you. . . . You can rest. . . . You're so safe you can go to sleep." His AIDS went into remission.[13]

Though developed for healing cancer, this form of visualization can be adapted for any dis-ease, from mild and temporary to serious and life-threatening. This is not a method to use only in desperate straits; it can heal mild dis-eases, easily preventing them from becoming more serious, and lessening their duration. It is the essence of psychic healing and self-healing. The battlefield imagery is unnecessary—people who accept and love their dis-ease (and themselves) more readily heal it than those who in fighting it fight their own bodies. Design your own imagery and use it in the meditative state for fifteen minutes several times a day. Use only positive images of what you want to happen; learn the anatomy of the dis-ease. The more vivid the image, the greater the success. Keep the images simple and have fun with them.

One important caution must be made here. If between visualization sessions you allow your mind to run wild with worst case scenarios, you have canceled the benefits of the healing. This returns to the concept of negative thought forms. What you think, you create. Any time fear creates these negative pictures, refuse them and replace them with the healing image immediately. See yourself well. This may not be easy but do it no matter how often it happens.

For some unknown reason the human brain is unable to distinguish between a real happening and a created image. It will act on what it sees, positive or negative, so make every image count. The images created by negative (and positive) emotions are just as powerful as those in the mind and reach directly into the sources of dis-ease. More is discussed on these later, but healing such things as resentment, hate, anger, guilt, blame, and self-loathing are also necessary for good health. Repeat the image of yourself in full, vital health again and again, and visualize yourself as loving and filled with love.

———— : : ————

Try a healing visualization of this type now. Sit in your meditative space, ground and center, and do full body relaxation. Bring the silver ball of light through you again, asking it to change to the color or sensory image that you need. It stops at an area of pain in your body. Fill the area with love and ask it what it needs to heal. Give it what it asks, if it is positive. Ask for an image of the dis-ease—it is weak and confused and wants healing. See it as drops of muddy water on the ground. Imagine the Goddess of your choice arriving. She is dressed all in pink and carries armfuls of white roses (white blood cells). She scatters the roses, they absorb the muddy water, and the Goddess carries roses and dis-ease away. She returns with a watering can, watering the area with healing light and perfect health. The Goddess is smiling and new pink roses are growing in Her garden. You are the garden. See yourself healed and blooming, celebrating a great achievement. Fill again with silver light and come back to now.

———— : : ————

Use your own images to symbolize dis-ease and healing instead of my example. If aggressive images suit you, use them, but gentler images may be healthier. Melt a breast lump that's a dirty snowball by bringing it in the warm (white cell) sun. Fill your body and dis-ease with love and tell the dis-ease it is safe for it to go away and leave you. Work on forgiveness and releasing painful emotions. Above all, love yourself, and love your dis-ease as part of you. It is there to be your teacher in its healing.

Affirmations are verbal visualizations. They are short phrases to say over and over, and to post around your environment, reminding you to keep positive thoughts. A few simple healing affirmations might be: "I am getting better and better," "I am healing rapidly," or "I am filled with love and healing—all is well." These are wonderful to use along with visualization imagery, but less effective alone than they are with sensory oriented techniques. Comparatively, mantras have more power than affirmations because they call on the names of Goddess and are repeated constantly. (Mantras are a wonderful help when the mind's negative worries just won't

quit.) Affirmations definitely help to reinforce visualization.

The basic ground rules for designing visualization imagery are also the rules for writing an effective affirmation. Both must be completely positive. Be careful what you ask for; you might get it. Remember that what you send out comes back. All imagery is in the present tense "now" form. Use "I am healing" instead of "I will be healed." "Will be" could be anytime in the future and a time that may never come; you want the healing immediately.

Also use "I have" instead of "I want" for the same reason, as in "I have perfect health." Avoid phrases using "not" and "no," saying "I am free of pain, I feel well" instead of "I am not in pain." The subconscious mind sometimes drops negative qualifiers completely, taking "I have no pain" for "I have pain." If the visualization or affirmation does not excite you, if you don't absolutely know that it is right for you, keep working to find the one that does. If the image becomes stale from repetition, choose another one. Both in the visualization and affirmation see/state the goal as already reached, yourself healthy and happy, while saying the phrase or before ending the imagery session.

The technique of visualization in the meditative state is the basis for all psychic healing methods. Like a muscle, the skill grows stronger with practice, and with it one's healing and psychic abilities grow strong. This technique coupled with emotional release is the art of psychic healing itself, and emotions are discussed in a later chapter. Every healing is a journey into the Goddess-within Void to uncloud the mirror and change mind from dis-ease to health. Visualization is women's access to the Mind that creates and defines all life. The next chapter discusses nonphysical psychic anatomy, the road map to the healing Void.

Notes

1 John Blofield, *The Tantric Mysticism of Tibet*, p. 240.
2 *Ibid.*, p. 84.

3 George W. Meek, Ed., *Healers and the Healing Process* (Wheaton, IL, Quest Books, 1977), p. 181.

4 Deepak Chopra, MD, *Quantum Healing*, p. 199.

5 LaUna Huffines, *Bridge of Light: Tools of Light for Spiritual Transformation* (New York, NY, Fireside Books, 1989), pp. 73–75.

6 Kenneth R. Pelletier, *Mind as Healer, Mind as Slayer* (New York, NY, Dell Publishing, 1977), pp. 264–265.

7 William Fezler, Ph.D., *Imagery for Healing, Knowledge and Power* (New York, NY, Fireside Books, 1990), pp. 75–91.

8 Stephanie Matthews Simonton, O. Carl Simonton, MD, and James L. Creighton, *Getting Well Again* (New York, NY, Bantam Books, 1978), pp. 6–12.

9 *Ibid.*, pp. 155–156.

10 Stephen Levine, *Healing Into Life and Death* (New York, NY, Anchor Books, 1987), p. 196.

11 Quoted in Marc Ian Barasch, *The Healing Path*, p. 270.

12 Stephen Levine, *Healing Into Life and Death*, p. 197.

13 Marc Ian Barasch, *The Healing Path*, pp. 271–272.

CHAPTER THREE

The Chakras and the Aura

J ust as the body is composed of bones, muscles, organs, cells, nerves, and blood vessels, it is also composed of layers and centers of energy connected by an encompassing energy field. Standard medicine ignores this energy part of Be-ing, though it is vastly larger and more important to life and physical health than the anatomy of the physical body. It is estimated that the part of each of us that is in our bodies is only as much as a fingernail's worth of the whole. Just as seemingly every solid object is made of fewer atoms and molecules than it is of the spaces between them, so, too, the human or animal body. Living Beings are primarily comprised of layers of seeming nothingness (the emptiness of the Void) filled with and held together by electrical energy fields (the Nonvoid), and created and directed by mind. We are made of much more light than solid stuff, much more thought and electricity than matter.

This "light" we are comprised of needs some definition here. Lately the term is used for nearly anything and everything positive in New Age metaphysics (darkness for the negative), while it has been rejected totally by some women healers as a racist term. Both are incorrect. We are all comprised of light (electricity, energy, information, thought) no matter what color skin we happen to have landed in for this incarnation. Everyone incarnates eventually in all the skin colors and all are positive. We also incarnate in other types of bodies than those on this one planet. I prefer to just use "negative" for the opposite of "light," as I believe in the many aspects of possible darkness, too. Negative also has no skin color.

Other sentient Be-ing planets may have bodies very different from the human form, and the Earth human male and female bodies developed from two different forms that were brought from other planets. People did not evolve on Earth, we were seeded (brought) here and genetically engineered. Barbara Marciniak in *Earth: Pleiadian Keys to the Living Library* (Bear and Co., 1995) states that the Earth body's DNA is a living trust of all the life forms of the universe. People colonized Earth from twelve different root planets, most of them in the Pleiadian Federation and a few from the Sirius and Orion star systems.

According to the channeling of Laurel Steinhice for my 1991 book, *Dreaming the Past, Dreaming the Future (Prophetic Visions of the Future)*, the Earth body was to be designed from the form of the people of Lyra. It was taller and thinner than current human form, may have been lighter skinned, and was meant to be androgynous, both male and female. When it was discovered that this body had hips too narrow to deliver the genetically engineered Earth child, something had to be changed. A race of black-skinned people already lived on Earth, genetically designed previously and brought here long before. They were closer to current Earth form and could birth humanity. The Lyrans became today's men, as they could not give birth, and the other tribe became the women.

The men were considered more spiritualized at the time but women soon surpassed them. The difference in the XX or XY chromosome that makes a fetus female or male is a continuation of the two species. We all come from African and black-skinned foremothers and we are all light. Unfortunately, the rivalry between our peoples—male and female, white and other colored, Lyran/Pleiadian and African/Earth—continues, too, and still needs healing.

Barbara Marciniak defines "light" as "information" (which is also thought) and I accept her analysis.[1] She describes Earth as originally designed to be a living library of all light/information and all species of the universe. This computer of living light was stored in human, animal, and plant DNA. Human DNA, today comprised of a double-stranded helix molecule, was once comprised of twelve strands and contained unimaginably more richness of experience and information. Somewhere along the way in a war between creator planets, human DNA was "unplugged" and its information was left present but not intact and scattered.

> Certain species took the existing species, which was indeed a glorious species, and retooled it for their own uses, their own needs. They disrupted the informational frequency inside human beings, changed the DNA, and gave you the double helix so that you could be kept in ignorance. Your frequency of accessibility was simply shut off....[2]

At this time of entering the New Age, human DNA is evolving again, to develop eventually into its full twelve-strand (beyond Earth levels) potential.

People are changing, growing in awareness, becoming psychic, discovering new abilities that sometimes frighten them but ultimately are positive. Our "light" is returning and we need all the "information" we can get in the quest for wholeness.

This light is not stored or accessed in our physical bodies, but is developing rapidly on nonphysical body levels. Women are becoming aware of these body levels, of the chakras and Kundalini channels, and lately even of a new chakra energy channel and a new series of chakras, the Hara Line. Our composition of light is extending, growing, deepening, and brightening.

Most women healers are aware of the four energy bodies closest to our physical levels. These are (1) the physical/etheric double, (2) the emotional/astral/Hara, (3) the mental, and (4) the spiritual bodies that surround the physical like the overlapping layers of an onion.

Beyond these bodies and beside them is a Body of Light with another series of layers, and further past that is the oversoul. All of this comes with incarnation and is formed by the time of birth.

The structure of the soul resembles the braided DNA helix but is multiple. Up to four strands of the braid may incarnate at one time, though the four resulting people rarely meet. They are called essence selves (simultaneous lives) and each essence self has many incarnations stored in her portion of the oversoul's DNA. Each incarnated essence self strand is matched by an unincarnated advisor, one's lifeguide. Most people also have many more guides. The oversoul has her own awareness. Some people who become aware of their oversouls call them angels, though not every angel is an oversoul. Goddess is the creator and life force beyond the oversoul and animating all the rest.

The energy layer closest to the physical body is called the *etheric double*. It is an energy twin of the dense body and a step-down transformer for energy handed through the line from Goddess down to physical body level. At each step the energy must be reduced to what light our two strand DNA still can assimilate and handle. On the etheric double level is the first layer of chakras that bring energy and light from the nonphysical bodies into the dense body. This is the Cho-Ku-Rei level in Reiki and these are the seven major chakras most healers know. I will describe them briefly in a moment. According to Barbara Marciniak, these seven chakras are now expanding to twelve centers.[3]

The etheric double aura is a direct energy copy of the physical body, reflecting its health. In the course of dis-ease, illness reaches this body last, just before physical manifestation. Psychics often see illness or pending dis-ease that has not yet reached the dense physical and can often heal it before it manifests. Likewise, healing through the other levels,

DIAGRAM 1
Soul Structure 1

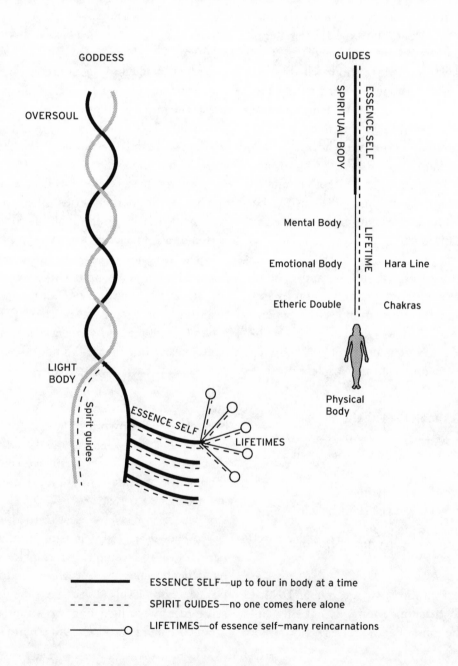

GODDESS

GUIDES

OVERSOUL

SPIRITUAL BODY

ESSENCE SELF

Mental Body

LIFETIME

Emotional Body   Hara Line

Etheric Double   Chakras

LIGHT
BODY

Spirit guides

ESSENCE SELF

LIFETIMES

Physical
Body

——————— ESSENCE SELF—up to four in body at a time

- - - - - - - - SPIRIT GUIDES—no one comes here alone

———————o LIFETIMES—of essence self—many reincarnations

especially emotional and mental, heals the etheric double before it reaches and heals the physical body. The chakras connect the etheric double to the physical body and transform the nonphysical energy (light) of health or dis-ease to the body. The chakras exist on an energy channel called the Kundalini or Kundalini Line.

The next aura body layer is the *emotional body*, also known as the astral body. It is the part that travels in and out of body experience or astral projection, and is the subconscious mind that can be made conscious through psychic growth and awareness. On this energy level is another energy line similar to the Kundalini, called the Hara Line, and another series of thirteen chakra centers. These chakra centers are long known in the East where the art of Ch'i Kung works to develop them. They are, however, just beginning to open in a universal way so that those working with energy are starting to psychically see them. Their opening is a highly important sign of DNA evolution.

We are just beginning to learn what these new chakras do, and will learn much more as they develop. Reiki attunements open and expand these chakras and the Hara Line energy channels, one reason why I believe Reiki to be vitally important for all psychic healers. The Reiki symbol for the emotional body is the Sei-He-Ki.

The emotional body in healing is all important, and emotional release is essential to healing. All of the damage that comes from living in a body—and a body whose potentials have been frustrated at that—are stored in the emotions. All human pain is stored in the emotions, and until that pain is cleared it negatively affects physical health. All energy that reaches the body passes through the emotional body before it reaches the etheric double and then the physical. It is the pain on this level that clouds the mirror of pure mind. Each retained painful emotion wreaks havoc on wellness, and everyone holds a quantity of emotional pain.

The Hara Line contains our incarnation's life purpose, which is frustrated by the clinging to emotions like fear, anger, rage, blame, depression, poor self-image, and inability to take action. The clearing and releasing of these negative emotions and then transforming them into positive feelings is the greatest factor in healing and in accomplishing life goals. The thymus chakra on the Hara Line connects the Hara Line to the Kundalini channel and is the place of accepting universal oneness. Negative emotions provide the separation that damages both spirituality and health, while positive emotions unite the woman to Goddess and Goddess-within. The Hara chakra on the Hara Line is our will to live and to complete our life's purpose, which has been determined before incarnating.

Next is the *mental body*, with another series of chakras as yet unnamed and unfathomed. They have not yet developed in humans. The mental body is the creative mind, the creator of the individual life from the Void by the electricity/light of the Nonvoid. There are two types of mind: individual mind clouded by the illusion of ego (emotion), and the unclouded and pure Universal Mind/Goddess and Goddess-within. The Universal Mind meshes with the individual mind.

The mental body at this level becomes the Light Body, joined to the universal mental energy grid, the collective consciousness, the Mind. The Duane Packer and Sanaya Roman audiotape study course *Awakening Your Light Body* (LuminEssence Productions, 1989, six audiotape sets) leads the meditator through the Hara Line in this energy level and into the Light Body itself. The series uses different names (sound forms) for the Hara chakras than those I used.

The previous chapter on visualization describes how important healing is from the mental level. It is through the mind that we create our own lives and realities, including our bodies and physical health. The Reiki symbol for this level is the Hon-Sha-Ze-Sho-Nen that accesses karma and the Akashic soul records. This level of healing can be used to reprogram the mind, healing past pain from this life and past lives, releasing it in the present and preventing it in the future. This is the level that holds life's negative patterns which can be healed into positive growth. This healing changes lives on far more than the physical level. Mental body healing must first transform the emotions before it can reach the dense body. Energy/light steps down (or up) in strict progression through the layers. Spirit guides are accessed through the mental body, as well.

The *spiritual body* may also have as yet undisclosed chakras. It reaches into the oversoul, soul, Goddess-within, and Goddess. This is the Buddhist Void, the place where ego dissolves and separation becomes oneness. There is no individual personality at this level, only participation in the All. The oversoul is the creating force of the individual, of a series of individual essence selves. These selves are a way for Goddess to experience all of Her Be-ing. The oversoul is like the mother of a family, but all the family members are herself.

Women beginning to make contact with their oversouls feel an overwhelming sense of joy and peace. One woman calls hers the Rainbow Lady, while another calls her oversoul Isis. These are not spirit guides. Perhaps each oversoul is one of the thousands of names of Goddess. My own oversoul, whom I have recently met and who is directing the writing of this book, has told me her name, Ariel. She is surrounded by light that streams horizontally from behind her in what only could be described as wings. Are what we call angels really our oversouls, or are our oversouls Goddesses—or Goddess, or Goddess-within, or all three, or none of the above? I honestly don't know. Meeting Ariel has changed and gladdened my life, however, and produced this book.

Reiki's spiritual body symbols are the Dai-Ko-Myo and Raku, that is—Enlightenment and Goddess Herself. The Dai-Ko-Myo is the woman freed of the need to reincarnate but who does so to help humanity. In Buddhist thought, this is the person who is free of ego; she ends separation in herself to embrace oneness and to heal. Her job on Earth is to heal others of pain and separation and to teach them the oneness of all life. She understands the joy beyond the emptiness of the Void and shows it to others. Kwan Yin and Tara are bodhisattvas, as are probably Mary and Christ. There are many bodhisattvas incarnated

on Earth at this time. They may or may not know who they are.

Spiritual healing means changing the template blueprint of a woman's life. Such healing usually results from grace, which I define as a combination and culmination of hard work with intercession from the oversoul and Goddess. Profound changes happen here, actual miracles. A woman gets up from her cancer deathbed and starts a new life, healed; a woman with AIDS suddenly becomes HIV-negative. Miracles happen every day and healers watch them frequently. I had a 10% curvature of the spine from adolescence that suddenly straightened when I was forty-four years old. I hadn't even asked for it to be healed. I didn't know such healing was possible.

I had a similar experience at thirty-five and became someone totally new. These are the mysteries of spiritual level healing. These healings come from the Void and beyond, from the Source. They are usually totally unexpected.

I will briefly list the etheric double chakras and discuss the Kundalini Line before going on to the less known Hara level. More advanced discussion on the outer bodies and the planes of existence come in later chapters. All the nonphysical body levels together comprise the aura, and each layer is anchored in very stepped down energy to a chakra (or more than one) on the Kundalini central channel. Hara Line chakras are anchored into the energy levels of the astral/emotional body.

The Kundalini central channel, called the Sushumna, runs vertically up and down the center of the human body at the etheric double level. In animals the chakras are lined in a triangle formation; for more information on them, see my books *Natural Healing for Dogs and Cats* and *Natural Remedies for Dogs and Cats* (The Crossing Press, 1993 and 1994). Beside and criss-crossing the central channel are two smaller channels, the Ida and Pingala. These begin at the root center (at the tailbone), and end at the left and right nostril. The seven chakras with body correspondences are located on the Sushumna in the loops between where Ida and Pingala cross. The energy movement of the two winding channels is very reminiscent of the shape of the two-strand DNA molecule.

The channels are the pathway by which Shakti rises from the root to meet Shiva at the crown. Shakti is the Great Mother of the Universe from which all form is born. Her image is a serpent coiled at the base of the spine, or the lightning rod Raku. She is the Void, the Goddess, from which Mind draws life and matter. Shiva, though considered the male principle, was originally deemed female, was created from Shakti and is *unmanifested* consciousness, the Nonvoid. The result of their union is the creation of

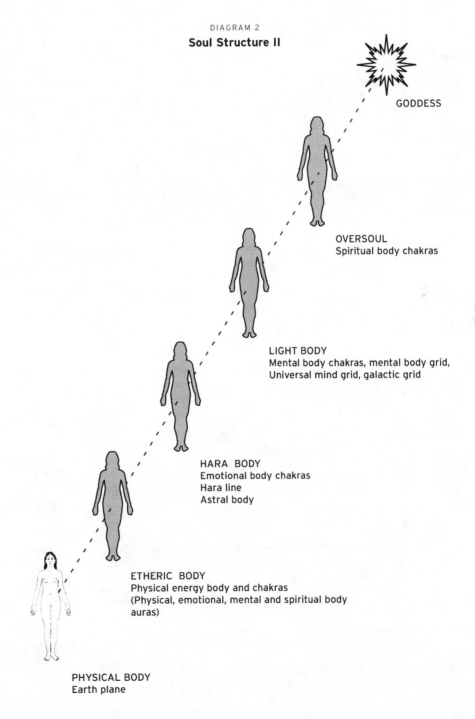

DIAGRAM 2
Soul Structure II

GODDESS

OVERSOUL
Spiritual body chakras

LIGHT BODY
Mental body chakras, mental body grid,
Universal mind grid, galactic grid

HARA BODY
Emotional body chakras
Hara line
Astral body

ETHERIC BODY
Physical energy body and chakras
(Physical, emotional, mental and spiritual body auras)

PHYSICAL BODY
Earth plane

DIAGRAM 3

Soul Structure III
Only a very small portion of self is in the body.

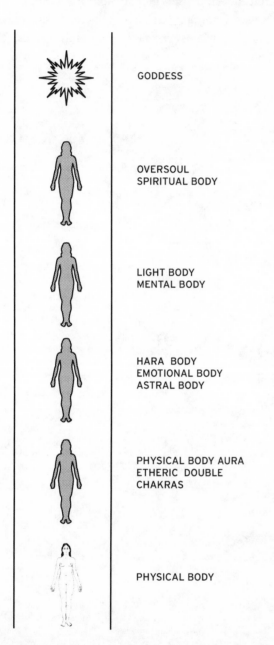

GODDESS

OVERSOUL
SPIRITUAL BODY

LIGHT BODY
MENTAL BODY

HARA BODY
EMOTIONAL BODY
ASTRAL BODY

PHYSICAL BODY AURA
ETHERIC DOUBLE
CHAKRAS

PHYSICAL BODY

The spiraled rise of Shakti opens and purifies each chakra as the Goddess passes through. Yoga and most Eastern meditation techniques are designed to stimulate this rise, but must be done with care to clear each chakra slowly and prevent a too forceful rush of upward energy. Though Kundalini rising is the Goddess' life force, too much movement too soon can cause unpleasant experiences and symptoms, including uncomfortable sensations: heat, electric current, tingling, sensations in the spine, dizziness, spaciness, emotional or physical release, inner sounds, visions, and hallucinations, out of body experiences, and even fainting spells.[5] Is the moving heat of menopausal hot flashes Kundalini rising?

These sensations can be frightening, and too much of this in a person unaware of the cause has occasionally resulted in a mental breakdown. Psychiatry refuses to understand this phenomenon and

DIAGRAM 4

The Kundalini Line
Central and Auxiliary Channels[4]

Major Energy Currents

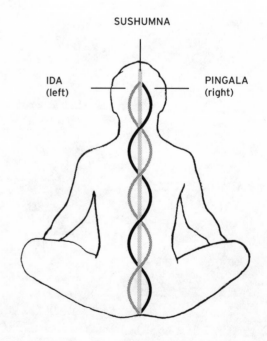

SUSHUMNA

IDA
(left)

PINGALA
(right)

the world and is the attainment of Enlightenment in the individual. To be Enlightened is defined as having an understanding of all things (oneness), which frees the seeker from the Wheel of Incarnation, from having to be reborn in a body. Note the similarities here between the Wiccan Wheel of Life and the Buddhist Wheel of Incarnation.

DIAGRAM 5

The Kundalini Channels and the Chakras [4]

"Ida and Pingala, as they rise from the region of the coccyx, entwine around the Sushumna, crossing from side to side at nodes between the chakras... The same spiral pattern is seen in the double-helix configuration of the DNA molecule..."

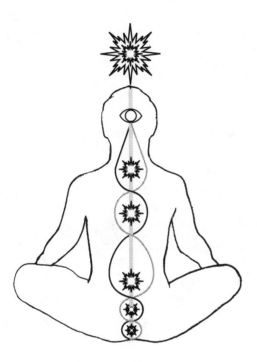

The double-helix configuration of the DNA molecule containing the genetic code of life.

becomes an important part of spirituality, psychic development, and healing. If the sensations become too intense, simply stop meditating for a few weeks. It is also the reason why beginning meditators are told to restrict their meditation periods to half an hour at a sitting. One important way to avoid Kundalini overheating is to end every meditation by grounding the energy, returning to the roots of the Tree in the center of the Earth.

Clearing each chakra, rather than focusing on the awakening of Shakti, is the safe way to start the Kundalini process. As the individual chakras are cleared of obstructing energy and healed, each center is able to hold the rising energy comfortably. This way of raising the Kundalini is a joyful experience. As the chakras open, the woman gains better health, emotional balance, and vitality, and as the energy rises naturally through this clearing process, psychic abilities open and develop. This energy is also equated with sexuality, creativity, manifesting, and cosmic awareness. Sexuality as Kundalini partakes of divine union which is the oneness of all life.

Kundalini moves upward through the chakras, the seven centers that are the progression of human life development from the Earthly to the spiritual. Each chakra measures a step in human growth, as well as a portion of physical anatomy and health, and a level of the four bodies and aura. The first three chakras, the root, belly, and solar plexus, are basic primary needs, those of survival, procreation, and will. The next three, the heart, throat, and brow, are more advanced and more mature, defining love, communication, and knowledge. The seventh center, the crown, is purely spiritual, connecting women with the mysteries beyond. An eighth chakra, the transpersonal point above the crown, though sometimes included with the Kundalini system, I now believe to be a Hara Line center.

The chakras begin at the base of the spine and finish at the top of the head. Located at the tailbone or coccyx in back and pubic bone in the front, the first center is the **root chakra,** represented by the color red. This center holds the basic needs of survival, security, and safety, and the ability to be

suppresses it with drugs. A yoga teacher offers more effective help. For most women, however, when the movement is done with awareness and common sense, Kundalini opening is safe and pleasant. It

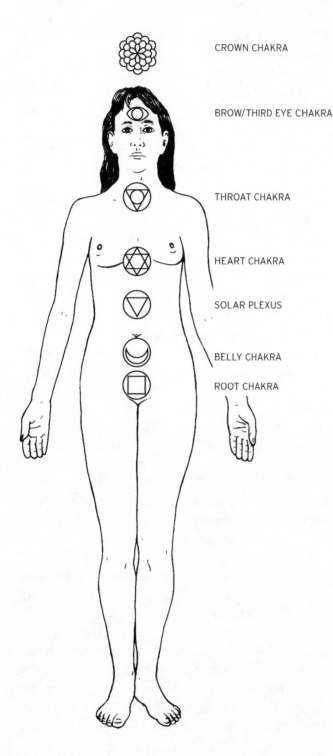

DIAGRAM 6

The Etheric Double Chakras[6]
The Kundalini Line
These are the seven major chakras. The etheric double is the closest energy level to the physical body and is called the physical body aura.

CROWN CHAKRA

BROW/THIRD EYE CHAKRA

THROAT CHAKRA

HEART CHAKRA

SOLAR PLEXUS

BELLY CHAKRA

ROOT CHAKRA

grounded into Earthplane existence in a body.[7] Energy blockages at this level include feelings of not belonging and not being home (no roots), not being able to make a living, and not being able to materialize goals. Accidents, homelessness, and suicidal tendencies are root center issues as well. Core identity is developed here: panic is root chakra emotion.

In the body, root center blockages manifest at the hips, legs, lower back, rectum, and uterus, for such dis-eases as constipation, diarrhea, colitis, painful knees, sciatica, and vaginal problems. Most uterine dis-eases are listed with the belly chakra, but I consider giving birth a root chakra concern. Women who are scattered and ungrounded, and those with adrenal exhaustion or chronic fatigue find healing at this level. Psychic abilities at this center include near death experience and past life regression—birth, death, and rebirth, the inside and outside of the womb. The root chakra's aura body correspondence is the etheric double, the energy twin of the physical body.

Next is the **belly chakra,** located between the pubic bone and the navel. All the chakras except the third eye/brow and crown are also rooted in the spine, extending from the front of the body to the back. Orange is the color for this center, and its basic needs are for sexuality, self-esteem as personal power, and power in the world. When emotional release opens past traumas, the pictures that are stored at this center are released from it. The need to control and hold on, and the healing ability to let go of these emotions are located here. Healing situations of this center include fear or difficulty surrounding menstruation and menopause, the need to mother others and to be mothered, relationship issues, and resentments over being manipulated or manipulating other people.

Belly chakra organs include the ovaries, uterus, fallopian tubes, pelvis, lumbar spine, kidneys, bladder, and large intestine. The dis-eases are those of the female reproductive organs: fibroids, endometriosis, sexually transmitted dis-eases, sexual dysfunction, infertility, spinal disc dis-ease, arthritis, urinary tract infections, and kidney dis-ease. Women who have been sexually abused manifest these dis-eases frequently. The dis-eases stop when the pictures of the traumas are cleared. The psychic skills of this center are clairsentience (feeling others' feelings), and out of body astral travel. The belly chakra is the stepped down energy of the emotional/astral body. One's unhealed inner child lives here.

The **solar plexus** is the third chakra, located at the level of the lowest ribs. Its color is yellow and this center is the body's receiver, distributor, and processor of energy and perceptual feeling. Earthplane life energy (light) enters the body here, to be sent through the whole organism on every level. Self-confidence and survival intuition, business sense, and material level learning ability are focused here.

This is the place of women's empowerment and willpower, and the ability to be materially successful. The center's yellow color also indicates the rational mind—math ability, studying skills, and concrete facts. Anxiety and fear are held at this chakra and released from it. Blockages at this level include fear of one's free will being violated, inability to free oneself from coercive situations, inability to accept responsibility, fear of criticism or of being ignored, psychic attacks, and fear of failure. This is an important center for us women, as it means taking positive control of our lives.

Digestion and assimilation of foods, ideas, intuition, and energy are located in the solar plexus. Organs include the stomach, liver, gallbladder, pancreas, and small intestines. Dis-eases include eating disorders, obesity, addictions, stomach ulcers, diabetes, gallstones, indigestion, motion sickness, nausea, and flu. Psychic skills for the solar plexus are dreamwork and conscious manifesting. The chakra is the first of two levels of the mental body aura.

The second mental body chakra, the center of the creative mind, is located at the **heart.** This is also the center connecting body and mind with spirit, or basic survival with mature needs. Located behind the breastbone between the breasts in front, and on the spine between the shoulder blades, the fourth chakra directs one's ability to love oneself and others, to give, and to receive. The healed inner child lives in the heart. There are two colors representing this center. Green is considered traditional but many women perceive this chakra in its astral color of pink or rose. Almost everyone in modern culture seems to have a hard, hurt, or broken heart, and it is no accident that heart dis-ease is the number one killer in this country. The heart is the center of compassion for oneself and others.

Pain in the heart comes from having been abused or abusing other people and animals, feeling unloved or unable to love, rejection, jealousy, grief, loneliness, and difficulties in relationships of all types. It also comes from witnessing these issues in the world. Deep heart hurts can result in aura obstructions called heart scars. When these release they raise quantities of old pain, but free the heart for softening, healing, and new growth. Dis-eases at this center include any of the heart, lungs, circulatory system, shoulders, and upper back. The psychic skills of the heart chakra are healing and the ability to feel emotion, compassion, universal love, and self-love.

The final three chakras comprise the spiritual body aura, the throat, brow, and crown centers. The **throat chakra,** located in the V of the collarbone at the lower neck, is represented by the color light blue. This is women's center of communication, expression, hearing and receiving others, and manifesting creativity. It contains the template blueprint of the body, mind, and emotions and represents the manifestation of the Nonvoid in the individual. Barbara Ann Brennan in *Hands of Light* (Bantam Books, 1987) calls the throat the Etheric Template.[8] This is possibly the most complex of the chakras as every possibility for change, transformation, and healing are located here, including karmic release. Most women have difficulties with the self-creation of this level; we have been stifled in our growth by a misogynist society. The throat is where women's anger is stored and finally released.

Difficulties of the throat center include being unable to speak for oneself; lack of accountability and cause and effect awareness; being unable to express feelings or sometimes even to be aware of them; the inability to listen to others; outbursts of rage, anger, crying, or abuse; exaggeration and lying; and the inability to cope or to take charge of one's own life. These manifest in the body as headaches and migraines, sore throats, laryngitis, thyroid problems, earaches, and deafness, bad teeth or gums, jaw problems (TMJ), stiff neck, or dis-eases of the cervical vertebrae.

Telepathy is the psychic skill of this center, along with the ability to change and rewrite the template through healing, hard work, and karmic grace. This is the place of clairaudience (psychic hearing) for connection with spirit guides. Much untapped information, creation/creativity, and psychic ability is stored at the throat chakra, which is now evolving in women and opening rapidly.

The indigo sixth chakra, located in the center of the forehead about the physical eyes, is called the **brow chakra** or third eye. The maturity level of this center is quite sophisticated, dealing with thinking and reasoning skills, intellectual concepts, ethical values, applying judgment to daily life, creating one's own reality, and understanding the meaning of life's processes and events. Women's power center is the brow, with its ability to perceive realities and unmask illusion. Men's power center is the solar plexus, with its material rather than conceptual reality base.

The third eye is the place of seeing beyond physical realities into realities considered psychic. Understanding nonphysical truth leads to spiritual and ethical awareness, and the third eye/brow is the individual's Mind (as opposed to mind in the mental body centers of the solar plexus and heart). The chakra's intellectual worldview aids in learning nonattachment and in transcending ego separation. There is no emotion at this level, only analysis and thought.

Energy blockages at this center include denial of truth or reality, paranoia and other mental disorders, refusal or fear of introspection, casting blame, negative thinking, and refusal to learn from life's experiences and past mistakes. The eyes, face, brain, and parts of the immune (lymphatic) and endocrine systems are third eye chakra organs. Physical diseases include cataracts, vision difficulties, hormone imbalances, mental retardation, recurrent infections, and such degenerative brain dis-eases as Alzheimer's and Parkinson's dis-ease.

Barbara Ann Brennan in *Hands of Light* calls the spiritual body aura layer of this center the Celestial Body. She describes it as the place of meditation, transcendence, ecstasy, and transformation, the place of perceiving oneness with Goddess and all that lives.[9] I define this as the center of the Goddesswithin, with the crown as Goddess. It is the combination of heart center feeling and unconditional love with the brow chakra's ability to think, analyze, and perceive Nonvoid potential that makes a healer. Healing is a combination of the information of these chakras. Clairvoyance, creating one's own reality, visualization, and psychic sight and knowing are third eye psychic skills.

The **crown** is the seventh Kundalini chakra, located just behind the top of the skull. Its color is described as violet, or clear with a golden core. The center is women's connection with Goddess and the Void, the place where life animates the physical body. The silver cord that connects the aura bodies extends from the crown, and the crown's continuation leads outward from the spiritual body to the Body of Light and the oversoul. The soul comes into the body at birth through the crown and leaves from the crown at death. This spiritual body center mirrors the root chakra as the two sides of the spiritual and physical life force. Birth begins and death ends at the root and crown and the Wheel of Life turns.

Qualities listed for the crown are often listed interchangeably with those of the third eye/brow. By this level in woman's development, she is fully a spiritual Be-ing and the chakras and aura levels overlap. Some cultures combine the two chakras into one. Brennan defines the crown as the mental (as in creation) level of the spiritual plane. In Buddhist terms, this is the Void, and in Wicca, the Goddess. Some Native American tribes would call it the Great Mystery.

This is the place of women's awareness of having a beyond-physical identity and a part in the universal plan. Attitudes and ethics, character, serving others, courage, wisdom, and spiritual challenges are the maturity level of the crown center. Blockages and fears at this level result in spiritual crises, karmic attachments, inability to understand and trust life as a holistic process, refusal of change and transformation, fear of aging and death, and fear of one's psychic abilities.

This can manifest physically in central nervous system dis-eases like multiple sclerosis, paralysis, muscular dystrophy, autism, spinal and bone degenerative dis-eases, osteoporosis, or karmic congenital dis-eases. This chakra is the last layer of the spiritual body that has physical placement and correspondences. Its psychic skills include mediumship, transcendence, and oneness with the Goddess and universe. The crown's auric field contains the life and life force of the individual's entire incarnation.

The Kundalini system does not end with these seven chakras; they comprise the trunk of the Tree of Life. This trunk has many branches and there are many smaller chakra centers throughout the body. There are chakras behind each joint, in the palms, soles of feet, and of course in the hands. The hand chakras become highly developed in healers as sensing devices and transmitters of energy. Some of the smaller chakras also exist on other aura body levels. Each of the hundreds of tiny energy vortexes of the acupuncture points may be considered a chakra.

In one further comment on the Kundalini Line, Barbara Marciniak describes the development of five new centers beyond the crown. This eventual total of twelve chakras will match the eventual reconnection of the twelve DNA strands. The centers continue along the straight central line of the Sushumna and reach from the individual to the universe. They are beyond the body and have no physical coordinates. Her eighth chakra, somewhat equivalent to the transpersonal point, accesses invisible psychic realities beyond the body; the center is located just above the crown, from a few inches to a few feet over the physical head.

Chakra nine, located as far outside Earth's atmosphere as the moon, connects the individual to the energy grid of the Earth, making that person a caretaker and steward for the planet. The tenth center

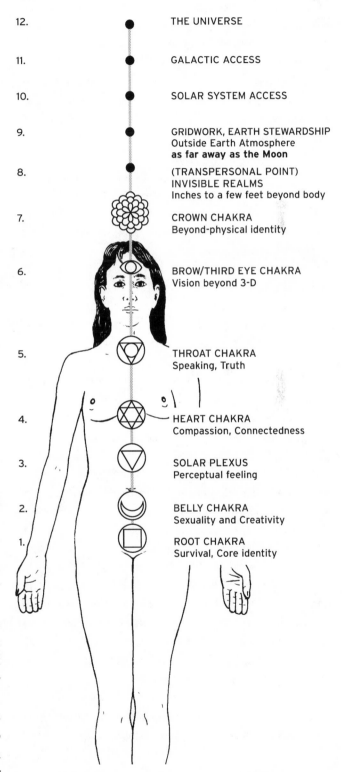

DIAGRAM 7

Twelve Strand DNA—The Twelve Chakras of Barbara Marciniak[10]

12. THE UNIVERSE

11. GALACTIC ACCESS

10. SOLAR SYSTEM ACCESS

9. GRIDWORK, EARTH STEWARDSHIP
Outside Earth Atmosphere
as far away as the Moon

8. (TRANSPERSONAL POINT)
INVISIBLE REALMS
Inches to a few feet beyond body

7. CROWN CHAKRA
Beyond-physical identity

6. BROW/THIRD EYE CHAKRA
Vision beyond 3-D

5. THROAT CHAKRA
Speaking, Truth

4. HEART CHAKRA
Compassion, Connectedness

3. SOLAR PLEXUS
Perceptual feeling

2. BELLY CHAKRA
Sexuality and Creativity

1. ROOT CHAKRA
Survival, Core identity

offers access to all the information of the Earth's solar system; the eleventh to Earth's galaxy; and the twelfth chakra gives access to the rest of the planets, and information of deep space and the universe. By the future development of these centers, we will truly become interplanetary Be-ings.[11]

Energy channels and chakra systems similar to the etheric double Kundalini Line exist on the other aura body levels. Until recently, most women have not had access to or awareness of these other systems, but as shown above, women are awakening and rapidly evolving in these Earth change times. Some women have begun to notice the opening of new chakras, and these are becoming evident as a series on a whole other level from the Kundalini. The transpersonal point above the crown was the first new center women became aware of. Next has been the thymus chakra, and a new evaluation of the Asian Hara.

I have watched these centers develop in myself, at first not realizing what they were. When my causal body first opened I tried to remove it—I thought it was something foreign that didn't belong there. A laughing spirit guide finally informed me it was part of me, and told me to leave it alone. Though my understanding of this level is still rudimentary, I am sharing what information I have. Giving this information will draw women's attention to these centers, and more information will then come.

I have named this astral/emotional body energy system the Hara Line from Barbara Ann Brennan's description of a three-chakra "Haric Level" in her book *Light Emerging* (Bantam Books, 1993). Her line and three centers match my perception, but I see a far more developed system than she describes. She defines the energy channel as "the level of your greater incarnational purpose and your purpose in any given moment."[12] The Hara Line indicates why we have incarnated for this lifetime. Clear understanding of this purpose leads to productivity, fulfillment, and peace of mind in one's life. Energy blockage on this level obstructs one's intentions and accomplishment, and the awareness of this purpose.

Brennan describes three chakras—three primary points on the Hara Line—where I now perceive a total of thirteen. The first of the three primary points is a clear-colored (all colors, no color) center above the head, which I have called the **transpersonal point.** It is a chakra familiar to many women who have placed it on the Kundalini channel. This is the soul's first manifestation into matter, the first opening of energy from the Goddess-Void. It carries the individual's reason to incarnate into her body, mind, emotions, and spirit. It individualizes the incarnating soul from Goddess, giving the woman a personal reality on Earth.[13] Katrina Raphaell, in *Crystalline Transmission* (Aurora Press, 1990) calls it the Soul Star and gives it similar properties. In the ancient Asian yoga called Ch'i Kung, this center is the source of heavenly Ki (Ch'i), or universal life force.

The energy line begun at the transpersonal point moves vertically through the body and enters deep into the Earth. Brennan does not describe this Earth terminus as a chakra, but I believe it to be one and have named it the **Earth chakra.** Katrina Raphaell calls it the Earth Star and places it six inches below the feet.[14] I feel it goes deeper, as deep as the person can ground herself into the planet and root her intention for being here. I see its color as shiny black. This is also a center known to Ch'i Kung as Earthly Ki, or the life force one draws from the center of the Earth. Both transpersonal point and Earth chakra are beyond the physical, above and below it as anchor points of the Hara Line. The rest of the centers have physical coordinates on the emotional/astral body.

Two more major centers are described by Barbara Brennan: one I have named the **thymus chakra** and the other is the Hara itself, which has been known in the East since ancient days. The first is located between the heart and the throat, and the second below the navel. Brennan defines the thymus (which she calls the Soul Seat) as a place holding "sacred lodging . . . very specific to our life task."[15] It is our drive and passion to fulfill the task we incarnated to accomplish. I perceive this center's color as aqua or aquamarine, and see it as connecting the

Hara Line and emotional body to the Kundalini Line and etheric double. More precisely, it connects a woman's emotions to her physical body.

On a physical level, this center protects the immune system, which is clearly affected by the emotions. (See the discussion of stress in Chapter 1.) The Greek word *thymos* means personality or soul and relates immunity to self-identity or life purpose. The thymus chakra is our emotional investment and wish to live and maintain the incarnation. Katrina Raphaell does not describe this center.

Ch'i Kung identifies this chakra as the acupuncture meridian Conception Vessel 17, which Stephen Levine in *Healing Into Life and Death* calls the "grief point." Find this point on the chest between and about three inches above the nipples, on the breastbone. When you find it, you will know immediately; it is painful and sensitive to pressure. *Gently* pressing this point "brings oneself wholeheartedly awake to the grief we have carried for so long and the vastness which awaits a merciful awareness."[16] Meditating on the sensations that come while touching this point opens the emotion of grief (which may include anger, resentment, fear, or other feelings) and releases them. By doing so, one learns compassion for oneself that translates into compassion for others. As Levine repeats frequently throughout this beautiful book, "not my pain, but the pain" (of the world).

The next primary chakra on the Hara Line, the last mentioned by Brennan, is the **Hara chakra,** the Hara itself. The center is known since ancient times in Ch'i Kung as the tan tien or Sea of Ch'i, and is located about two and a half inches below the navel, above the Kundalini belly chakra. It is golden orange-brown in color, but may deepen during healing, even turning hot and red. Women's physical balance center is at this place on the body. In Ch'i Kung, all energy work starts and ends at this center, which is the source of incarnation and the place that the life force emanates from to the rest of the body. The Hara chakra connects one's will to live with the life-sustaining energy of the Earth at the Earth chakra. Says Barbara Ann Brennan:

It is with your will and this one note
that you have drawn up a physical body
out of the body of your mother the Earth.
It is from this center that healers can also
connect to a great deal of power to regenerate the body, provided that the healer
grounds the haric line deep into the
molten core of the earth.[17]

The next three Hara centers are placed between the primary chakras above. The causal body chakra is located between the transpersonal point and the thymus, the diaphragm center between the thymus and the Hara chakra, and the perineum chakra between the Hara and the centers in the knees. They are all Ch'i Kung positions. (None are mentioned by Barbara Ann Brennan, and only the causal body is described by Katrina Raphaell.) The first of these is the **causal body chakra** located in the base of the skull where the neck meets the head at the back. This is the chakra I tried to remove—it looks like crimson yarn wrapped around a golden core.

Raphaell sees this center as blue and defines it as silent peace, the winter Earth that surrounds a seed before it germinates in the spring. She describes it as all potential (the Nonvoid) and the receiver of impressions from the transpersonal point/Soul Star. From this place spiritual energy moves through other centers, "connecting and aligning the impersonal with human thought."[18] The center must be activated and balanced to achieve its purpose of bringing mental commitment to one's life purpose. Is it this activation into life force that changes the color?

I for the most part agree with Katrina Raphaell's definition of the chakra. I also see the causal body chakra as the place of manifesting one's spiritual life purpose, as embodied in the entire Hara Line, into Earthplane physical reality. The "human thought" that is all potential is of course the Mind that creates life and reality from the Void through the Nonvoid. The center is also a major transformer of nonphysical information into consciousness as in channeling, automatic writing, and working with spirit guides

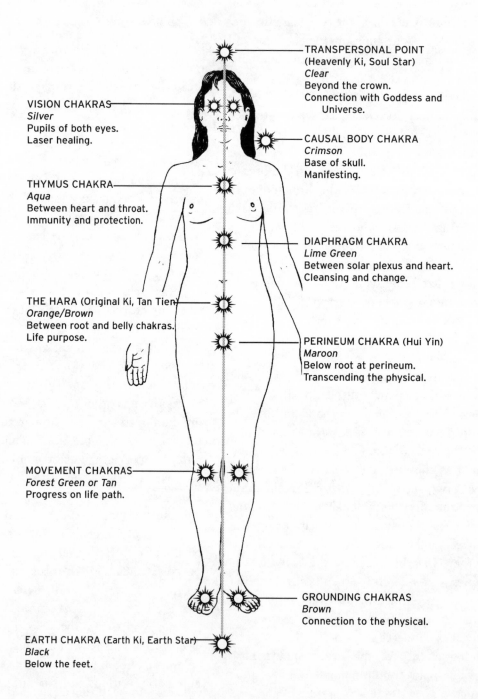

DIAGRAM 8
The Hara Line

TRANSPERSONAL POINT
(Heavenly Ki, Soul Star)
Clear
Beyond the crown.
Connection with Goddess and
   Universe.

VISION CHAKRAS
Silver
Pupils of both eyes.
Laser healing.

CAUSAL BODY CHAKRA
Crimson
Base of skull.
Manifesting.

THYMUS CHAKRA
Aqua
Between heart and throat.
Immunity and protection.

DIAPHRAGM CHAKRA
Lime Green
Between solar plexus and heart.
Cleansing and change.

THE HARA (Original Ki, Tan Tien)
Orange/Brown
Between root and belly chakras.
Life purpose.

PERINEUM CHAKRA (Hui Yin)
Maroon
Below root at perineum.
Transcending the physical.

MOVEMENT CHAKRAS
Forest Green or Tan
Progress on life path.

GROUNDING CHAKRAS
Brown
Connection to the physical.

EARTH CHAKRA (Earth Ki, Earth Star)
Black
Below the feet.

for psychic healing. As such, it is an important center for healers to activate, but this must be done with all the Hara Line centers together. Exercises for this are included in the next chapter, and this is the purpose of the Ki Exercises used in Reiki II training.

The **diaphragm chakra** is located between the thymus and the Hara chakra, at the level of the physical diaphragm muscle, approximately just above the solar plexus. Its color is lime green. It is also the Triple Warmer (T-11) acupuncture point, the adrenal gland center. Duane Packer and Sanaya Roman in their *Awakening Your Light Body* tape series show a membrane dome of energy at this location, which they name by the seed sound of mumin (moo-min). The dome is a filter, separating spiritual from material energies and allowing only what is finer-tuned to pass through. I perceive the activation of this center as causing or providing a clearing and detoxification of any obstructions to the fulfillment of one's life purpose. This is a cleansing of the entire Hara Line.

This detox for me was very intense, traumatic, and often frightening, a deep purging of much astral/emotional garbage. It felt like a ripping away of many aspects of self, with the basic emotion that of fear. Morning after morning for weeks I awoke to overwhelming sensations of fear and panic, sometimes with "pictures" to explain them but often not. Since the primary emotion of much of my earlier life had been fear, I considered the process an intense releasing. When it ended, much of my excessive daily stress and anxiety permanently eased.

I have spoken with others who have gone through this activation; they have variously named the center the "garbage chakra" or "vomit chakra." The best method I found of going through the process—which ultimately is positive but may not seem so at the time—is simply to allow it. Watch the sensations and let them go, neither fighting, resisting nor trying to change them. Welcome the clearing and send love.

The last of the major Hara Line chakras is the deep ruby or maroon **perineum chakra.** It is familiar to Reiki II students as the Hui Yin position; to Indian meditation and yoga students as the moolband or root lock; and to acupuncture and Ch'i Kung as the "gateway of life and death" (Conception Vessel 1). This energy point is located (though on the emotional body) between the openings of the vagina and the anus, where episiotomies are performed in childbirth. This is the energy gate through which Earth Ki (or Ch'i) is brought into the body, up the legs, into the vagina, and then taken and held for distribution at the Hara center. It is the place of activating and anchoring one's life intention and purpose into physical plane reality. Taking the Hui Yin position, drawing closed the vagina and anus to lock the perineum chakra, results in circulating and clearing Hara Line energy through the entire Hara system. More on this in Chapter 4.

Three smaller chakra pairs complete the Hara Line centers as I now perceive them. These are a pair of silver centers behind the eyes, called **vision chakras;** a pair of forest green centers behind the knees I call **movement chakras;** and a pair of brown centers in the soles of the feet called grounding chakras. The pair behind the eyes pave the way to using the eyes as lasers in healing. Those at the knees direct movement forward on one's life path. The **grounding chakras** on the feet root the Hara Line into Earth Ki and root one's purpose into physical direction and manifestation. The acupuncture point of the feet chakras is Kidney-1, Bubbling Spring. All of the Hara Line centers have Ch'i Kung and acupuncture identifications.

Besides the chakras, the Hara Line itself is comprised of a double flow of energy. One channel moves from the perineum chakra up the back, over the top of the head, and down the face to the upper lip. In acupuncture and Ch'i Kung this channel is called the Governor Vessel (GV). The second energy flow starts at the lower lip and descends down the front of the body to end at the perineum. This is called the Conception Vessel (CV) in acupuncture and Ch'i Kung. Auxiliary flows move energy through the legs and arms into these channels. The channels are connected by placing the tongue on the roof of the mouth and contracting the perineum. Movement of energy through this circuit involves circulating Ki (life force) through the connected channels and the Hara Line chakras. This is called the Microcosmic Orbit, or Large and Small Heavenly Cycle, and is the basis of the Ch'i Kung discipline.

The next chapter explores this energy flow as well as energy through the Kundalini Line and chakras. It also discusses other aspects of energy that healers need to know and work with.

Notes

1 Barbara Marciniak and Tera Thomas, Ed., *Bringers of the Dawn: Teachings from the Pleiadians* (Santa Fe, NM, Bear and Company, 1992), p. 42.

2 *Ibid.*, p. 28.

3 *Ibid.*, pp. 55–56, and Barbara Marciniak, *Earth: Pleiadian Keys to the Living Library* (Santa Fe, NM, Bear & Col., 1995), pp. 34–35.

4 Ajit Mookerjee, *Kundalini: The Arousal of the Inner Energy* (Rochester, VT, Destiny Books, 1982), p. 21.

5 *Ibid.*, p. 71.

6 *Ibid.*, p. 11.

7 The analysis of Carolyn Myss influences this version of the seven chakras. See C. Norman Shealy, MD, and Carolyn M. Myss, MA, *The Creation of Health*, pp. 93–119.

8 Barbara Ann Brennan, *Hands of Light: A Guide to Healing Through the Human Energy Field* (New York, NY, Bantam Books, 1987), p. 47.

9 *Ibid.*, p. 53.

10 Barbara Marciniak, *Bringers of the Dawn*, pp. 55–56, and Barbara Marciniak, *Earth*, pp. 34–35.

11 Barbara Marciniak, *Bringers of the Dawn*, pp. 55–56, and *Earth*, pp. 34–35.

12 Barbara Ann Brennan, *Light Emerging: The Journey of Personal Healing* (New York, NY, Bantam Books, 1993), p. 29.

13 *Ibid.*

14 Katrina Raphaell, *The Crystalline Transmission: A Synthesis of Light* (Santa Fe, NM, Aurora Press, 1990), pp. 38–42.

15 Barbara Ann Brennan, *Light Emerging*, p. 28.

16 Stephen Levine, *Healing Into Life and Death*, pp. 116–117.

17 Barbara Ann Brennan, *Light Emerging*, p. 29.

18 Katrina Raphaell, *The Crystalline Transmission*, pp. 35–36.

CHAPTER FOUR

Energy

Healing means working effectively with energy, the source substance of all life. Energy can be neither created nor destroyed; it is used and returned to the Earth and universe. It can be used well or wasted, used optimally or ineffectively, and used wisely or misused. Like electricity, it can be used for both good and harm. This chapter is about understanding energy flows, protection, color, and healer's ethics for some of the possibilities of using energy and healing well. Energy is the cosmic glue of all matter and the body, as well as of molecules, the nonphysical bodies, and the planet. Every culture has a name for this. In India the term is "prana," it is "Ki" or "Ch'i" in Japan and China. Barbara Marciniak calls it "light." I usually call it energy, the Goddess' life force. To willfully misuse it is to violate the Goddess and to use it ineffectively is to miss Her opportunities and gifts.

One of the first rules of Wicca is to "harm none." The second of Wicca's very few and very simple ethical statutes is "What you send out comes back to you many times." Some say three times and others say ten times, but the principle is the same. These two seemingly simple ideas are the basis both of Goddess Universal Law and of the ethics of healing, as well as pretty much everything else in life. The rules are simple: no one is to be harmed (includ-ing oneself, others, animals, and the planet) by anything you do, and energy returns in like form to the sender. Send energy (light, the life force) wisely; give what you wish to receive.

That healers are not to cause harm seems simple enough but has many ramifications. What is harm and what is good? Who is to define harm or good? Some situations are fairly simple and evident—healers have good intent. However, other situations are not so simple. Any manipulation of another's energy or will without that person's express consent may seem to be good—the rationalization is that it'll help her to heal—but is not. No healer may ethically perform healing for another without her permission. That permission is most easily obtained by asking her. If she cannot be asked on the physical Earthplane level, ask astrally in meditation. To do this, meditate on the person and visualize her, then ask her in your mind. You will receive an answer, and if the answer is "no" it must be honored. This method also works with animals, infants, and children, and with adults who are unconscious.

In a healing situation, if what you think a woman needs differs from what she chooses to have you do, the receiver's free will is paramount. To violate her will invokes the manyfold law, with consequences immediate or later and karma for future lifetimes. If what the receiver wants is something the healer feels is wrong for either or them or unethical in any way, the healer has the right to refuse. Rule one in healing is to honor free will, harming none.

This also means that everyone involved in a healing situation must benefit from it or not be injured by it. If a situation is between two people and one of them comes to you for healing, the effects of the healing cannot harm, manipulate, or violate the free will of either. Even in the case where someone feels she is being injured by the other person, the solution must benefit both. For example, if a woman need protection from someone who is physically or psychically threatening to her, injuring the woman's opponent in any way is still a violation. It is correct to use shielding and protecting techniques, to shut the other party out, but to do no harm. (See below.)

I hope no Wiccan or psychic I train ever misuses her abilities or manipulates, "hexes," or harms anyone. The manyfold law assures cosmic retribution for those that do wrong, and the law is very clearcut. Let the universe/Goddess do the retribution—it is not for humans to touch. To take this into our own hands is to tie ourselves to the other person, to share or sometimes even to take on their karma. A healer's work is not to effect this or any other kind of punishment or to judge in any way, but to heal and, if necessary, protect. Anything else is a misuse of the life force energy we are entrusted with.

Harming oneself also violates Goddess Law, which is also the law of energy. Any act that harms anyone including oneself is a violation. The healer must protect herself from being negatively affected in a healing by the receiver's dis-ease or pain. The receiver is not doing harm by releasing negative energy—that is precisely why she came for healing in the first place. It is up to the healer, however, to know how to handle releasing energy, to clear it

without it hurting her. Some healers take on others' symptoms, deliberately or not. Taking Reiki I is the easiest and most effective way I know to stop this permanently from happening.

Other techniques include surrounding yourself with light before beginning a session, running energy after it (see below), and/or making a conscious choice and affirmation before starting, stating silently or aloud, "Only what is mine remains with me." When stripping off negative energy, attachments, space junk, etc., in the session, place it in a visualized fire or in a cosmic garbage can to be transformed. That way it no longer can hurt anyone. I also usually prefer not to send pain energy into the Earth until it has been cleansed. Further polluting the Earth violates the rule of harming none. If pain energy is sent into the planet, simply visualize it being transformed to something She can use positively, like compost. Before starting any healing, place a bubble of protecting light (energy) around yourself, the receiver of the session, and any animals or plants that may be in the room.

To overly identify with another person's pain is to invite it in. Yet healers inevitably draw to themselves people who have dis-eases and situations similar to their own. Such healing can teach the healer how to help herself, but overidentification with the receiver hampers the work for both of them. Begin any healing with light protection, and during the session enter the meditative state and step outside of ego. Put your own issues aside, outside the healing for the time being. At the end of the session make the affirmation again, "Only what is mine remains with me." In any healing, put the receiver first.

Women often ask me, "If I do healing for someone and take away her dis-ease, am I violating her karma?" In my opinion, no, for several reasons. First of all, a healer doesn't heal anyone other than herself. What happens in a healing session is a three-way agreement between healer, receiver, and the Goddess (or her assisting spirit guides). Healers don't do the healing; they are simply channels, hands transmitting the Goddess' will and energy. What the Goddess chooses to do through the healer's hands is

Her blessing and choice. It is *Her* will to change and heal a person's karma. Many are receiving this release at this time. When someone receives this grace, it is because it has been her karma to do so. Otherwise, the change would not have happened.

The healer's participation in this blessing also affects her own health and karma. As in the case of negative energy, positive energy also returns; as in the case of a negative karmic tie, doing good may affect positive karma:

> We cannot really help others without becoming in some way one with them. . . . The real healer of illnesses and other troubles clears the channels that connect the personality with the inner Spiritual Self. The result is a flow of power that adds to strength and well-being.[1]

Every time we ethically do healing for someone else (including animals and the Earth) we heal ourselves and our own karmic debts.

All healing is self-healing, too. No one can heal any body but her own. The wisdom is in the body, and healers channel only nonphysical (not body) energy. What a healer does with that channel and transmission of energy is to facilitate the body's repair of itself, or probably, more accurately, to aid the Goddess and the receiver in repairing it. The receiver's body, emotions, mind, and spirit choose how to use the energy that is sent. In a self-healing situation, the healer and receiver are the same person. The woman asks to receive the energy she needs from Goddess Source. Spirit guides act as intermediaries between the healer or self-healer and Goddess. They direct by energy transmission much of what happens in any healing. The woman's desire to heal is vital for results.

Healing is a cooperative act, not the action of a healer doing energy work *to* another, but *with* her. Along with permission to do the healing, the receiver needs to cooperate and work with the healer (or at least not block the energy) if any real gain is to be made. I learned this the hard way. For a year I participated with another healer in weekly sessions for a woman who had breast cancer. When I first saw her, I felt she needed medical attention; the three lumps were very large and visible, one almost as big as a lemon. She refused and asked for healing, saying that she knew she would die within a year if she went the medical route. So we began.

During the sessions, I often made suggestions of things for her to do: what to focus on in meditating, how to release and come to terms with past traumas and emotions, ways to move energy through her body. Sometimes I suggested a vitamin or herb, castor oil packs or compresses to help, often giving her the items. I asked her each week to call me in a few days and let me know what was happening. She rarely did anything I asked and even missed some of our sessions without calling to tell me she wasn't coming.

When we asked her if she truly wanted to heal, she always said "yes." At least once every healing, however, she made some reference to being "tired of being here," or "ready to check out," or "not really caring what happened." Confronting her didn't help. I often questioned my involvement in this process, but the lumps in her breast were clearly shrinking. After about nine months of this work, they were gone, and we did a closing healing ritual and stopped the sessions. I didn't hear from her for awhile and assumed all was well.

About a month later, word came to me that the woman was in the hospital. The lumps had returned with new complications, and she had decided to go the medical route after all. She was placed on chemotherapy, to which she reacted immediately and repeatedly with life-threatening crises. After each emergency she went back to the chemotherapy. In less than a year she died. While it is every person's right to decide whether or not she wants to live, I feel a healer also has a right to decide how to spend her energy. Spending quantities of time and energy on someone who cannot cooperate helps neither healer nor receiver.

Women ask frequently about the ethics of charging for healing. I myself do not charge anyone, but consider it an individual choice. Many women make a living at one type of healing or another, massage therapists, for example, and a few as psychic healers. Be very careful of legal concerns, which vary from state to state. A massage therapist's license or a reverend's papers (from a Wiccan or Spiritualist church) may be required for legal safety. Never diagnose and never prescribe, never promise "cures"—the medical system calls this "practicing medicine without a license" and it carries a jail term. I have no problem with women charging for healing. They are expending time and energy, and money is also a form of energy exchange. Some exchange may be needed for the receivers to value what she receives.

I do have a problem, however, with charges for healing or teaching that are excessive or that make it unavailable for average women. The $10,000 Traditional fee for Reiki III training comes to mind. We live in a world of pain where everyone is in need. To withdraw healing from those who need it because they can't pay or can't pay high fees, is I feel an ethical violation and a violation of the energy of healing. Women have been both poor and excluded from the benefits of society far too long and to repeat this exclusion with Goddess energy is inexcusable. When deciding whether or not to charge and setting fees, please keep this in mind. Accepting barter and offering scholarships are often appropriate.

Another healers' ethic is to refuse to blame others for their pain. It has become a New Age "thing" to do this, but I feel it a real ethical violation and misuse of energy. The basis for this ethic is an over-simplification of the very complex laws of karma. We do not consciously or directly choose our own dis-eases, nor can we always directly choose whether or not the dis-ease can be healed. In the case of the woman with breast cancer, she made choices about her dis-ease and healing, the right of every human being. However, no one "chooses" breast cancer. Certainly not the one woman out of seven who develops this cancer today.

The laws of karma set up a series of learnings for a lifetime that are agreed to by the soul before it incarnates and then forgotten at birth. There is no conscious in-body participation here, it is like the programming of a computer before the file is printed.

The learning must manifest in some way, but not necessarily in dis-ease. Dis-ease can be avoided or healed by many things: changes in emotion and thought patterns can accomplish the lesson without it. When dis-ease or pain manifests, it does so because the preset program activates and nothing has yet changed it. There is little real controllable choice in the matter by that time, but there may be much inner choice to prevent a dis-ease from activating or to heal it when it does, by accomplishing the learning in another way.

A healer who tells someone "you have this dis-ease because you chose it" is wrong, and moreover defeats any chance she may have had of helping the person heal it. The receiver of this judgment automatically shuts down and in doing so shuts out any good the healer could have accomplished. Too many healers use the emotional sources of dis-ease information in Louise Hay's *You Can Heal Your Life* or *Heal Your Body* (Hay House, 1982, 1984) and Alice Steadman's *Who's the Matter With Me?* (ESPress, 1966) in this way. Instead, make these definitions into a question, using them only to give the receiver a handle on the why that she can accept or reject. The definitions are also as often wrong as right for any given individual. Use them for insight and information, not for blame or judgment.

In *Healing Into Life and Death*, Stephen Levine calls for a change from thinking oneself responsible *for* dis-ease to being responsible *to* it. No one is a failure if she is ill or if she cannot heal herself of illness. To harm none, also the Buddhist concept, is a pledge not to inflict useless pain. It means compassion in the face of suffering, and who should be compassionate if not a healer? As Levine puts it: "Judgment breeds a tightness that stresses healing. Mercy and awareness breed a wisdom capable of finding its own way through."[2]

Judgment is a misuse of healing energy and to my mind is the biggest ethical misuse today's healers perpetuate. Judgment is ego, whereas compassion is oneness and Goddess. It is only compassion that heals. A healer who cannot be compassionate has too much still to learn to be a healer at all.

Healing based on blame, ego, or judgment can do great harm to both the healer and receiver.

In one more ethical concern, I urge healers to be available to help each other at need. All women are isolated in the patriarchal culture as a way of keeping us powerless and under male control. We healers give of our energy to help others, sometimes many others, but when it comes to ourselves, we seem to be even more isolated than other women. There just aren't enough of us, and our networks sometimes are scattered over a wide area. Few healers live in any one city and even fewer in rural areas. I always take any healer's request for help (and every woman's, in fact) very seriously, and rarely if ever refuse it.

Healers need as much help as anyone else. Because we heal others does not make us exempt in any way from our own dis-ease, pain, abused pasts, or karmic lessons. Most healers who seek help look for others at their level of expertise or beyond it, and there may be little likelihood of finding the appropriate person near where we live. Many times I have needed help and healing beyond what I can do alone. Sometimes it has been there and many times it has not. Spirit guides work virtual miracles but sometimes need to work through human hands. I urge women to form a cordial network with other healers where they live and to offer help on request. When a sister needs it, don't be too busy to be there for her or judge that she can to it herself. This does not invite women to take undue advantage of others' caring; healers must make every effort to do what they can alone.

Let's move on to the concept of energy as protection. We are made of energy and so is everything else on the Earth and in the universe. Thought is energy, the energy of creation, and thought can be used to protect one's personal energy field. I gave a few brief examples earlier: surrounding oneself with light before starting a healing, refusing others' symptoms, and dealing with releasing the receiver's pain in a healing session. Some meditation exercises follow. As a woman begins to expand her psychic energy, situations arise that need to be understood and dealt with in effective and ethical ways. "Bugs fly to the light." As your abilities grow, undesirable energy may occasionally test your light and your ability to protect it.

——————— : : ———————

Enter the meditative state, ground and center, and do full body relaxation. Imagine yourself first surrounded by energy/light and then filled with it. The light can be clear, gold, or the color of your choice; ask it to be your most optimal color for protection. Visualizing light in other sensory modes like music or fragrance is fine also. Mentally play with the energy ball or bubble you are now in. Is it wider at some places than others? Brighter or thicker at some places than others? Is the overall color strong and bright, or weak and dull? Are there breaks in the bubble or gaps, thin places or dark spots?

Now visualize more light filling and strengthening the bubble overall, then look again for areas of weakness. Taking these one by one, draw more energy in through your crown into your body and project it out to heal these damaged areas. Send it from your eyes, hand/s, finger/s or from your third eye/brow chakra. When the light shield is fully bright, with no breaks or dull areas, sit within the bubble and notice how it feels. This is your protection shield, which can be activated at any time you feel exposed to negative or threatening energy. Negative energy can be a perceived psychic attack, an uncomfortable feeling while walking on the street, or an onslaught of cigarette smoke or other people's emotions in a restaurant or crowd. Activate the bubble each time you leave home for work or other activities. Use the bubble before healing sessions to protect yourself from taking on others' pain. (This is not to suggest that the *woman* receiving healing is negative.) To recreate the shield at other times than in meditation, just think of it or ask it to be there.

You can also program the shield for permanent protection, and this needs to be thought out carefully. A shield should not be a wall or barrier. A wall blocks out all incoming energy including what you need and would like to have come in. A wall will very quickly become extremely uncomfortable to live behind. In a shield, energy moves in and out. I like a shield to block out harmful or negative energy, but let the positive and helpful energy in. Likewise, I ask that my shield releases and removes as much negative energy from me that it can. This way, what is harmful or negative from within me is released and is cleared. Every human being has their own negative energy, we all have pain.

Think what you want the shield to do, then state it in your mind, while you are still in the meditative state. Examples: "Only the positive may come in and anything negative must leave." "Only what is mine affects me. Release all that may harm." Visualize the shield around you and come back to now. The programming needs reinforcement from time to time; New Moons are a good time to repeat the meditation. It also can be changed as your needs for protection and healing evolve.

———————— : : ————————

Chakra shields are a variation of this. Sometimes needy people attach themselves to another's energy, and as healers are powerful and often help such people, they are often targets. The person doing the draining probably does not consciously know she does it, but many emotionally imbalanced people are "psychic vampires." To protect yourself from this and stop it, first enter the meditative state and check for cords into the chakras (more on this in Chapter 6). Remove all negative cords before setting up a shield.

Then visualize a shield of usually golden energy forming over one or more chakras. The belly chakra, solar plexus, and throat most frequently need shielding. Program this shield like the previous one, allowing negative energy already within to be removed and preventing more from entering. Allow positive energy and one's own energy to pass freely through. Choose the wording for this carefully, be careful what you ask for. Use the affirmations above or similar ones. Note how the shield feels and how your own energy changes with the shield in place. The person draining you is never mentioned, but she may be very angry with you afterwards, because you no longer will let her drain you of your energy.

———————— : : ————————

To make sure your shields are strong, renew them from time to time. You can also set up shields around your home, car, and pets. Again, be very clear that only negative influences are screened out, and that your own energy may pass through. I believe that careful protection is essential for every healer, preventing much disturbance, energy drain, and even illness.

———————— : : ————————

Try some exercises for clearing and healing the chakras, running energy, and activating the Hara Line. Sit in meditation, ground and center, and do a full body relaxation sequence. By this time in meditation, you may be able to enter the alpha state just by shifting into it, and the preliminary techniques may no longer be necessary. Begin the Tree of Life exercise, grounding your roots into the Earth, but this time when raising energy through the tree trunk, stop at each chakra, beginning with the root center.

See the root chakra filled with golden Earth energy that turns to red as the energy pours in. The color is beautiful, bright, and clear, and the chakra remains "lit" though your attention moves past it. If the center appears dull, fill it further with Earth Ki until the color clears. Now draw golden Earth energy one step higher, into your belly chakra, and watch the color change in that center to vibrant orange. Move through the seven centers in turn, activating their colors and stopping to meditate for a few minutes at each. The root chakra is red, belly chakra orange, solar plexus yellow, heart green or rose, throat light blue, third eye dark blue indigo, and the crown is violet (or white and golden).

When you pass the crown, watch the Tree branch and flower. Draw the falling petals back to Earth; they create a protective bubble of light around you as they fall. The colors of the chakras fade to golden, one by one from the crown moving down to the root center. Ground the energy fully into your Earth roots and the core of the planet before stopping the meditation.

———————— : : ————————

When doing any form of Kundalini rising energy work, this is extremely important. Always bring the flow of energy back into the planet. The energy for healing that is needed in the body and aura levels will remain there, only the excess drains out. This grounding prevents negative symptoms like spaciness or feeling wired from occurring.[3]

———————— : : ————————

In another meditation, choose one chakra only to meditate upon for the entire session. Try starting with the root and each day thereafter moving to the next higher center on the body. Always ground the energy in the Earth before stopping. In the session, notice the color of the center and if it not bright and clear, fill the area with light and color to heal it. If the chakra seems off center, move it into place; if cracked or broken looking, fix it with whatever visualization seems appropriate. Ask if there is an emotion to be healed at the center, or any past events that need releasing. View the situations and emotions, and then let them go. Send love to the situation.

Ask if there is a person (or people) stuck at this center, release them one at a time and let them go. If forgiveness is in order and you are ready to forgive, do so. Otherwise send the universal Goddess love that heals all things. Send forgiveness to yourself and healing love. Use the visualization of your choice for these images of forgiveness, love, and healing, in any or all of the senses. Try the word association meditation described in Chapter 1; look at and release the ideas that arise. Fill with light through all the chakras and then come back to now. In the next meditation session do this for the next chakra, until all seven have been explored. In doing this, you will learn a lot about yourself and accomplish much clearing and releasing. Notice how you feel after each session, and how you feel as the sequence of sessions progresses.

——————— : : ———————

Drawing light through the chakras and Kundalini energy channel is called "running energy." It is done for the same reason that a daily shower is done on the physical level, but works on the nonphysical anatomy of the etheric double. Everyday life offers a myriad of encounters with energy, some of which may include negative energy. These include worries, fears, frustrations, stress, and other people's overflow of emotions around you. Energy draws to energy and some of your or other people's negative stuff can stick. Imagine it to be like dust on a table. Energy also is depleted as it is used and must be replenished: the human Tree of Life needs to be fed and watered. Replenishment also happens in sleep. Running energy clears the aura of this collection of emotions passing through and passing by. It refreshes and refills the etheric double and the chakras.

Use the technique when tired, before a healing to increase your energy levels and afterwards to refill them, and use it to clear yourself of difficult emotions or of holding others' symptoms. Using it daily helps to keep the etheric double free of the effects of stress and negative emotions that could otherwise result in dis-ease. It helps to clear the chakras of blockages from every level, aiding better physical health. Running energy is an optimal stress reduction method, and since cleared chakras are free to expand and develop, it is a good method to aid spiritual growth and increase psychic awareness. Done before bed, it aids restful sleep and positive dreams, and done in the early morning it helps to balance one's emotions for the rest of the day.

——————— : : ———————

The meditation with the silver ball of light is a basic running energy meditation, as is the Tree of Life. Do the silver ball again, this time visualizing the chakras. Change the color of the ball and the light entering the Kundalini channel to each of the chakra colors in turn. Run each color steadily for awhile through all of the centers, the Kundalini Line, and the aura bubble. Notice the qualities of each chakra color moving through; each color has its uses in healing. Add the colors of silver, gold, black, and clear/white in turn and notice how they feel. Black is used for grounding and protection, and each of the other colors has its own characteristics. Each color seems to settle in its own particular chakra, but will carry the qualities all through the body as well. When finished with the exercise, change the color running through to silver again and let the light and movement fade.

——————— : : ———————

Interior decorators are well aware of the effects of color energy on human emotions and well-being. Their use of colors is often the use in healing. Some ways of doing this are by running energy with the color, sending it to fill another person's aura or your own, wearing it, using gemstones of the chosen color, or even use colored light bulbs in a room. These often have intensive cleaning and detoxifying effects; sit with colors for about twenty minutes once a day, no longer. Color is another form of energy and of healing light.

There are the chakra colors. Red is hot, exciting, and energizing. Use it to warm, to increase circulation and red blood cell production, to bring on menses, and to increase life vitality and the will to live. Orange is brightening and mood raising, another active hot color. It heals the reproductive organs, raises sexual libido, and stimulates orgasm. It ends procrastination and initiates action. Yellow adds determination, self-confidence, and courage, and speeds digestion, elimination, and detoxification processes. It is cooler than red or orange, but still warm and active. Heart chakra green, neutral in temperature and activity, is used to normalize and soothe. It calms, heals infections, and balances blood circulation, respiration, and the emotions. Green is a good color for growth and overall healing.

The other heart center color is pink or rose. This color feels slightly warmer than green, and less neutral emotionally. It aids the emotional heart and the processing of emotions, stimulating trust and a sense of feeling loved and cared for. Like green, light blue is an all-healing color. It is cool, calm, peaceful, and creative, heals the throat, eases stage fright, and encourages expression and opening. Blue helps when an emotional release is needed to clear the air and get the healing moving. The dark blue of the third eye is cold, analytical, and astringent. It is used in healing infections, clearing the lymphatic system, and balancing nervous system processes. This is the original "clear light of reason" energy.

Violet or purple is calming and stress reducing. It induces sleep and rest and is often used for insomnia, restlessness, and nervousness. It also connects the woman using it with her sense of spiritual wellness, of being part of a plan and purpose, and in this way it is all-healing, too. Clear light contains all of the natural colors, and is a good energy cleanser, but healing with color is more accurate. Neither fluorescent nor standard incandescent light bulbs are actually clear light, but the new natural spectrum light bulbs are. Gold is an intensely detoxifying energy, as is silver, with the difference that gold is hot and silver cold.

Colors carry emotions for women, so if blue means peace to you, use it to bring peace inside you when running energy. Typical color connotations may be green for abundance or growth, orange for action, pink for universal love, and red for sexual love. Healing can mean green for one person, but blue or gold for someone else. Experiment with color and emotions in meditation, including the Hara Line colors. Each dis-ease state or painful emotion may call for a different color energy, and therefore I always let the light become what it needs to be in a healing. What is most optimal for the receiver's aura is the color that the energy then becomes.

The astral colors of the emotional body include the colors of the Hara Line chakras. These are almost indescribable in Earthplane terms; they are not colors as we know them and have named them. As far as I know, these colors have no names, and trying to name and describe them gives only an approximation of what they are. These color energies are unearthly and beautiful. Often in a healing when light is sent without specifying color, the energy becomes one of these astral colors. It is partly to invite them that I do not designate color in healing, but let the energy turn into whatever color is needed at the time. The Hara Line colors are clear (transpersonal point), silver (vision chakras), red-gold or silver blue (causal body), aquamarine (thymus), lime green (diaphragm), orange-brown (Hara), deep ruby or maroon (perineum chakra), forest green (movement), brown (grounding), and black (Earth).

These can be visualized when asking to see the Hara Line in meditation, and they can be sent (or will appear) in healings. Other astral colors I am aware of are a rose-wine color I call red-violet, a deep purple, and a blue I can't define. There may be more. Each of the Earthplane chakra colors has an astral color counterpart. These colors also appear in the chakras of dogs, cats, and horses (see my books *Natural Healing for Dogs and Cats* and *Natural Remedies for Dogs and Cats*).

Working with the Hara Line begins to open these colors for healing. Hara Line energy work is the Asian, usual Taoist, discipline of Ch'i Kung. The basic Hara Line energy circuit is called the Microcosmic Orbit in the West, or the Small and Large Heavenly Cycle, and is similar to raising Kundalini through the chakras. Whereas energy in the Kundalini Line moves upward to exit through the crown (and must be consciously insisted upon to ground again), Hara Line energy is circular with built-in grounding. The completed circuit prevents problems and symptoms from electrical overload and is safer and simpler to do. A lot of energy can be generated quickly without risk or discomfort. It is another mode of running energy. The Sanaya Roman and Duane Packer *Awakening Your Light Body* tape course raises phenomenal healing and self-healing power, using this Hara Line.

In Ch'i Kung, where the energy pathway is directed in a circle rather than upwards only, the goal is to use the life force efficiently for health and long life. Spiritual awakening comes later. Practicing the energy circle daily is said to be a cure for almost any dis-ease because it heals energy blockages and weaknesses anywhere in the body, and brings Ki (energy, light) to all the organs. Ch'i Kung works with the Conception and Governor Vessels (comparable to the Ida and Pingala on the Kundalini Line), instead of the central Kundalini Sushumna that is focused upon in India. There is a grounded ending to each session, rather than a heavy one-way push of Ki into the upper chakras. By moving energy in a circle, any excess of energy is safely grounded or released.[4]

There are two moving channels of the Hara Line. The Governor Vessel or Channel begins at the perineum chakra and travels up the spinal column and back of the body. It moves in a straight line over the head and down the face to end at the center depression in the upper lip. The Conception Vessel begins at the center of the lower lip and travels down the front of the body, through the Hara chakra to end again at the perineum. These are two straight line energies that are not connected and not a circle or a circuit. They must be connected and joined to

DIAGRAM 9

**The Microcosmic Orbit
Small Heavenly Cycle**[5]

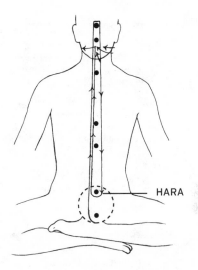

Front view of the Small Heavenly Cycle

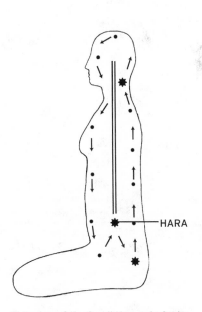

Side view of the Small Heavenly Cycle

activate the circular flow that is the basis for Hara Line healing and Ch'i Kung.

This connection is made by what is called in Reiki the Hut Yin position, and in Kundalini yoga

DIAGRAM 10
Circuit of Ki in the Body[6]

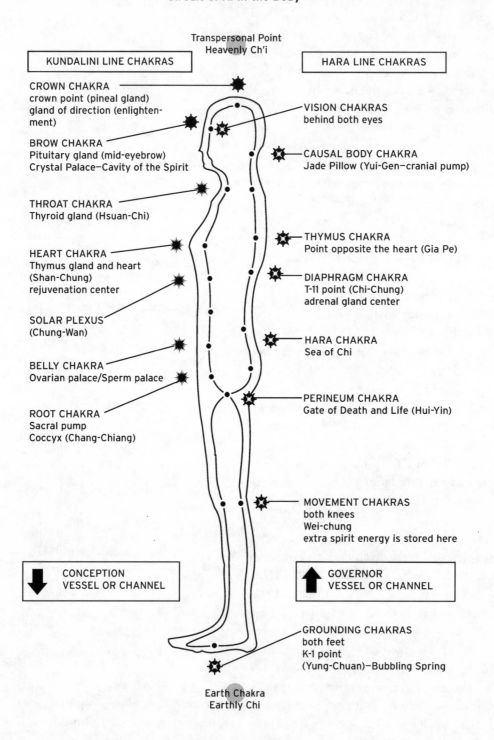

Transpersonal Point
Heavenly Ch'i

KUNDALINI LINE CHAKRAS

HARA LINE CHAKRAS

CROWN CHAKRA
crown point (pineal gland)
gland of direction (enlightenment)

BROW CHAKRA
Pituitary gland (mid-eyebrow)
Crystal Palace–Cavity of the Spirit

THROAT CHAKRA
Thyroid gland (Hsuan-Chi)

HEART CHAKRA
Thymus gland and heart
(Shan-Chung)
rejuvenation center

SOLAR PLEXUS
(Chung-Wan)

BELLY CHAKRA
Ovarian palace/Sperm palace

ROOT CHAKRA
Sacral pump
Coccyx (Chang-Chiang)

VISION CHAKRAS
behind both eyes

CAUSAL BODY CHAKRA
Jade Pillow (Yui-Gen–cranial pump)

THYMUS CHAKRA
Point opposite the heart (Gia Pe)

DIAPHRAGM CHAKRA
T-11 point (Chi-Chung)
adrenal gland center

HARA CHAKRA
Sea of Chi

PERINEUM CHAKRA
Gate of Death and Life (Hui-Yin)

MOVEMENT CHAKRAS
both knees
Wei-chung
extra spirit energy is stored here

CONCEPTION
VESSEL OR CHANNEL

GOVERNOR
VESSEL OR CHANNEL

GROUNDING CHAKRAS
both feet
K-1 point
(Yung-Chuan)–Bubbling Spring

Earth Chakra
Earthly Chi

the root lock or moolband. In a seated position, placing pressure on the vagina indirectly closes the perineum chakra and creates a posture called in yoga Siddhasana, the posture of accomplishment. It is considered the optimal meditation position for spiritual growth and a way of spiritualizing the sexual life force energy. The pressure is made by placing the heel of the foot (or a pillow, crystal, tennis ball or any other object) against the vagina or anus, or the perineum between them.[7]

The closing can also be done by drawing in the vaginal and anus muscles and holding them tight, something that takes practice to hold for more than a few moments at a time. This contracting of the Hui Yin (perineum chakra) brings Earthly Ki upward into the Hara, while at the same time drawing Heavenly Ki downward to the Hara chakra as well. When the two energies meet, they generate heat that first moves to the base of the spine (coccyx, root chakra), releasing Hara Line energy through the body.

The second part of the position is to place your tongue on the roof of your mouth, just behind the teeth. This connects the Conception and Governor Vessels at the top of the body, as the perineum contraction does it at the bottom. There are three possible placements on the palate to do this from, but the simplest is the furthest to the front, just behind the teeth, called the Wind Position. Only light pressure is needed; just touch the palate with the tongue tip and keep it in place.

———————— : : ————————

Try this in meditation position, placing pressure on the vagina and tongue on the roof of the mouth. (Men can contract only the anus.) It is probably easier to contract the anus muscles first: the vaginal muscles will follow. Contract the anus as if you are trying to draw your rectum up into your body. Contract the vaginal muscles, as if trying to stop the flow of urine. If you have ever done Kegel exercises after childbirth, for bladder incontinence, or to stimulate orgasm, the exercise is familiar. The contraction happens anatomically in the pubococcygeus muscle. When both openings are contracted correctly, it feels like air is entering the body through the rectum. Hold this position for as long as possible and comfortable, then release. Repeat it several times.[8] Then hold it closed or place pressure against the vagina to hold it for you.

———————— : : ————————

Ki immediately begins to move upward in the body along the Hara Line, and energy can no longer move downward to leave the body through the feet and internal organs. Connection is made to Earth energy (Earth chakra, Earth Ki), which is drawn upward through the legs into the Hara center. With your tongue also held in place, the light circuit is closed and the Conception and Governor Vessels are joined at both ends. You will feel the Microcosmic Orbit/ Small Heavenly Cycle begin almost immediately moving through the Hara Line. Now Ki moves from the transpersonal point (Heavenly Ki) downward, as well as from the Earth chakra upward. The Hara Line is activated, and the energy cycles through the body in what feels like a moving circle.

Practice the Microcosmic Orbit described further below while connecting the two ends of the Conception and Governor Vessels into this energy circle. The Hui Yin position makes the Microcosmic Orbit possible. This orbit is the basis in Ch'i Kung for all Hara Line and Hara chakra energy work. For serious work with the Microcosmic Orbit, I recommend two books by Mantak Chia: *Awaken Healing Energy Through the Tao* (Aurora Press, 1983), and Mantak and Maneewan Chia's *Awaken Healing Light of the Tao* (Healing Tao Books, 1993). My information on Ch'i Kung is mostly from these sources. The path of energy movement in the Microcosmic Orbit is also the beginning and basis of the Reiki Ki Exercises.

———————— : : ————————

The orbit is done in meditation, with the energy and attention focused inward. Begin by placing your awareness on the Hara chakra. When warmth (energy, Ki) begins to build at the Hara, move it by mind intent down to the perineum chakra then up into the spinal cord. Stop for a moment behind the Hara (at the Kidney point, called Ming-Men), then raise the energy slowly up the spine, past the causal body chakra to the top of the head or the transpersonal point.

Follow the energy/light flow, but do not force it. Hold this energy at the top of the head, or transpersonal point above the head, for up to ten minutes. Then direct it downward through the forehead (eyes/vision chakras). Flow the energy down the front of the body, through the thymus and diaphragm centers, to the Hara/navel again. Hold it at the Hara chakra until the warmth collects there, then start the orbit again, moving it next to the perineum. Repeat the circle several times. Increase gradually with practice to thirty-six orbits per session.[9]

———————— : : ————————

When you are proficient with the above, include the legs and Earth connection for the Large Heavenly Cycle. From the Hara chakra, direct the energy flow to the perineum center (Hui Yin), then divide it into two channels and send energy down the back of the thighs to the movement chakras at the backs of the knees. From there it flows down the calves of the legs to the grounding centers on the soles of the feet. The Kidney-1 (K-1) acupuncture point on both soles is the location of the feet chakras. The point is called Yung-Chuan, Bubbling spring, and is the body's electrical connection with Earth energy (Earth chakra).

Once warmth builds in the soles, move the energy flow to the big toes, then up the front of both feet to the knees, drawing it from the Earth chakra through the grounding centers. Continue the flow up the insides of the thighs and back to the perineum. Return the flow up the spine and divide it again for the arms at a point between the shoulder blades. Send Ki/energy down the insides of both arms to the middle of the palms, where energy flows from when doing hands on healing. Concentrate on the sensation, then follow the flow along the middle finger and up the outside of the arms. When it reaches the shoulders it returns to the main circuit and flows up the spine and neck, past the causal body chakra to the top of the head/transpersonal point again. Continue the energy orbit along the central channel, returning it once more to the Hara.[10]

———————— : : ————————

You may feel the flow of Hara Line energy/Ki, see it, or only sense its presence by tingling sensations. At the beginning, you may not even be aware of a moving flow at all. You may or may not see the Hara

chakra points and colors. In time, as the circuit of light activates, clears, and develops the Hara Line, you will become more aware of all of these. The chakras do not all open at once in most women. Including the legs and arms for the Large Heavenly Cycle is wonderful for healing sciatica, lower back problems, and arthritic knees, and it also helps in overall grounding.

———————— : : ————————

When finished with moving the energy, complete the Microcosmic Orbit meditation by grounding it. This is extremely important and must be done at the end of every session, whether you have done one energy circuit or many. With the energy at the starting and stopping place of the Hara center, place your fist lightly over your navel area. Rub it in a spiral of no more than six inches width. Women move the spiral counterclockwise thirty-six times, then reverse it to go clockwise twenty-four times. Men move it in the opposite direction—clockwise thirty-six times, then counterclockwise for twenty-four. This grounds and collects the energy, preventing electrical overload and discomfort.[11] If uncomfortable sensations develop in daily life from the energy opening, decrease the use of the orbits or stop using them completely for a few weeks, until your body adjusts to the energy.

———————— : : ————————

Practice the Microcosmic Orbit in meditation daily or twice a day, the first thing in the morning and the last thing at night, starting with periods of a few minutes and increasing to half an hour (thirty-six orbits) per session. The Hui Yin/perineum chakra must be contracted and the tongue placed on the roof of the palate at all times in the exercise. As you practice for longer periods, a sense of total well-being becomes part of your daily life and many physical and emotional problems begin to clear. Doing the exercise releases endorphins in the brain, causing a natural high. It removes energy blockages, reduces stress, increases spiritual awareness, and develops the body-mind-spirit connection.

Asian practitioners of Ch'i Kung consider this energy orbit the source of all healing and credit it with the ability to heal any and every dis-ease. It was developed by a man with terminal tuberculosis who used it to heal himself fully. It heals far more than the physical body. For women who wish to explore the Hara Line and Hara chakras, this is the place to start.

All healing is energy work in some form or another. This chapter is just a brief beginning to the art of using energy for healing and life. Ethics, protection, Kundalini work, running energy, color, and the Hara Line energy orbit and chakras are all healing uses of energy. I have tried to show optimal ways to use this Goddess life force well. The next chapter teaches women to access nonphysical Be-ings, spirit guides, for help in using other nonphysical resources in healing.

Notes

1 Alfred Taylor, "Can We Avoid Karmic Debts?" in V. Hansen, R. Steward, and S. Nicholson, eds. *Karma: Rhythmic Return to Harmony* (Wheaton, IL, Quest Books, 1975, 1981, 1990), p. 211.

2 Stephen Levine, *Healing Into Life and Death*, p. 267.

3 The following source has a lovely version of this traditional meditation: Alma Daniel, Timothy Wyllie, and Andrew Ramer, *Ask Your Angels* (New York, NY, Ballantine Books, 1992), pp. 119–122.

4 Mantak Chia, *Awaken Healing Energy Through the Tao* (Santa Fe, NM, Aurora Press, 1983), pp. 6–7.

5 Earlyne Chaney and William L. Messick, *Kundalini and the Third Eye* (Upland, CA, Astara, Inc., 1980), pp. 32–33.

6 Dr. Stephen T. Chang, *The Tao of Sexology: The Book of Infinite Wisdom* (San Francisco, CA, Tao Publishing, 1986), pp. 182–182.

7 Mantak Chia and Maneewan Chia, *Awaken Healing Light of the Tao* (Huntington, NY, Healing Tao Books, 1993), p. 170.

8 Dr. Stephen T. Chang, *The Tao of Sexology: The Book of Infinite Wisdom*, pp. 105–106. I have seen these exercises in several sources.

9 Mantak Chia, *Awaken Healing Energy Through the Tao*, pp. 73–74, and Dr. Stephen T. Chang, *The Tao of Sexology*, pp. 181–196.

10 Mantak Chia, *Awaken Healing Energy Through the Tao*, pp. 60–61.

11 *Ibid.*, p. 59.

CHAPTER FIVE

Spirit Guides

Perhaps the greatest joy in healing work for me has been opening to and working with spirit guides. I first discovered them while reading Laeh Maggie Garfield's book *Angels and Companions in Spirit*

(Celestial Arts, 1984) but only began working fully with them for healing after receiving Reiki II. Their humor, love, and awesome expertise makes every healing session a learning process and a new wonder. They are friends and teachers beyond compare and a real salve for loneliness. They are an avenue of learning for the student who has not been able to locate an Earthplane healing instructor. With spirit guides at work and the opportunity to make use of them in many healing sessions, no other teacher is actually needed.

My first awareness of my own guides was Helen, who appeared in my first spirit guide meditation in about 1985 or 1986. She had bright red hair and red lipstick, and was dressed in a black flapper's outfit of the 1920s, fringe, rhinestones, and all. She carried a foot-long cigarette holder with no cigarette in it that she swung around forcefully for emphasis. She said she had been a happy prostitute and was in my life to teach me about sex and love. Standing behind her, not speaking yet, were a nun I later knew as Theresa (and much later learned was Theresa of Avila) and a blue light form that later still became

known to me as Grandfather. These others did not become prominent in my life until Helen had gone. When she left to reincarnate, I missed her terribly and felt very alone for about a year. She tried her best to find me a lover but only temporarily succeeded, and my lover of that short time saw her as well. Helen interviewed her thoroughly and outrageously on her love-making ability. I had reports later from both of them about each other and the reports were hilarious.

In 1988 Theresa began the work of teaching me to heal and to heal myself. I was told that she had also been one of my past lives but didn't know at the time who she was. Expert in both herbs and energy work, she often appeared carrying a large basket of fresh picked plants, roots, and bark. When I asked her advice she was the voice of common sense—I hear my guides much more often than I see them. She had a wise, wrinkled face, an always neat habit, and a no nonsense attitude. She got the job done and that was that. As my healing became more advanced she appeared in the sessions, an extra pair of hands and a presence clearly felt. Women I did healing with talked to her in the sessions as much as I did. When negative energies needed to be released, or an entity became frightening, or I just didn't know what to do next, she appeared and took over, and I learned something new every time. She monitored my body when I wrote and did healing for me that I could get nowhere else. She always had answers, even when the questions seemed unanswerable, though sometimes I didn't understand those answers then.

When a student of mine wrote a college term paper on Theresa of Avila in 1992, she asked for the saint's direct help and I agreed to try. As Theresa swung my pendulum, answering yes and no questions, she started giving me more complete information in sentences and finally spoke through me in my first channeling. We learned things about her life I never would have thought to ask, which were verified in my student's later research. At that time I had not read Theresa of Avila's book.

The energy was so strong in the room that the air seemed to mist and shimmer. My two dogs left quickly, their neck hairs on end, though they later grew to like her presence. At the end of that one-hour session, I was too dizzy to walk for the rest of the evening. Occasionally after that, Theresa would speak through me in a healing, if my hearing her words and then repeating them got too slow and frustrating for her. I was always quite dizzy at the end. She also channeled through me during some types of workshops, especially workshops on natural remedies. I was told that she is a group guide, focused on bringing information and teaching to healers.

As my ability to work with spirit guides grew, Grandfather became more visible and more active. He had been the channeler of all my books to that time, though I was not always aware of him, and finally started to show himself as a Native American shaman of the Ojibwa tribe. It was difficult for some time for me to work with a male guide and his energy is very male and very intense. He is not the great talker that Theresa is, but Theresa moved to the background as I made more contact with Grandfather and only rarely appears to me now. Grandfather has been instrumental in healing me and in helping my

writing, but does not do healing for other people. Instead, he helps to bring in other guides when they are needed in healing, and has helped me to access spirit guide healing teams.

One of those teams was Bharamus, a group of at least six entities, male and female. One male voice was prominent but I never had a visual image for him. Others in the group included a middle-aged woman, an elder woman, a man with an Irish accent who said he was a barrister, and at least one who was a doctor. When I asked them once where they went when they were away from me, they said they lived on a spaceship circling Earth. They appeared and disappeared in healings for me and in healings I did with others for about three years and then they left, as Theresa had, at about the time I began to work more consciously with Grandfather. They were never as dominant or as clear in my life as Grandfather or Theresa.

The other prominent healing team is built from the information of Machaelle Small Wright's amazing book *MAP: The Co-Creative White Brotherhood Medical Assistance Program* (Perelandra, 1990). MAP is a way of accessing a personal spirit guide team for self-healing. Following the book's simple directions, I readily made contact with my team and promptly began quizzing them about who they are and what they do (and where had they been when I'd needed them all my life). I asked immediately about the name "Great White Brotherhood," which is outrageous to me, and was told I could change the name to "The Society of Illuminated Minds," which is more appealing. "Great White Brotherhood," they said, is a total mistranslation of the group's name in India. I made other substitutions to the core process and designed my own team with their guidance.

Working with MAP is amazing and has changed my life. This is a group focused totally on self-healing and on every aspect of it from menstrual cramps to damaged core souls. They straightened my back and have done much other physical level work, but are also available for healing emotions and helping in sticky situations, clearing entities and attachments, establishing protection shields, and giving me information on herbs and flower essences. A branch of my personal team heals animals and other people, and another group aids in karmic release work for myself, pets, and those I do healing with. My current version of MAP brings nonphysical healers from other planets, including a surgical team from Jupiter with a wry sense of humor, into healing and self-healing sessions. Work with spirit guides gets more and more interesting.

My favorite nonphysical guide is not a spirit guide at all but a Goddess who appears to many women and is a planetary healer. In 1991 I did a weekend workshop in Omaha and my friend Carol came to it with a magnificent photograph. The picture is of a lovely, very young woman with ancient deep eyes. She has a heart-shaped face, reddish fuzzy hair to below her shoulders, and a body filled with golden light. She holds yellow daisies or sunflowers and what seems to be a rattle in one hand and long string of beads in the other. She wears a wreath of roses in her hair. My reaction to the photo was that I couldn't look away from it. I was looking into a living woman's eyes of total love and beauty, and my own eyes started to tear.

Carol, seeing my reaction, told me to put the photo beside my bed that night. I did, and almost as soon as I began to relax I made meditative contact with her. Since the photo had been taken at Medjugorje in Bosnia, where there have been psychic sightings of Mary since 1982, I first asked if the woman was Mary. She said "No." I asked then, "Are you Persephone?" since her flowers and youth suggested the spring Goddess, and was told, "No, but that's close. Call me The Maiden for now." She asked if I would like to be her priestess and said she hadn't had a priestess for a thousand years. She wanted to be invited into rituals and healings, but said she would only participate when she was needed. I invited her into the ritual I led the next day, and she began appearing to me nightly. Carol gave me the picture, and I brought it home.

About six weeks later during a healing, the lady gave me her name. "I'm Brede," she said. I didn't hear her clearly and asked her to repeat it. "Brede,

Brede. Are you disappointed?" How could I be disappointed. Brede (Brigit, Bride, Brete) was and is the Maiden Goddess of Old Europe. In our nightly conversations, she told me that she is a planetary guardian here to "heal separations between people and countries." She is incarnated in a body in another dimension, actually looks like her lovely photo, and says that coming to Earth to do healing is her job.

She is the figure that appears in many of the supposedly Mary sightings that are happening all over the world. She has been seen in Rwanda, South America, Spain, England, and a dozen or more other places, as well as in Georgia, Texas, Colorado, Florida, Pennsylvania, California, and more. Women in several other cities have given or shown me photos of her taken in various places. Many women are also seeing her, some for years, in their meditations and healing work. One woman who is now thirty told me that a vision of Brede crying when she was eighteen led her to join a convent. "I thought she was Mary, and that was where to find her," the woman said, "but I didn't see her again until I left the Church."

When Brede joins me in a healing, the room fills with powerful green light, and life changes happen in the session. She brings a gentle aura of total peace and unconditional love, trust, and joy. Sometimes she needs healing herself, and I give it if she will accept it from me. Sometimes she needs hugs and love. She leads me into, and protects me, doing Earth healing and healing for those passing over in Earth change mass deaths. She has promised me that at my own death, she will be there to take me.

Working with Brede, and being the Lady's priestess, has been one of my greatest joys. Her message for this book: "Tell them to love one another. Tell them to heal." Where Mary is the spirit of the old age on this planet, Brede is the spirit of the healed Earth now being born in such pain. In pre-Christian Europe, she was the Goddess of birth, inspiration, healing, and love, and she continues her job today. Invite her into your meditations and healing work; often she will come. She is not an individual spirit guide, but a healing guide for the planet and for all who wish to work with her.

When the fragments of a large comet hit the planet Jupiter on July 14, 1994, a wealth of new healing energy began to reach Earth. As I understand it, Jupiter is an other-dimensional center of university for trained leaders of this and other galaxies. Earth has been quarantined from other planets since the war between Orion and the Pleiades, and the resulting invasion of human DNA by Orion, began in the time of Atlantis. The event of the comet has signaled the partial end of this quarantine and released the interplanetary healers on Jupiter to help us on Earth. They are healers, teachers, and openers of evolutionary growth and change in those Earth people able to accept and work with them. They first appeared to me and to several other healers about a week after the comet hit.

I was on a plane and very sick when I first met Aura, who appeared as a small, quick flashing ball of blue light. She asked me if I wanted her to be male or female, told me her name, and asked me what was wrong with me. By the end of the two-hour flight I felt fine. I did some very intense soul retrieval work that weekend, some of the longest and most intensive healing with others I have ever done, and she assisted all the way. I participated in a full moon ritual, was asked to lead the meditation, and took the women flying out to meet their "little blue fairy healers." Everyone in the group found a friend, innocent as children, who gave themselves names like "I-need-Ja" and "I'm Here," and names of flowers and women. The cat of the house also walked around all evening in a ball of blue light, and was extremely proud of herself and her new friend.

These Be-ings have a group consciousness, what one knows all know, and at the beginning they had very little understanding of Earth life. On my trip home, my suitcase stayed behind at the airport. When I asked her why later, she said, "You left it with that man (baggage claim) so I thought that was where you wanted it." One woman's little blue spirit exploded her vacuum cleaner when she complained bitterly about not wanting to do the housework.

They are learning about Earth, however, and if they didn't understand daily life at first, they have advanced understanding of aura work and core soul healing. Things that hadn't budged in years of trying to heal them suddenly healed easily and smoothly for me and others with Aura and her friends. Aura was with me for a few months and then moved on—her work with me was done. Other Jupiter spirits are healing extensively here, and her people are on the planet primarily to help healers. Ask in meditation if one of them would like to work with you.

Another in the collection of spirit guides I have known is an astral acupuncturist named Helena (different from my flapper guide Helen). Helena was introduced to me by my friend Robyn Zimmerman, whom she had helped with menstrual difficulties when Robyn wanted to conceive a second child. On Robyn's suggestion, I tried to contact her for my own menopause problems but was told, "Helena doesn't make house calls, you have to find your way to her." I finally asked MAP to take me to her and they did.

I found myself in a large hall with a group of women wearing what was either a sort of Eastern veil or habit. They put me on a table, and I felt one of the group bending over me. Then I felt what could only have been an injection in my arm, followed by a series of needles (more strange than painful) in my abdomen and later in my lower back. No one spoke. I landed in my bed wide awake with a jolt exactly two hours after I'd begun. I went to Helena nightly for about ten nights. Sometimes I felt the needles and was aware of the process, and sometimes I only felt the initial injection. I always woke up exactly two hours later and had trouble sleeping for the rest of that night. My uterine and hormone imbalances began to heal, as well as a five-year-old lower back disc injury incurred while moving to Florida.

Another friend did channeling to find out who Helena is. Her story is fascinating. She was born in Southeastern Russia in the nineteenth century, and was a nurse. When her mother died because of medical ineptitude, she knew there were better ways of healing people and wanted to learn them, but women were not permitted medical training at that time. Her father, however, accepted her need to learn and sent her to China where she was trained in Asian medicine, acupuncture, and herbs. Returning home, she began her practice for women and children against much patriarchal opposition, which grew as she became an increasingly sought after healer.

Eventually to save her life she had to hide her face, and she entered a convent. She trained other women, ran a healing center and hospital at the convent, and was a well-known and very much loved underground women's secret. She wrote books which have not survived, destroyed by the male medical system that wouldn't accept female competition or a new form of medicine. She is one of the foremothers we have lost. Other women may go to Helena as I did, and several have done so with wonderful results. She specializes in women's dis-eases. Ask your guides or healing team to take you to her if you need her help. Helena doesn't make house calls and she's getting very busy.

One further guide in my series, and the newest, is Ariel. There has been much focus on angels in the metaphysical community, but I have never paid much attention. I assumed that angels were simply a Christian name for spirit guides, not realizing them to be a separate group of Be-ings. A friend I do healing with, however, works with angels and kept telling me, "Ask your angels to do that for you." Then Copper, my unflappable Siberian husky dog who sees everything but refuses to believe any of it, started telling me about "those things with wings that hang around here but don't exist."

I am perhaps too brave and open in sharing healing information that some others have power or a money interest in keeping secret. Sometimes I come under attack for it, and frequently I have felt the need for psychic clearing or protection from negative energy (my own and others). My friend kept saying, "Talk to your angels. You aren't making enough use of them, and they can help you." When I finally did so, four more than human-sized glowing Be-ings entered my bedroom. At first they didn't speak to me, they put a shield around my house,

dogs, and myself. They closed a negative energy portal that had made my home before the current one a trap for unwanted entities. That done, they found me a new place to live with better energy, moved me into it within days, and shielded it completely. Next they pulled several old psychic attacks from my aura and healed the damage. I finally believe in angels. Copper says, "Their wings are made of feathers, but they don't exist!" They delight in teasing him.

One night I asked for a piece of core soul healing that I knew still needed to be done, but didn't know how to do. When I called in my version of MAP, I added my angels to the team. A woman who introduced herself as Ariel came and did the healing, and when I asked her if she would stay with me, she agreed. She has done the channeling for this book and more healing work for myself, my dogs, and others. Alma Daniel et al. in *Ask Your Angels* (Ballantine Books, 1992) says Ariel is an Angel of Healing. She has also introduced me to the Angel of Wiring, who with the Jupiter surgical team, is healing much of my vision problems and neurological damage.

Some other infant energies have come to me and to my pets and home. One gives presence to a china collie dog with a puppy that I keep in my office. My dog Kali was immediately and unusually interested in her and said she was her mom. The presence is highly nervous and becomes anxious when I do healing in the room. "I have a puppy to raise," she said, "you're disturbing my puppy." When no amount of reassurance quieted her, I finally asked her if she'd like to go back to the antique/junk store where I'd found her. "I'll be good," she said, "don't send me back." Now she joins in healing more constructively or at least doesn't interfere. Other people in the room have been aware of her on several occasions.

Two more of these energies have joined me recently; they seem to be baby angels. At a toy store at Solstice I found two soft, white furry stuffed toys, a cat and a dog about eighteen inches high. Both are dressed in pink pajamas and bunny slippers, and each is carrying her own stuffed teddy bear. They're ready for bed and adorable. I didn't initially buy them, and they seemed to be with me all that night asking me to. The next day I went and got them both and set them on a chair in my bedroom. It was clear they weren't to be separated. They seemed to have a presence from the first, and people to whom I showed the pair felt it immediately. I finally started making psychic contact with both of them. They are protective energies and energy cleansers for my home, healers for my dogs (who accept them and don't say they don't exist), and they make me laugh. They are childish and childlike and very cute—and probably much more powerful than they look.

Obviously there are lots of types of spirit guides, and it is universal law that no one comes to Earth or lives here all alone. Personal guides are part of our core souls, and everyone has a life guide that remains for the entire incarnation. Grandfather is my life guide. Other guides may be psychic energies that come for a period of time, or until a specific level of learning is reached, and then they move on. Some come for a specific job or purpose that may also be temporary. Some may only come in for a healing, while others stay for years or decades or permanently. A guide can be a past or future incarnation, an angel, Goddess, animal spirit, planetary healer, or extra-terrestrial helper. Everyone has both guides and angels, and some angels may be our own oversouls or Light Bodies.

We are not alone on Earth, and were never meant to be out of contact with our nonphysical partners and helpers. A technological society that divides mind and body and ignores the spiritual and nonphysical has also deprived women of this comfort and help. As the energy vibration of Earth increases and develops, however, women's psychic abilities and openness to receiving guides are strengthening. Part of Earth's quarantine has lifted and healing is entering the planet. These changes are bringing people back into contact with the nonphysical, other side of Be-ing, and returning the partnership of women with their spirit guides. Children's imaginary playmates and the helpful, quiet voices in our heads are real.

Only the joyful and positive ones are guides, however. Anything negative, harmful, denigrating, or offering unethical advice is neither an angel nor a guide. Any Be-ing that makes decisions for you or tells you what to do is not a guide. I challenge all new psychic energies, "if you are not from the Goddess leave immediately." If what is not a guide and has negative or critical characteristics says it is a part of you, and you know that to be so, see the information on subpersonalities in the chapter on Soul Retrieval. These are also not spirit guides or angels.

My first reaction upon meeting Helen as my first spirit guide was, "Of course I know you; you've been there all along." When a new voice enters my awareness, I ask it immediately, if it is not obvious, "Who are you? Are you from the Goddess, from the light?" If they are, they are energies to trust. If not, insist that they leave, asking your real guides to help you should they refuse. Those Be-ings that are truly guides are always fully respectful of free will. They will not mind being asked to prove their intentions. If a Be-ing is not a good spirit and you ask it, it must tell you so or show you. Many who are not of goodness simply leave when asked.

Once I have checked the intentions of a new energy, I begin asking it who it is and why it is there. Spirit guides come with a job to do, anything from keeping you entertained, to healing your anger, to helping you write a book. If you have a specific need—finding a new home, for example, or energy protection for your car—ask to be put into contact with a guide or angel who would like to do the job. Some guides are very specialized and won't do anything outside of their self-determined limits. Grandfather heals me but won't heal anyone else. Helena heals only women's dis-eases and only when the women find their way to her convent hospital. Angels are powerful protectors with specific jobs, including some who are healers.

Some guides appear in nonhuman form. Shamanistic totem animals, each of which represents its entire species, are such guides. Some women are aware of a pet dog or cat that has passed over and become a guide for them. Despite a furry appearance, these Be-ings can be high-level spirits with more than human awareness. They are often human spirits showing themselves as animals, and are sometimes advanced sentient Be-ings of other-planet origins. Occasionally a human spirit guide will incarnate into an animal body on Earth, if it is the best way for that guide to be close to and teach his or her human charge. Witches call these more-than-animal pets familiars, and the relationship often continues beyond the animal's death. The woman involved is usually aware in some way that her pet is not just a dog or cat. Treat these Be-ings with great respect; they have sacrificed much to be with us.

A woman who is very attuned to cats has a Siberian tiger as one of her guides, a big cat. Another has a golden dragon that does not allow her to bring images of other dragons into her home. Says Linda Page:

> I had a friend tell me I had a golden dragon friend. I thought, sure, right. Several other people told me the same thing. Then one time he showed himself to me. He scared me, but less than if I hadn't had someone tell me about him. He's quite a gentleman, actually.[1]

She was at her wits' end when the dragon started bringing baby dragons along with him. They were rambunctious and clumsy, and things started breaking in her house. It was like having elephants playing football in the living room. Finally she had to ask her dragon friend to leave the kids at home.

Some nonhuman appearing spirit guides are energies from other planets, allowed now to help us on Earth. It is an honor to be thought mature enough to perceive them in their alien forms, and an honor that they join our healing sessions. Earth has a poor record at accepting diversity, and if we can't tolerate a different religion or skin color, how will we react to a healing helper that looks like a lizard? Usually such Be-ings take on human appearance for us, but sometimes they show themselves to those women who can work with them as they are. They are not personal guides but planetary healers. My Jupiter healing team have egg-shaped heads and large round black eyes, and seem to have hands different from ours as well. They understand humans as energy fields and are highly advanced healers, far beyond what they call "Earth's primitive medicine." They use diagnostic tools that are totally foreign to this planet.

Our personal spirit guides, however, the nonphysical partners that participate in our daily lives, are virtually always human entities from Earth. Most have been in bodies many times and are usually members of our own oversoul group. They are a portion of the oversoul, an essence self strand that remains unincarnated in the other world. They are assigned to us to aid our growth, evolution, and spiritual learning for this lifetime. By their work with us, spirit guides also learn, develop, evolve, and grow. The relationship is one of mutual benefit, giving and receiving on both sides, human and guide.

Each essence of self incarnates again and again, and may have eventually hundreds of lifetimes. Her life guide teachers incarnate with her over and over, and other members of her soul family when not in body can also be among her spirit guides. A soul does not become a guide until it has reached a spiritual level clear enough to allow it to be an effective guardian and teacher. Not all advanced souls become guides.

A very evolved spirit may be a group guide rather than a personal or individual one, and some can be spirit guides for more than one person. I was delighted to meet a woman in California who told me that Grandfather is also her guide. Joy recognized me first, and I felt on meeting her that I'd always known her. She is probably of my soul family. Theresa, on the other hand, is a guide for groups of people. She likes to work in workshops, and I share her with many other healers. Brede does healing for the entire planet: many of the women to whom I have shown her pictures now work with her for healing or in their own lives. These are more than personal spirit guides.

Everyone has a life guide, plus a series of other personal and group guides, permanent and temporary. Even if a woman is unaware of them or of some of them, they are there. Spiritually advanced women have spiritually advanced guides. As a woman's level of growth increases, her guides change to match her awareness level. A person's interests are matched to her spirit guides as well: healers have guides with expertise in healing. A woman who is a musician will have guides who can advise and teach her about music. As her healing ability (or musical ability) grows and changes, new guides come in to help her at each level. Her former guides may leave or withdraw to the background for less frequent contact.

A guide's purpose is to assist the individual in helping her complete the learnings and purpose of this incarnation, whatever they may be, and aid in the soul's spiritual growth. They keep the individual from losing sight of these goals. They direct, teach, and influence the individual but never order or control. They are not permitted to make choices for us, they can advise on choices only when asked, and they are not permitted to violate free will in any way. Spirit guides are agents and messengers of Goddess. They are instrumental in supervising and overseeing our learning processes, providing protection, bringing gifts, aiding our life's work, and helping any work we do for others.

In doing healing sessions, a healer always has guides as helpers, if she invited them to be there. The receiver's guides will also participate if invited, and guides' presence make all the difference. I have frequently done healings that felt like the room was full of people. Sometimes I see them, and other times only feel them. Sometimes the receiver of a healing thinks my hands are still on her when they've long been removed. She may feel several pairs of hands. Being aware of spirit guides' presence, inviting them in, and thanking them for their help, is the beginning of work with guides in healing. Other guides besides the personal ones will come in this setting.

Often guides give me information in a healing that logically I have no way of knowing. When such information arises, it is because it is important for

the session. I have never found such information wrong, and virtually every time that the message seems odd to me, the receiver will confirm its validity. Most of my psychic information comes by clairaudience. I heard it in words, and since this is my best perception, this is how it is given. It is as if someone who knows much more than I do is standing beside me, offering what I need to be most effective as a healer and cheering the receiver and me on. When I feel spirit presence, I know that the healing is an important one. Much in the way of emotional release, past life resolution, and entity clearing happens in such sessions.

For someone who has never worked with guides, meeting them may come as a gradual awareness or it may come in an intentional, focused meditation. For any psychic healer, it is almost inevitable that you will start working with guides at some fairly early point. When in a healing you hear a voice directing you to send green or ask about her sister, it is definitely a spirit guide. I once thought the voice I heard was my guilty conscience, and discovered it to be Theresa. Spirit guides make healing a joy and a wonder. Their presence causes miracles to happen, both in healing sessions and in daily life. Personal spirit guides and angels add a dimension to living that is a joy to experience.

To begin working with these nonphysical teachers, first be aware of them. When you hear that quiet voice, pay attention to it. When there are extra hands in the healing, thank them. At the start of a healing or self-healing session, invite them in. State your request for "all positive healers, angels, and guides who wish to help" to come. Once they know you are aware of them and trying to make clearer contact, they begin helping you do so. Once you begin to acknowledge your guides' presence and thank them for it, they become more noticeable. Ask to be shown how best you can work with them in healings. In meditation, ask their purpose in being with you. Some women hear guided information, as I do. Others may feel their presence, while still others receive visual impressions. You will see them or see colors or light forms in the room. Some guides come with a fragrance of flowers or incense: Brede comes with the scent of roses. The appearances are always a delight, they are never meant to frighten you.

Always treat these Be-ings with respect. They are not to be worshipped, but they come from Goddess and have far more information than we in bodies do. Once you are fully certain that your psychic contact is a high-level healer, ask how you can work with her or him. Guides are to be trusted; they always do good and will never cause harm. Be careful what you ask for in a healing, however, making sure that what you specifically ask them to do is what you really want and need. They will confer with you on choices if you request it. Some healings may be karmic and not allowed, or not allowed yet, and some are learnings that must be completed first. Ask your guides to work gently; they may not have been in bodies for centuries, or maybe not at all, and may not remember how it feels and what a body needs. Some guides are learning to be spirit guides and may not be infallible. It is never wrong to question your guides, but do so respectfully. If you yell at them or demand, they will withdraw.

———————— : : ————————

Try an exercise for meeting your life guide. This is extremely simple to do and tremendously rewarding. Like most spirituality work, it is done in meditation. It initially requires a more deeply relaxed meditative state than most healing and visualization work and a more protected meditation space. I like to do spirit guide meditations, at least the first time, as a Wiccan ritual with a cast circle to make really sure that only Goddess energy comes in. Light candles and incense if you wish to; the fragrance of burning sweetgrass draws positive spirits and candlelight is a good meditation focus. Smudge the room and yourself with sage for clear energy.

Make sure you will be undisturbed; this meditation may take longer than your usual meditation. It can also be done at the end of a session after completing other psychic work or running energy. Cast a simple circle, bringing in the protection of the four directions (North, South, East, and West) plus Above and Below. Make the affirmation, "Only the highest level energy enters here." Now ground and center, and do a full body relaxation process, tensing and relaxing your body's muscles from feet to head. Once completed, though you feel relaxed, repeat the process. If you begin your contact with guides after another meditation, the relaxation may not be needed. Unlike most meditations, which are seated, this time lie on the floor with your knees raised and bent, so your feet make contact with the Earth.[2]

Once completely relaxed, make the following affirmation within your mind: "I am ready to consciously meet my life guide." Lie alert with a quiet mind, and be open to what comes. Listen carefully for the presence has always been with you and is so familiar you may miss it if you aren't completely open. When you make contact (this can happen by sound, vision, fragrance or touch), ask for information. If you hear your guide and want to see her, ask her to appear to you. Ask her name, who she is, what her purpose is in your life. Listen for the answers; you may hear or just know them. There may be several guides present, ask them to come forward one at a time rather than all at once. It may take several meditation sessions to teach you how to contact them in the easiest daily way.

———————— : : ————————

When I first did this meditation, I was amazed at how simple and easy it was to contact my guides. Helen, Theresa, and Grandfather appeared for me the first night, all eager to talk to me. I heard and saw Helen in my mind very clearly, with Theresa as a non-speaking visual picture only, and Grandfather as a bright blue light form. I was totally delighted. The process felt completely loving and safe. Each night after that first experience, I used my nightly meditation to talk with them and learn more about them. I still do this now.

As these first guides told me their purposes in coming to me and taught me how to work with them, I included them in my life more and more. The relationship is cooperative, we work together. After a few sessions, full meditation is no longer required to make contact with your spirit guides. Just talk to them and they are there. I work with my guides and angels in every aspect of my daily life, in self-healing, writing, teaching, and in healing others.

Try the above meditation at another time, this time asking to meet your healing guides. If you are a

Reiki healer, at least a Reiki II, you have a team of Reiki guides who may act as your healing team as well. Again, ask who they are, what they do, and how you can best learn to work with them for healing. Ask any other questions you may have. When doing healing sessions, invite the guides to join in at the start and be open to the manner in which they participate. Both your life and your healing work will broaden considerably with this contact. It is a richness not to be missed, a joy, and a vital part of being a healer.

In another spirit guide meditation, ask to meet your angels. They may be harder to contact. Be fully relaxed. I saw mine visually, and Copper saw them months before they began to speak to me. They will not come into your life or speak unless you invite them, and they will not do anything for you until you ask specifically. It was harder for me to understand what angels do and why mine were there and what help I could ask of them. They are more distant and less personal, more awesome, than spirit guides, but they do many of the same things that spirit guides do.

Alma Daniel, Timothy Wyllie, and Andrew Ramer in their book *Ask Your Angels*, helped with this:

> Ask your angels to be with you as you go
> through your daily life. Ask them to quiet
> or guide your hands when you are doing
> something that requires skill or accuracy.
> Ask them to lead you to suitable and
> comfortable lodgings or an eating place
> when you are in a strange city. Ask them
> to insure a safe journey and return and to
> facilitate connections when you, or people
> you love, are traveling. Whenever you
> want to expand your knowledge, capabil-
> ity, or skill, remember to ask your angels.[3]

I have begun to work with angels in healing, and an angel is channeling this book. They have more power than guides: they can be asked to do needed healing work in another place. During a psychic healing by telephone, I recently asked them to clear the energy and place protection around a woman and her apartment a thousand miles away. I asked the angels to teach the woman how to make contact with her own healing spirits. I asked them to lift a negative attachment from a friend at a time when I did not feel well enough to do the job myself with my guides. Angels are more autonomous than spirit guides and will work alone, as guides do not. In an early angel contact, I asked to leave a house I hated and felt helpless to change for a better one and it happened almost immediately.

Ask your own angels and each of your guides what their purpose is in your life. When invited into healing sessions, their presence brings change and transformation in sometimes funny and often astounding ways. If you need something specific in a healing or in daily life, you only have to ask. Whoever can do the job will do it, if it is positive for you and for the good of all. When doing self-healing, guides and angels take the place of other human hands. Ask specifically and clearly for what you wish to do. Occasionally, however, human contact seems to be required. Other healers may be needed, especially in times of crisis or when it seems that progress has halted for a while.

Reiki teacher Laura Gifford describes working with guides and angels in healing other people:

> One type of communication I receive from
> my guides is where there is no verbal or
> visual clues, they simply move my hands
> or raise my arms . . . . There are times
> especially when I am working within the
> emotional body of the client that I feel
> a presence standing behind me. It feels
> like an angel walks up behind me and
> connects to me by securing my arms
> to its outstretched wings, and (directs
> the healing).
>
> I have a guide that likes to poke me in
> the area the client needs special attention.
> For example, I may feel a sensation in
> my knee to prompt me to work on the
> client's knee.

Then I have the guides who, if all else fails and I haven't paid attention, "yell" at me. It's usually something like "I can't believe she's not listening. We set this up for you, you know, you asked us to help, here it is now do it, speak up, say something NOW!" . . . I feel they are actually speaking through my heart.[4]

My team of surgical helpers from the Jupiter healing college have a similar sense of humor. In one healing, we asked them to heal at the source of the receiver's long-standing hiatal hernia. They pulled something that looked like a moldy cork out of her chest, leaving a gaping hole. Even on the psychic level it seemed raw and unfinished to leave it that way. "Aren't you going to close it?" I asked. They slapped a bandaid over it, a child's bandaid with stars. Their response to my surprise was, "Well, you said you wanted it closed." I answered that I wanted the hole healed; they said it would take a few days. I am learning that in most healing, instead of asking merely to heal the dis-ease, it is best to ask to heal it at the source. Much more is accomplished toward permanent change that way.

My dogs were in the room during this session, and the Jupiter guides wanted to know, "What class of sentient Be-ing is this?" When they didn't know what dogs are, I tried again. "It's an animal, do you know what animals are?" They then asked if I ate them. Copper said, "They don't exist," but seemed to like their teasing. While I call this bunch the "Jupiter Comedy and Surgical Team," other guides tease, too. Brede and Theresa have both teased me many times about my impatience. (I want it healed NOW.) Despite the silliness, amazingly good things happen in these sessions, and there is no disrespect.

When doing healing with animals, invite their own guides into the session. Domesticated pets have personal guides, while wild animals have nature devas as personal protective spirits. Animals have higher selves and oversouls as well. There is an Overlighting Deva, species oversoul, for each animal, bird, insect, fish, and plant species. A witch's

familiar may be a human spirit in a pet body and belong to her human guardian's oversoul group.

Any Goddess that is associated with a particular animal type may be asked to help in the healing. Bast is a healer of cats, and Hecate or Diana of the Hounds (Artemis) may help in healing dogs. Saint Francis is another animal healer, as is Kwan Yin. Also ask into the session those angels who are nature or animal healers, plus Mother Earth or Mother Nature Herself. I urge women who work frequently with animals to learn psychic communication with them. The pets can then participate in their own healing, and animals often are also active in healing people.

Many of the countless names of Goddess will also enter into healing sessions. There are many healer Goddesses like Brede/Brigit, Kwan Yin, Isis, White Buffalo, Calf Woman, Mary, and Yemaya. Where something old or negative needs to be torn down or released, call in Kali, Ma, Oya, or Hecate. Despite their fierce reputations, they are fierce against injustice and dis-ease but gentle with women. They are not to be feared, only loved. Where much wisdom is needed, call in the Wise Mothers: Hecate, Copper Woman, Old Woman, The Grandmothers.

When doing healing for someone with traditional belief systems, ask into the session energies she can relate to and trust. Angels are usually well accepted, universal in most religions and cultures. Mary is always a powerful and loving healer in any situation. Saint Theresa of Avila is very wise and a great problem-solver. The receiver may also have a favorite saint to call upon. Jesus will enter healing, as will Meher Baba or his Kwan Yin energy wife, Maheira. None of these or the Goddesses are personal spirit guides, but they are group and planetary healers and will come. They bring great peace into a healing session, and when they do, much growth and learning can happen for healer and receiver. When such high-level energies participate, both healer and receiver benefit. The healer may be surprised at the healing she receives from them, while doing her work for another person.

Though a healer in a healing session may call upon many guides, angels, and Goddesses, her own and the receiver's, they never seem to conflict with each other or get in each other's way. There is perfect cooperation with the energy best suited to help doing the work. Most spirit helpers other than personal guides will come into the session only if they are needed or will only participate at need as Brede does. The healer's healing guides and receiver's spirit guides will almost always be present for any session, however. Angels will be there, but can only participate if they are invited in. When a woman's higher self is invited into the session, it is her astral energy body that appears.

Spirit guides are obviously very special Be-ings and we have a very special relationship with them. They are perhaps the closest and most intimate relationships of our lifetime, particularly for those women who learn to work cooperatively with them. The relationship is that of student to teacher, more in the Eastern than the Western sense. In Buddhism, the male or female guru is the student's example of the Buddha on Earth, and the guru in that setting is honest and takes the responsibility seriously. The guru is the "outer teacher." One's "inner teacher" is the Buddha nature within oneself, her Goddess within, represented by one's inner guide or life guide.

Says Sogyal Rinpoche in *The Tibetan Book of Living and Dying* (HarperSanFrancisco, 1993):

> When we have prayed and aspired and hungered for the truth for a long time, for many, many lives, and when our karma has become sufficiently purified, a kind of miracle takes place. And this miracle, if we can understand and use it, can lead to the end of ignorance forever; the inner teacher, who has been with us always, manifests in the form of the "outer teacher."[5]

Such a relationship of perfect love and perfect trust is what one's spirit guides, angels, and nonphysical, healing helpers are, whether inner or outer. They are women's spiritual healers and teachers on the Goddess path of growth and soul evolution. Incarnated or not, they are the Goddess' love. As each of us dies and leaves our bodies and the Earth behind, our guides are there to meet us as we leave, and they will continue to teach us on the other side. They are with us through lifetimes, deaths, and uncountable rebirths, through trauma, pain, happiness, change, and joy.

Hypnotherapist Michael Newton takes clients into the between life state and has made a study of death, rebirth, and reincarnation. In his book *Journey of Souls* (Llewellyn, 1994), he describes cases where women's spirit guides have incarnated with them into their present lifetime. He asked why a particular soul, beyond being spiritually advanced and having a desire to teach, is chosen to be a guide:

> They must be compassionate without being too easy on you. They aren't judgmental. You don't have to do things their way. They don't restrain by imposing their values on you. . . .
>
> They build morale . . . and instill confidence—we all know they have been through a lot themselves. We are accepted for who we are as individuals with the right to make our own mistakes.
>
> They never give up on you.[6]

A relationship of this quality can only be treasured and honored. Discovering my guides has probably been the most important learning breakthrough in my growth as a healer. When I teach other healers, I believe it to be the most important thing they can learn, and the most necessary thing for successful healing for oneself or with others. It is also one of the most loving and joyful learnings on the spirituality path. Having given the tools of meditation, visualization, energy work, and nonphysical guides, in the next chapter I will finally begin to describe an actual healing session.

Notes

1 Linda Page, Personal Communication, January 4, 1995.

2 The following process is from Laeh Maggie Garfield and Jack Grant, *Angels and Companions in Spirit* (Berkeley, CA, Celestial Arts, 1984), pp. 38–43.

3 Alma Daniel, Timothy Wyllie and Andrew Ramer, *Ask Your Angels*, p. 254.

4 Laura Ellen Gifford, "How Do I Know? Learning to Trust in Your Reiki Guides," in *Reiki News*, Winter 1995, p. 9.

5 Sogyal Rinpoche, *The Tibetan Book of Living and Dying* (San Francisco, CA, HarperSanFrancisco, 1993), p. 134.

6 Michael Newton, Ph.D., *Journey of Souls: Case Studies of Life Between Lives* (St. Paul, MN, Llewellyn Publications, 1993), p. 112.

CHAPTER SIX

Hands on Healing

I t is interesting to me that though hands on or laying-on-of-hands healing is the basis of all direct healing in every culture, very little has been written about the process. This is perhaps because the work is so simple that very little teaching is needed, and a person only learns by doing the healing herself. Once you have learned to work with spirit guides, little more is required; they do the healing and the work. Perhaps modern culture shies away from anything profound and spiritual that it can't explain in material-technical terms. Perhaps patriarchy today doesn't need or want an explanation of hands on healing in a world that separates body from mind, emotions, and especially spirit.

The dark unknown that patriarchy and technology shuns is the realm of women, as it always has been. It has been women's way of healing, or one of them, since the time of the Goddess matriarchies. Since the patriarchal takeover, the European Inquisition, and the world conquest of indigenous peoples by Christianity, healing has gone underground. All of the patriarchal religions have tried hands on healing and failed, and dropped it from their dogmas. To allow healing for everyone is too threatening a concept. It is too feminine, too whole, too empowering.

Healing is one of the foundations of Wicca, both nonphysical healing and the physical healing with herbs and other natural remedies. The Goddess worldview is one of unity of body, emotions, mind, and spirit, and holds the concept that we are much more than our bodies. Though this is so, our bodies are still important as vessels for the soul that is part of Goddess. All the healing we do comes from who we are as incarnated in-body spirits. Despite this philosophy, only a small percentage of witches (or other women) are healers. It takes a very special person to go beyond modern technology and patriarchal conditioning and reject the mechanistic dogmas of current thought. It is a special woman who chooses to help others.

Buddhist philosophy takes a different path. In the time of the Buddha, his wife Yasodhara and their early Buddhist disciples, many miraculous healings happened. Someone in need of healing would look for a wandering Buddhist monk or nun, usually to be found meditating under a tree, and ask for help. There were so many healings that the Buddhist's reputation for them grew far and wide. The sheer numbers distracted the people from their work at spiritual growth, until the early teachers decided that healing was a distraction from the higher spiritual life. Therefore, they made an effort to discourage both seekers and healers.

Because of their recognition of human suffering and their awareness of the primary Buddhist principles of compassion and service for all living Be-ings, they could not ignore the need for healing or the monks' and nuns' psychic and spiritual development that made them healers. The Buddha's life was devoted to learning and then teaching others to heal the source of all suffering through spirituality, the Buddhist idea that healing one's nonphysical Be-ing is the only answer.

If people are all a part of the Buddha nature, they are already perfect and already healed. By showing them their perfection and helping them to understand it, full healing (Enlightenment) can be attained. On the emotional level this healing begins by teaching women to let go of what holds them trapped in painful emotions. On the mental level, it means "unclouding the mirror," to open the free choice of realities and release karma. Full healing, and the only healing in Buddhism, comes from understanding and releasing the limitations of mind (ego, separation, what clouds the mirror) in order to fully perceive oneself as Buddha/Goddess.

This is Enlightenment, which is a knowledge of oneness and how the universe works. When it is attained, there is no further need to reincarnate in a body and therefore no further suffering. However, Enlightenment can only be attained while incarnated in a body. The body is the key to the healing of emotions and mind, and it is only in the body that karma can be released. From this seeming catch-22, Buddhist philosophy comes to Wicca—the body is to be honored and cared for as the temple of the spirit, the place of the perfect Buddha nature or Goddess-within.

Hands on healing begins with the body, and reaches from and through it to the nonphysical levels, the emotions, mind, and spirit. In a hands on healing (or direct healing) session, energy or light drawn from Goddess flows through the healer and into the receiver of the session. The healer is a chan-

neler or focus of this life force energy, not its originator. The energy enters the receiver through her physical body, but it moves through and into all the energy levels, manifesting last in the physical. The factor of spirit guides is the wild card that turns the session into anything can happen, and enhances every aspect of the work and its results. The guides use the energy and our hands.

Healing does not come from the healer but through her. The Navajos call this becoming a hollow bone. The healer cannot predict what will happen in a healing, other than that it will be positive and do no harm. Legally, she is not permitted to predict or diagnose, and she is not permitted to offer cures in or out of any session, unless she is a licensed medical doctor. Ethically, a healer is unable to predict because she has no way to know. Anything can happen in a healing from nothing to actual miracles, to anything in between. The healing may address things altogether different from the initial need of the recipient that prompted the healing session.

The energy for the healing comes from the Goddess through the healer, it does not come *from* her. A healer who feels drained at the end of a healing session needs to learn to root herself more firmly to the Earth and open her crown to run energy in both directions. Establish the flow before beginning and use it to refill at the end of every session. Likewise, a healer who absorbs the receiver's pain can run energy and send the symptoms away; she can affirm, "Only what is mine remains with me."

Those healers who are drained in a healing session are not connecting with Goddess and must learn to do so. Some of the problem comes from ego. It reads "my healing," rather than "the Goddess' healing." Letting go of results and expectations in the sessions also makes it easier to be a clear channel and stand aside from self so the Goddess can move through. For any healer who has a problem with feeling drained or taking others' symptoms, the easiest remedy is Reiki training. These things were problems for me until I received Reiki I, from which point they stopped immediately. The Reiki I attunement has also released them permanently for dozens of women I have trained. Practice running energy in the meantime and accept yourself as simply the Goddess' hands, a hollow bone for spirit.

The life force energy for healing enters the healer at her crown. It leaves through her hands when she places them on someone else or on herself with the intent to heal. A light meditative state is needed to make the connection between Goddess and receiver and to start the flow. The deeper the meditative state the healer can access, the more profound the healing, as in deep meditation the transmission of energy/light and connection with Source is greater. The more practiced in meditation, visualization, and running energy the healer is, the greater the amount of this electrical force her body can hold and bring through. The life force energy is limitless; the limit is in what the healer's energy circuits, her Kundalini and Hara Line, can allow. She will not be permitted to overload her ability to safely channel this energy. The more spiritually and psychically developed the healer becomes, the more energy she can handle, and the deeper her connection with guides and Goddess. Therefore the more profound the possible results of her work.

The deeper the meditative state a healer can sustain in an energy session, the more access she gains to nonphysical Be-ings, her spirit guides, angels, spirit teams, etc. These are the real agents of the healing, and the deeper the meditative state, the higher the level of guides and the more ability they have to work through you to effect change. With deep connection to guides and a cooperative effort, the healer only has to put her hands down and the guides do all the work. The cooperative relationship is learned by inviting it, by getting out of the guides' and helpers' way, and by experience in working with them.

The cooperation must also include the receiver. She must be willing to accept the energy and desire to heal herself. She must be willing to do the work of inner change, releasing emotions, adjusting her outlook, and letting go of things that are holding her back. She must be willing to risk change in her life and be willing, and at least partly able, to trust in herself, the guides, Goddess, the healer, and the process. A healer and receiver who do not trust each other cannot be successful together.

A receiver unwilling to participate and cooperate will not change or heal, no matter how experienced and skilled the healer. If the receiver has decided that she doesn't want to heal or can't be healed, there will be no healing. If she is only going through the motions because her loved ones want her to or she thinks she should, instead of by her own desire and choice, she also will not heal. The cooperation between healer, receiver, and Goddess (with her spirit guides) is essential. The Goddess and guides are always willing, but what happens in a healing session also very much depends on the healer and receiver involved.

Healing is serious but does not have to be somber. It is always loving and gentle, no matter how difficult or harsh the issues or dis-ease being addressed. Respect is essential: respect of healer for the receiver and her dis-ease and life path, and respect of the receiver for the healer's efforts to help and her abilities and skills. There needs also to be respect for the life force energy present in the session, and for the Goddess and guides who join it. A healing is a sacred occasion, but remember that joy and sacredness go together. As the "Charge of the Goddess" states, "All acts of love and pleasure are the Goddess' rituals." Healing is an act of love.

It is also an act whereby compassion is the catalyst for transformation. Without compassion, nothing heals and only harm is done. The first Goddess law is to harm none. In a healing situation the traumas and pain of lifetimes are often brought forth for release and change. The stories a healer may have to hear can be disturbing. Healing is a safe place, a totally safe space, in which such painful stories can be opened and cleared. The receiver needs a place of total safety in which to do this. Judgment and blame are not safe and do not belong in any healing situation. The healer's job is to listen and be compassionate, never to judge. Her job is to comfort, and to encourage the receiver to express, open, and clear her pain in fullest safety. Anything less is not healing, but is harm.

Healing is also a safe place for the receiver to cry or to be angry, to release emotions she may never have allowed herself to feel before. Again, the healer's job is to listen, to be completely nonjudgmental, and to encourage the receiver to express what she needs to let out. Telling her not to cry or "don't feel that way" prevents a letting go that needs to happen. While this is occurring, the healer continues her hands on session, quietly so as not to interfere with the release process. By the end of the session and usually within ten or fifteen minutes, the release is done. When something of this sort happens in a session, the healing and change have been profound. The receiver has made a breakthrough into new growth, and old pain that has hampered her life is gone.

Confidentiality is also essential, and it is a healing ethic. Whatever happens in a healing is between the healer, receiver, and the Goddess with her guides. It does not leave the room without the receiver's express permission. To violate this is to violate a deep trust, and healing without trust cannot happen. Women are violated repeatedly in patriarchal culture, and healing is something that has to be very different. Women have been violated again and again, lifetime after lifetime in our bodies, emotions, minds, and spirits. To betray trust, compassion, or confidentiality in the healing situation is spiritual abuse. In teaching and writing, I often describe healings I have witnessed to use as examples; the women's names and identifying characteristics are always changed unless I have their permission to do otherwise.

When working with spirit guides, the healer in a session may receive a lot of information. Women often ask me how much to tell the receiver. In my opinion, the receiver has the right to all that will not frighten or harm her, and all that she can understand. I probably would not tell a suspicious born-again Christian, as an extreme example, about her past lives. A woman who is open to knowing, however, will be told what I see. I feel that psychic information is given for a purpose, to direct the healer's work or to give the receiver what she needs to resolve her dis-ease or pain. If I am not sure about transmitting a piece of information, I ask the guides before speaking.

There are some situations where I feel information is inappropriate to relate. If I am told that a woman has a serious or life-threatening condition, and she has not indicated to me that she knows it, I will usually not tell her. I may, however, suggest she get medical help and "find out what's really going on." Diagnosing is illegal, and it can also be irresponsible. It can cause unnecessary fear and harm, even if correct. Continue the healing in these situations, whatever diagnosis you intuit. I have seen many a malignant tumor turn benign or disappear by the next medical check-up.

If I feel someone may be dying, again unless she indicates to me her own knowledge of it, I will not tell her. I have seen women approach death and retreat from it to go on with living. I have experienced these times in myself as well. A woman who seems to be dying may not be physically going to pass over. She may instead be dying to an old way of life and thinking before being reborn to something new. We go through these rites of passage, these initiations, many times in a lifetime. The woman who may seem to be dying from the information I receive in a healing session may have passed the crisis by the next one or later on. The possibility of reincarnation while still in one's body is real in these Earth change times.

Self-Healing

All healing is self-healing, and though the hands on technique is something usually done with others, it can be done alone as well. Visualized meditation is a very powerful way to heal when working alone and I will deal with this in a later chapter.

———————— : : ————————

Your own hands are a powerful healing force. There are a number of ways to do this, both simply and in a more formally structured manner. For a simple method, go to your meditation space, light a candle, ground and center, and get fully relaxed. Put a circle of light around you and ask your guides and angels to come in. Talk with them for a moment, telling them what is wrong and what you need. There is no need to speak out loud. Then lie down on your back, with arms and legs uncrossed, and place your two hands palm down on your body. Let your intuition and your guides determine where each hand goes. One hand over your heart and the other on your abdomen are likely places, or both hands over a pain area. Always use both hands, opened palms down. Keeping your mind alert and quiet, let the energy and healing flow into and through you. When the light flow or the sensations stop, thank your guides and the healing is done.

—————— : : ——————

I recommend doing this just before bed, because the guides often will continue healing you while you sleep. Take a shower before starting and wear loose or no clothing for the session, but keep a blanket nearby to pull over you. Your body temperature may drop as your meditative state deepens. You may go out of body and you may feel cold. Wait until after the healing to allow yourself to sleep, if possible. Sometimes the guides will put you to sleep in order to work on you.

Another way to do hands on healing for oneself is to use the Reiki I hand positions. When the full sequence of these is done, you have brought light/Ki/energy and healing into all of the Kundalini and Hara chakras, as well as all of the organs of the physical body. The session front and back takes about an hour if all the positions are used. It can be done from a sitting position or lying down. Doing it in bed means you are likely to fall asleep before finishing it. This is fine, but be careful not to leave candles burning; it may be best not to light any candles for this healing.

If you have had Reiki training, this method will be the most obvious to you to do, but even if you haven't had the attunements the positions are helpful and effective. They are the basis for most hands on healing/laying-on-of-hands work. If you cannot comfortably reach one or more of the positions that follow, skip them and do those that you can. If you feel comfortable only doing the positions on the

front of the body, this is positive as well. There is no right or wrong way to place your hands for any healing; one basic guideline is to put your hands where your body hurts or as close to that place as possible.

—————— : : ——————

This is a full body self-healing. Begin from a sitting position or lying on your back, and keep arms and legs uncrossed so the energy moves through you unobstructed. Calm and center yourself and call in your guides before starting. If you are lying down, place a blanket on top of you and move your hands under the blanket. If you need pillows under your head and/or knees, position them before you start. I like to do this form of self-healing skyclad, but if you wish to be dressed, wear something light, loose and nonconstricting like a sweatsuit or a nightgown. If lying down, try to keep from falling asleep as long as you can.

The illustrations (pp.84–88) show the hand positions for self-healing from my book *Essential Reiki*.[1] They are numbered for easy identification. The session starts at the head and moves to the feet on the front, and then continues from head to feet on the back. The first three positions are on the head. In the first, place your slightly cupped hands gently over (but not pressing on) your eyes. Hold the position until the heat, tingling or energy sensations that develop stop. This may take up to five minutes, so give it time. The first position balances the left and right sides of the brain, and is wonderful for headaches and eyestrain. It covers the brow/third eye chakra.

Next (position 2 and 2a), move your hands to the sides of your face. Your thumbs rest just beneath your ears, and your palms cover your cheeks. Again, wait for the energy cycle to be completed. This is an almost instinctive way to place your hands and it is extremely comforting. In the third head position (3 and 3a) move your hands to the back of your head, cupping the occipital ridge. This covers the crown chakra, and also the third eye from behind, as well as reaching the causal body chakra. Give the energy time to flow through.

Now go to the throat chakra (4 and 4a). If putting your hands over your own throat brings on a panic reaction—it is less likely when you use your own hands—place your hands instead over your collarbone below it. Position five (5 and 5a) is over the heart. Put your hands over your breastbone,

DIAGRAM 11

Reiki I Hand Positions Self-Healing
The Front—Head Positions

1. Over the eyes.

2. Over the cheeks, thumb is just under the ears.

2a. Alternate second position.

3. Back of the head, over the occipital ridge.

3a. Alternate third position.

DIAGRAM 11 (CONTINUED)

Reiki I Hand Positions   Self-Healing

4. Over the throat.

4a. Alternate throat position.

5. Over the heart—breastbone (self only).

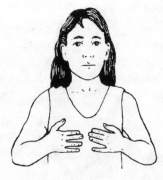

5a. Alternate fifth position (self only).

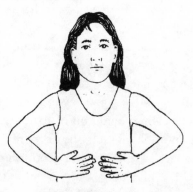

6. Over lower ribs below breasts.

DIAGRAM 11 (CONTINUED)
Reiki I Hand Positions   Self-Healing

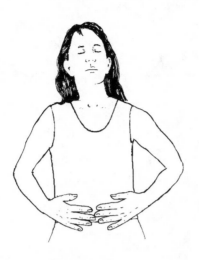

7. Over middle abdomen.

8. Over pelvic bones—lower abdomen.

9. Hands in center above pubic bone (not touching genital area).

9a. Alternate ninth position—over pubic area (self only).

or even over your breasts if healing is needed there. The solar plexus is next (6). Place your hands in opposite directions with fingers facing over your lower ribs, just below your breasts. Anatomically, your right hand is over your liver and gallbladder and your left over your pancreas, spleen and stomach. Your may hear some internal rumbling at this position and will also be very relaxed with the process.

With your hands held in the same way, move next to the middle abdomen at about the waist or just below it (7), then lower once more to cover the pelvic bones (8). The energy reaches the intestines from this position, and the belly chakra. The last of the torso positions is with the hands brought together in the center of the lower abdomen, one above the other, just over the pubic bone (9 and 9a). On yourself, you may cover the genital area if you wish. This

DIAGRAM 11 (CONTINUED)
Reiki I Hand Positions   Self-Healing
The Front—Knees, Ankles and Feet

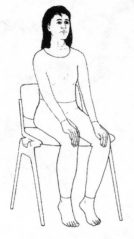

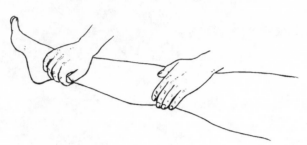

10. Front of both knees.

10a.-11a. Knee and ankle done together. Do both legs.

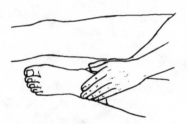

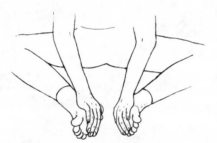

11. Front of both ankles.

12. Bottoms of both feet—or 12a.

12a. Bottom of one foot then the other.

DIAGRAM 11 (CONTINUED)
Reiki I Hand Positions   Self-Healing
The Back

13. Back of the head—one hand over occipital ridge, one hand over crown (top).

13a. Alternative head position for the back.

14. Back of the neck and over top of shoulder muscles.

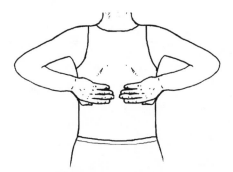

15. Over ribs, below shoulder blades, back of heart.

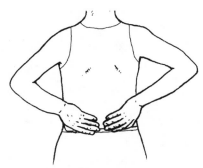

16. Middle back.

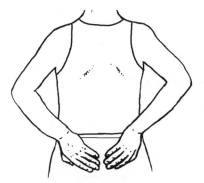

17. Lower back over sacrum.

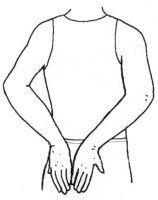

17a. Alternate or additional position for lower back.

18. Backs of both knees. (refer to figure 10, but do position from back).

19. Backs of both ankles. (refer to figure 11, but do position from back).

19a. Hold back of knee and ankle at once on same leg. Repeat with the other leg.

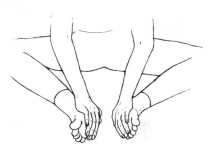

20. Bottoms of both feet.

position is for the root chakra and covers the uterus and ovaries, bladder and vagina in women, the bladder and testes in men.

Next move to the knees, ankles, and feet. The hand placements here serve to balance and ground you, reconnecting you with Mother Earth, and also to integrate and bring through the energy of the healing. If you are going to sleep after the session, these positions are less important. For the knees and ankles (10, 10a, 11, 11a) first put your hands on both knees for the time of energy flow, then do the same at both ankles. You may have to reach to find a comfortable way to do the ankles. An alternate choice here is to put one hand on the right (or left) knee and ankle at the same time, then move to the other leg's knee and ankle. Do the feet

last, bending your legs and placing your hands on the bottoms of the soles where the chakras are. Put one hand on each foot (12), or both hands on one foot then move to the other (12a). Again, keep your hands in place while the energy sensations continue.

Then go to the back. There is one position only for the head (13), but since you have done three head positions already this one is optional. Place one hand on the crown of your head and the other at the back (causal body chakra). It can be done alternatively with both hands at the crown (13a). Next, place your hands over the back of your neck or on top of the large trapezius muscles between neck and shoulders at the back (14). These muscles are tension-holders for many women. They constitute the throat chakra at the back, but are not as sensitive as the throat center front is.

Turn your arms around now if sitting, or turn onto your stomach if lying down, and reach upward to below your shoulder blades (15) covering the back of your heart. Your hands point toward each other as on the front torso. Next move lower to the middle back, holding your arms and hands in the same way (16), and do one position lower yet (17). These positions cover the solar plexus and belly chakras. An alternate or additional placement is over your lower back (17a) with hands positioned downward for the root center. From a sitting or lying position on your side, repeat the knee and ankle placements (18 and 19 or 19a), but this time put your hands at the back instead of the front. To finish, do the bottoms of both feet again (20).

———————— : : ————————

This full body healing takes some time but is a wonderful luxury and gift to oneself. Pay attention to the emotions, thoughts, and guided messages that happen. Keep your mind clear to listen for these and follow the directions of your spirit guides and angels. If you don't go to sleep afterwards, drink a full glass of water. When ending the session move slowly; you may feel spacy for a while, or even the next day. The same position can be used for a full body healing with another person, but respect body privacy.

Healing with Others

In doing hands on healing with others, the setting is as important as it is in self-healing. Your meditation space is a good place to start, but it may not be large enough for two people, and the healer needs room to move around. Both people need to feel physically comfortable, as a session takes at least an hour or more. A massage table with space around it and a rolling office chair for the healer is the most ideal. Next is a carpeted floor. Place a blanket and pillows under the receiver, and the healer will need a pillow to sit on.

A bed may be comfortable for the receiver but is difficult for the healer, but in some situations it is necessary to work this way. The easiest way to do this is to place the receiver diagonally on the bed, her head at a bottom corner with the healer in a chair at the foot of the bed. The healer may need to stand, or sit on the bed, to reach some of the positions.

Though this is not a meditation space, any healing needs to be quiet and uninterrupted. Some healers like to play soft music, but I find that a distraction. There should be no ringing telephones, no children or pets moving in and out. Only the healer and the receiver should be in the room. The room needs to be warm and to feel safe. During the healing, the receiver drops into the same meditative state as the healer and both may feel cold in what seems to be a warm room. Have an extra blanket handy, tissues in case of an emotional release, and glasses of pure (not tap) water available at the end.

———————— : : ————————

Both healer and receiver are usually dressed in loose and comfortable clothing. Ask the receiver to remove her shoes, tight belt, and eyeglasses; contact lenses are usually not a problem. Some healers prefer all jewelry be removed from both parties, but I do not find it necessary. Make the receiver very comfortable. She lies on her back on the massage table, floor or bed, and in a full body healing she will turn over later. Place pillows under her head, and under her knees if she needs them. The healer's touch is very light at all times, barely in contact with the receiver's body. Place a circle of protective light around both participants.

The hands on healing session for others is the same as a full body self-healing, with two exceptions. First, because the hands reach out rather than turn in, there will be some change in how the positions are done. The healer needs to do the session in such a way that her own body is totally comfortable, or the reaching can cause considerable strain. Do not cross your arms or legs or allow the receiver to do so, as it blocks the flow of moving energy. Second, be very aware of body privacy. Touching another's breasts or genitals is an invasion of body safety unless the person is yourself or your mate. Be aware of this for children as well as adults. One out of three women in American has been raped and probably half to three-quarters of women have experienced incest or otherwise been violated. Healing sessions must be safe spaces for women.

When the receiver is settled and comfortable, take a few moments for the healer to ground and center herself and to enter the meditative state. Establish protection and begin running energy. Ask for the presence of the Goddess and of guides and angels belonging to both participants, and ask that the work be for the greatest good of all. The positions for this sequence are again those used in Reiki I and from my book *Essential Reiki*.[2] The healing is done quietly, with a minimum of conversation, unless or until the receiver or healer needs to talk about what's happening in the process.

To begin the healing, do the head positions standing or sitting behind the person receiving the session. You will remain there through three head positions, the throat, and probably the heart. The hand positions are again illustrated and numbered. Always put both hands on the body at once, palms down. Begin with your cupped hands placed gently over the woman's eyes, not pressing on them (1). Feel the energy sensations cycle and when the sensations stop, move to the next position. This first position balances the left and right sides of the brain. The woman receiving the

healing may become restless, but when you move to the next position she will become quiet.

Position two (2) is over the cheeks, with your little finger placed just beside the ears. Where position one covered the third eye and vision chakras, position two reaches the crown and third eye. The person receiving the session most often becomes quiet here and may seem to go to sleep or out of body. To do the next position (3), the healer lifts the receiver's head (the receiver usually helps), and slides her hands underneath. Cup your two hands under the curve of the back of the head, the occipital ridge. You'll know the place because your hands feel comfortable there. Crown, third eye, vision, and causal body chakras are covered. The head positions treat the skull, brain, eyes, ears, and central nervous system.

Reach forward to the throat center (4). Because so many women panic when hands are placed over their throats, I never place my hands directly on it. Instead put your hands below the throat and over the collarbone. You can also hold

DIAGRAM 12
Reiki I Hand Positions   Healing Others
The Front—Healer stands or sits behind person receiving healing

1. Hands cupped gently over the eyes.

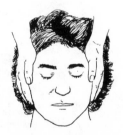

2. Over the cheeks, healer's little finger rests lightly against ears.

3. Hands under the head—healer does the lifting.

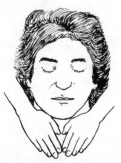

4. Hands rest lightly over the collarbone—slightly below the throat.

DIAGRAM 12 (CONTINUED)
The Front Healer comes to side of person receiving healing.

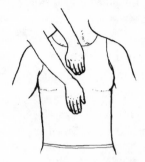

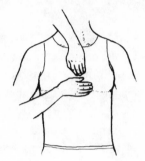

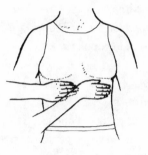

5. Between breasts—optional position. Use with respect not to violate women's body privacy.

5a. Alternate of fifth position.

6. Below breasts over lower ribs.

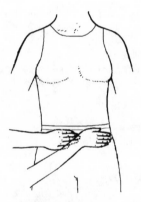

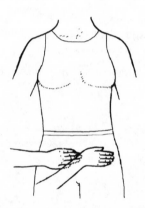

7. Just below waist.

8. Across pelvic area above pubic bone.

your hands tent-wise above the throat without touching it, but this is an uncomfortable strain for the healer. In past lives, many of us who are healers today died at the stake, usually strangled before the flames reached us. Therefore, the phobia.

Extend your arms further forward or move to either side for the heart and thymus (5 and 5a). Never place your hands over the breasts of a woman you are not intimate with, unless you have consent to do so. (If the woman has cystic breasts or breast lumps, you might ask her if it is o.k.) Usually, however, place your hands above the breasts, between them if there is room to do so, or skip the position completely. Healing energy goes where it is needed, and no benefit is lost by skipping this position. Again, wait for the energy to climb and fade, a period of up to five minutes,

then move your hands to the next position. You need to be at the woman's side instead of behind her now. The solar plexus (6) is located just under the breasts and covers the upper digestive organs, the liver, gallbladder, stomach, and pancreas. It also includes the diaphragm chakra.

With the torso positions, you have a choice of how to place your hands. They can be held in a horizontal line across the body, the fingers of one hand almost touching the heel/wrist of the other. Alternatively, and sometimes more comfortably, place your hands side by side (thumb almost touching thumb). To find the positions with this, imagine the receiver's torso divided into four quarters and place your paired hands over each quarter in turn. See the illustration on page 94. Do the upper right side, upper left side, lower right side, then lower left side. Bring both hands to the center

DIAGRAM 12 (CONTINUED)
The Front—Healer moves further down the side.

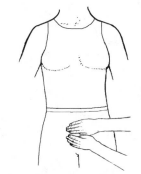

9. Both hands across lower
   abdomen above pubic bone.

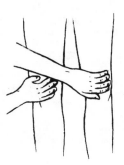

10. Front of both knees.

11. Front of both ankles.

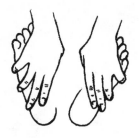

11a. Ankle and knee at once. Do both
     legs. Preferred position—
     combines 10 and 11.

Healer moves to bottom, facing feet of person receiving healing.

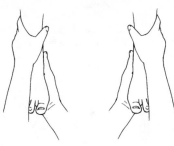

12. Bottoms of both feet.

12a.-12b. Alternate of twelfth position.
Bottoms of both feet done one at a
time.

of the woman's lower abdomen last. Start from either side, it doesn't matter. Do this on the back also if you choose to.

To continue with the torso, position (7) is just below the waist and covers the belly chakra and Hara, with the next hand placement just below it (8) above the pubic bone and over the pelvic area. Place your hands either horizontally or side by side. Then bring both hands to the center of the receiver's lower abdomen (9), just above the pubic bone (root center and perineum). The hands are placed one above the other on the body. These positions cover all the abdominal organs.

The knee, ankle, and feet positions are more important here than for self-healing. For the past half hour or more, the woman receiving the healing has been lying quietly (unless she has had an emotional release). She may appear to be asleep or just "out there somewhere," out of body. The

hand positions on the legs and feet begin to bring her back to Earth now.

To do them, the healer must move again. In doing the torso placements, the healer stood or sat on one side of the receiver. There is no need to move from side to side, just reach across the woman's body to her opposite side. Now move further down so you can reach her legs. Do the tops of both knees (10) and then the tops of both ankles (11). Alternatively, place one hand on her knee and the other on her ankle of the same side (11a)—this is the preferred way. Complete these positions by again waiting for the energy sensations to fade. Finish the healing with the bottoms of the feet (12). Do one foot at a time (12a and 12b), or both feet at once, which is preferable. If you are continuing the healing by doing the back of the body, you may choose to skip

DIAGRAM 12 (CONTINUED)

Healing Others
The Front—Healer returns to the head of the person receiving the healing.

13. Optional head position—One hand on crown and other hand on back of head (at occiput). Person receiving healing will have her head turned to the side.

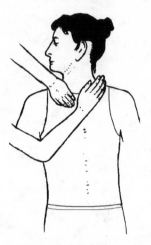

14. Back of neck. (Healer moves to receiver's side.)

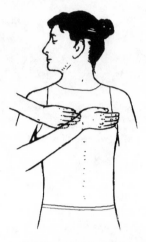

15. Over shoulder blades.

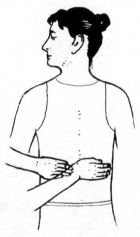

16. Middle back.

17. Lower back below waist—over sacrum.

the feet positions until the end of the session. Now ask the woman to turn over and move to her head again.

With the receiver's head turned to the side, optionally do the one head position for the back (13). One hand is placed on the crown and the other on the back of the head at the occipital ridge/causal body chakra. The next position is the back of the neck (14). I have not met anyone sensitive to the throat position from the back. Placing your hands over the trapezius muscles, the big muscles where the

shoulders meet the back, is an optional alternative.

Move to the woman's side again, and do three positions down the back (15, 16, 17). The hands may be placed end to end or side by side, as on the front torso. These positions cover the heart/thymus, solar plexus/diaphragm and belly chakra/Hara centers. They also reach the kidneys, and are wonderful for tension, stress, and back trouble. If the person has a particularly long back or much lower back pain, do one more position further down, where the buttocks

DIAGRAM 12 (CONTINUED)
Reiki I Hand Positions   Healing Others
The Back

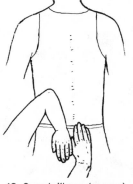

18. Over tailbone (coccyx)—
optional position.

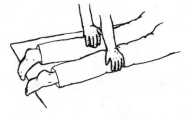

19. Backs of both knees.

20. Backs of both ankles.

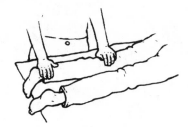

20a. Hold back of one knee and
ankle together. Do both legs.

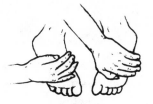

21. Bottoms of both feet.

begin (root/perineum). An optional way to do this is with one hand facing in each direction (18).

Next go to the legs and feet, and this time it is extremely important to do these positions thoroughly. They help the receiver ground—she has been "out" for a long time. Move beside her legs and do hands on healing on the backs of both knees/movement chakras (19) and the backs of both ankles (20). A preferred way to do this is to place one hand on the back of the knee, and the other on the back of the ankle of the same side (20a). Wait for the energy, then repeat on the opposite side. Make sure to do both legs.

The last position of the healing is the bottom of the feet. Whether working on the front or back of the body, the feet are still held on the bottoms, where the grounding chakras are located. You will feel streams of energy moving through the feet, and the energy may continue to move for several minutes. This position integrates the session's energy and completes it. The receiver of the healing will be far from

grounded when she gets up from the massage table, but she will be functional. Without the feet positions, she would be much too spacy.

By the time the healing is finished, much has happened. Thank your guides and nonphysical healers and let the receiver lie quietly as long as she needs to. The guides and angels may keep on working, and it can take the receiver a few minutes or even half an hour to fully integrate the session and be ready to sit up. If she falls asleep during the healing, simply tell her you are done, then give her time to wake up. She may feel very spacy or too relaxed to move for a while. Help her to sit up if she needs your help. Give her a glass of pure water (bottled or filtered, not tap water full of chemicals). The healer needs a glassful, too. Do not allow the receiver to leave or drive until she is fully present and grounded.

———————— : : ————————

DIAGRAM 12 (CONTINUED)

Reiki I Hand Positions   Healing Others

Optional Hand Placement Alternative

Optional hand placement alternative for torso and back. Place hands side by side instead
of end to end. Replaces hand positions 6, 7, 8 and 9 on front and 15, 16, 17 and 18 on back.

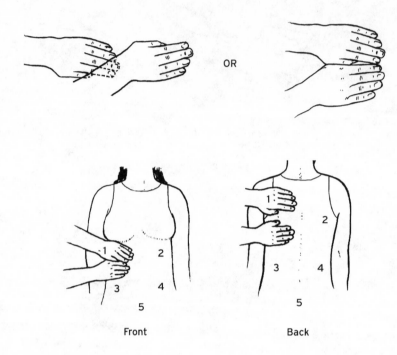

Front   Back

The receiver may feel overly relaxed or spacy for as long as a few days after the session. She may go through a detoxification process with symptoms like diarrhea, frequent urination, runny nose, sweating, unusual body odor, or thirst. She may wish to fast. Tell her to honor her body with what it craves that is positive, to drink lots of pure water with or without lemon juice in it. She should be told not to stop the process of healing with remedies of any kind. The healer may feel hungry, needing protein or complex carbohydrates. She may crave sugar or chocolate. I like to use cottage cheese or yogurt instead; corn chips or crackers also help. The healer may need to run energy for a while and may also feel ungrounded, but she should otherwise feel well.

The hand positions used here are the Reiki I positions for a full body healing. Where your hands actually go in a hands on session is optional but these positions and sequence are tried and true. If your intuition or guides tell you to skip a position, do something out of order, or put your hands on other noninvasive areas, do what they tell you to do. Guides' participation may be apparent in these sessions, with many pairs of hands on the receiver's body and in her aura. Sometimes it feels like a roomful.

The guides may tell you to stay at one position or your hands may feel glued there for a long time. The guides may also move your hands, and even move them out of the healing completely for a period while they do the work. Get out of their way and do as you are told, even if what they do seems odd or you don't understand their reasoning. The team from Jupiter does this with me frequently, and they aren't always polite about it—but they get a good job done every time.

When your hands are on each position, you will know when the energy flow is finished and when it is time to move them. Reiki healers get a distinctive energy cycle of sensations; non-Reiki healers may get the same cycle but the sensations will be fainter or the healers may feel other things. Either way, you will know when to move. With Reiki the sensations start as feeling simple body warmth. From there they change into a variety of feelings—intensified heat or cold, a ripple effect, waves of sensation, colors, or even less pleasant feelings like fingers falling asleep or aching. In most cases the sensations are subtle rather than blatant, but they are definitely there. When these sensations stop and become an awareness of body warmth, it's time to move your hands. In Reiki this takes about five minutes per position.

For women without Reiki, the same things may happen or other things. The healer may feel nothing but just know when to move. She may suddenly feel her hands being pushed off of the receiver's body, or feel them lifted by her guides. She may hear her guides tell her when to move her hands or she may ask their advice. The receiver, too, may feel strange sensations or she may feel nothing. She may or may not feel the same things the healer does. The sensations may change at each position for both women.

The information received from the guides and angels will always be what is needed for that healing. The receiver and healer may both get impressions or instructions, or only the healer or receiver. These may come in words heard, emotions felt, or pictures shown to either woman of what the guides are doing or what the woman needs to know. They may come as colors or sensations, or the guides may do their work without communicating. Pictures can be of earlier in this life or past life information, especially if the healer asks in the healing to release the source of the dis-ease.

The receiver may react in a variety of ways, too. She may remain quiet or even go to sleep, or she may be very active. She may or may not describe what she sees—I ask them to. She may begin to cry or need to talk; releasing pain by reliving it temporarily is positive and a letting go. Reassure the woman that she is

welcome and safe to do this. The first few times a healer experiences an emotional release it will scare her, but all she needs to do is be supportive and let the receiver do the work. Continue the healing while it is happening without distracting her from the release. By the end of a session, the receiver will be quiet and calm, will feel good, and sometimes years' worth of old pain is gone.

Not every healing is the optimal full body sequence described above. Sometimes constraints of time and place require a quickie where the receiver may not even be able to lie down. In this situation, have her sit in a straight chair and do what you can. It may be possible only to put your hands on the woman's head or her shoulders and so one position that way. If your hands can be placed on the pain area, this is another positive position.

Before starting, calm and center yourself and ask in your guides and angels, even if the healing is happening in a restaurant or at a party. Deep meditation will not be possible here, but you have learned by now to shift into light trance easily and that is all that is required. Run energy if you can. Emotional releases are unlikely to happen in front of other people, and usually should not be sought unless you can find a quiet place for a fuller session. Surprisingly positive results can happen even in minimal healings like these.

Hands on healing sessions an also be done for babies and animals, and there are some differences from working with human adults. First of all, your hands may cover several positions on a small body and less formal positions are required. On pets try placing hands on their crown or sides of head, on the upper back or side at the front shoulder area, the lower back just before the start of the tail, and on the belly. Even this may be too many placements. You may simply put your two hands somewhere on the body, anywhere that the pet is willing to hold still for.

This is also true with infants and small children. Try the sides of the head and one position at the center of the abdomen for infants. Use very gentle touch and no pressure. For older children, add other positions. A baby may be held in the mother's arms or placed on top of the mother's body to calm it for the touch. Both children and animals fill with energy rapidly and even these basic placements may not take long. Your guides will work quickly and probably continue after your hands are lifted. Pets get up and leave and babies or children get restless when they've had enough. Their attention spans are short; don't force them to stay longer than they choose to. Pets that need the help may ask for the energy, returning to push themselves against your hands repeatedly. Give it when they ask. Do the same with children, short (very short sometimes) sessions repeated frequently, even several times in an hour or a day.

With full body adult sessions, one healing may be enough to clear less serious dis-eases. For chronic dis-ease (including emotional pain) once a week is good for intensive work, once or twice a month to take things slowly. Healing sessions can open a lot of emotion and cause detoxifications that a woman with much to clear may not wish to do quickly. For serious, acute dis-eases, healings can be done daily or even more often in crises. This is for full body healing with others. For self-healing, follow your intuition, but nightly may not be too often for most

women and issues. In self-healing, the amount of energy coming into you is also the amount your body can comfortably handle. In healing with others, the healer's transmission of energy may be stronger than the receiver's usual energy flow.

This has been a basic beginning of hands on healing techniques. The only way to really learn and become expert at this or any other type of healing is to do sessions frequently. The real learning is in the doing. It is experience that makes a cooperative working team of you and your guides and angels. Doing many healings also presents many different situations, dis-eases, women, and their reactions that give the healer a background of knowledge to work from and with. Healing cannot be learned from a book; doing the work for oneself and others is the only way. The next chapter describes methods of clearing and releasing painful emotions from oneself and others.

Notes

1 Diane Stein, *Essential Reiki: A Complete Guide to an Ancient Healing Art* (Berkeley, CA, The Crossing Press, 1995), pp. 36–39.

2 *Ibid.*, pp. 44–46.

CHAPTER SEVEN

Emotional Release

This chapter is about using the power of the mind to heal the emotions. Every one of life's many traumas remains in the aura until it is healed and released. Each of these affects the individual at all the body levels, including the level of physical body health. The emotions are at the bridge between the physical body and the all-creative power of the mind. Life traumas are the central factor in the clouding of the mirror of the mind, which then obscures the woman's knowledge of herself as Goddess. By releasing these obscuring emotions, a woman's nature as Goddess-within is revealed, and separation is changed into oneness.

The mind draws matter, change, health, and transformation from the perfection of the Void/Goddess. It attempts to create health, since women's bodies are programmed to know what health is and to seek it. Negative thought forms prevent the mind from transmitting good health: we are what we think. Likewise, negative emotions held in the emotional body, Hara Line, and belly chakra prevent good health from manifesting at the physical level. The purpose of emotional release is to use the aware, positive mind to clear these past traumas and heal the emotions and their negative effects on women's lives.

The emotional body is a record of sensations and feelings, a storehouse from the past. Currently active emotions, feelings, pictures, and impressions are brought into the body through the belly chakra and held there until released. Long-standing ones move to the emotional body aura, where even when the causative events may be forgotten, the emotions are held and remain. A new situation may invoke an old emotion, even though the reason why it is invoked may not be immediately or easily apparent. Every reinforcement of a negative emotion, every life trauma that generates it, great or small, seats that emotion more deeply into the emotional body aura layer and beyond.

Deeply seated emotions lodged in the emotional body become our emotional healing issues in this life and next lifetime's karma, carrying forward to our next incarnation if they are not healed in the present life. They are carried forward until they can be released. Likewise, much of women's karma is comprised of emotions left unresolved from past lifetimes. These emotions reincarnated from the past have to be replayed to be healed. In order to do this, the woman in this lifetime finds herself in trauma situations that may repeat those that started the emotion in a former life. This karmic patterning is held in the aura at the Hara Line, the place of one's life purpose for this incarnation. This is because it is so crucial to heal these emotions and patterns that doing so becomes a part of one's life purpose.

All of this has profound implications, particularly for the issues women are facing today. Women in the past few years are talking about and healing such things as rape, incest, child abuse, alcoholism, and battering. They talk about "breaking the chain" so these abuses will not happen to them again, or become patterns carried on by their children through them. The chain that is broken, however, goes backwards and forwards, and the healing means something far deeper than most women comprehend. Healing these traumas in women's lives is likely also going to heal patterns from past incarnations, and their completion changes lifetimes to come, for themselves and often for others.

I will use the example of my own life. I was severely physically and emotionally battered as a child, with a great deal of neurological, visual, and spinal damage from the experience. My emotional and physical patterns when I began my active healing process were also those of a woman had experienced incest. Yet in several years of healing, therapy, and trace work the sexual abuse didn't surface, though I expected it to, though I was ready, and was looking for it.

When I began to receive past life information, the traumas surfaced. I was born in this lifetime in 1948 and my past life ended just a few years previous to my current birth year. In that latest lifetime, I died in Germany at the Buchenwald concentration camp. I was female there, a Jewish lesbian, and an older teenager as I died in the medical reproductive experimentation that was done on women in the camps. I also experienced repeated beatings, abuse, and rape there, which my determined resistance made only worse. Before I was taken to the concentration camp, my grandfather had abused me sexually for several years.

With knowledge of the source of the trauma, I was able to heal myself of the damage. I had sought

through every this life emotion and trauma as far back as the womb and done tremendous amounts of emotional healing. The pattern, however, could only be released from the karmic level as held on the Hara Line and outer aura bodies. It could not be released from those higher levels until the work on this life's traumas was completed. With this final piece of understanding, the healing is now being finished emotionally and in my body. There have been many changes on every level, and I will manifest no further abuse in this lifetime nor in the lifetimes ahead.

The information of this chapter discusses how to heal emotional pain and damage from this lifetime. Karmic reprogramming and release to heal past incarnations is discussed in a later chapter; it is more advanced work. Karmic reprogramming cannot be done until the work is at least initiated from the emotions of the present. Likewise, to complete emotional release for this lifetime's traumas, the woman must be aware of what happened to her to cause the damage before she can heal it. She can discover this in meditation or in healing sessions if she does not already know.

There is a major advantage to healing painful emotions and this life past traumas through psychic healing. Women who have done it through therapy, support groups, the medical system, etc., have discovered how drawn-out and discouraging a process it can be. When I tried it, I found myself left three years later with a knowledge of all this life's wrongs and problems, a deep depression, and rage, without a clue about what to do. When I asked my Gestalt therapist, who at that point decided she was done with me, her reply was: "When you're angry hit telephone books. It will gradually fade." But it didn't, and I found myself disempowered and less and less able to function.

With psychic healing I did by myself and with the help of other healers, I learned what to do. More relief and release happened in any psychic healing session than in therapy and I started to find answers. Once I figured out the process and techniques, the healing happened rapidly, sometimes even more rapidly than I could easily assimilate. (Brede and

Theresa say I'm impatient and they're right.) Things came together, if not always gently, and healing that never seemed possible occurred. My life is very different now from what it was five years ago or at any time before, and the techniques have proved effective in healing work with others. This healing releases pain as therapy cannot, and releases it to far deeper levels. The methods are explained below, and in fact are the basis for all the techniques in this book. There was no healing until I accessed the spiritual path and looked for healing in that context.

The idea that dis-ease in the body is caused by negative emotions in not a new one. I use the terms *negative* and *painful* interchangeably here; negative emotions does not mean that a woman is negative for experiencing them. We are all survivors if we are female and in bodies in this lifetime. Buddhism describes unfinished emotions as the force that chains people to the Wheel of Incarnation. As unhealed emotions reincarnate with the person and can only be healed in bodies, they force the woman to reincarnate again and again. Each incarnation, however, adds new emotional attachments, continuing the process.

By using the mind to heal and release the emotions, the cycle ends. Emotion is a factor of ego or separateness and letting go of emotions leads to one's Buddha nature/Goddess-within and the understanding of oneself as a part of the unity of all life. Healing the emotions unclouds the mirror, allowing one to see the reality that the mind has created. Freeing the emotions and the limitations of mind means Enlightenment. With this understanding, a woman need no longer reincarnate.

The concept that emotional pain results in disease was also known to the ancient Greeks. Paracelsus, the man trained by wisewomen who is deemed the father of medicine, wrote about this two thousand years ago. Hildegard of Bingen's medicine written eight hundred years ago includes it. Women's knowledge of healing has long since been dropped from organized medicine but it is quite alive. Trance channeler Edgar Cayce, known for his thousands of long distance healings through home remedies, nutrition, and naturopathy, also spoke of emotions and dis-ease. He was aware of stress, karma, and attitude as factors, things not medically validated in his time. He is credited with returning many lost female ideas to Western awareness and founding New Age metaphysics before his death in 1945. Many of the suppressed rural and immigrant midwife/healers of his era could probably have duplicated his work but were not consulted or listened to.

Cayce stated:

> Anger creates headaches or indigestion, depression results in weariness, emotional turbulence triggers asthmatic conditions and so on. He said, "no one can hate his (sic) neighbor and not have stomach or liver trouble" and "one cannot be jealous and allow anger of same and not have upset digestion or heart disorder."[1]

Alice Steadman, in her 1966 book *Who's the Matter With Me*, was probably the first modern woman to codify this theory into a healing system. She dedicates her book "for the sick and tired who are sick and tired of being sick and tired." In it, she speaks of people as spiritual Be-ings with a purpose in being on the planet, and the need to love and respect one another. People's thoughts and fears create dis-ease in the body, and by examining and changing these mental-emotional negatives, health is regained. Dis-ease is caused by friction between body and soul; not knowing oneself as Goddess, not following our incarnational life purpose, or denying one's spirituality.

> The places on and in your body that are consistently sensitive are trying to tell you that you are going against your soul purposes. As your mother tapped your hand that was reaching into the forbidden cookie jar, so our soul spanks us with pain in the part of the body that is the symbol of the wrong thought or act.
>
> We must stop reacting blindly to stimuli; we must become aware of the associations between emotions and bodily reactions.[2]

She describes lower back problems as the imbalance of power between marriage partners who should be equals, and women's breast or uterine tumors as frustrated desires around love and creating a home. Stomachaches and ulcers are a need for love and security. Colds are the result of helplessness and suppressed anger, inner crying over something you can't change or fix. Blood clots and strokes are the withholding of love and affection, and a heart attack is a call to return to openheartedness and tenderness.

Probably the best known writing on dis-ease thought forms and emotions is from Louise Hay in her books *You Can Heal Your Life* and *Heal Your Body* (Hay House, 1984 and 1982). The concept here is similar to Alice Steadman's (though it seems harsher), and her definitions are quite similar. She discusses emotions and beliefs as the core of dis-ease and releasing negative thoughts and emotions as essential for healing. Not believing oneself good enough is a major dis-ease source, along with self-punishment and self-blame. She describes resentment, criticism, fear, guilt, and blame as being personal patterns that draw others to us who treat us accordingly and that finally manifest as dis-eases in the body. Resentment may become cancer, criticism arthritis, guilt manifests as body pain, and fear as everything from ulcers to hair loss.[3]

She states that to release past traumas and these negative emotions and thought forms means to forgive. All dis-ease manifests from a state of unforgiveness, and all healing comes from forgiving others (everyone) and oneself. Forgiveness does not mean condoning abuse, but simply a willingness to let the abuse, the past and the negatives hurting our lives go. This is a process of positive self-love that can heal all things.

> We need to choose to release the past
> and forgive everyone, ourselves included.
> We may not know how to forgive, and
> we may not want to forgive; but the very
> fact that we say we are willing to forgive
> begins the healing process. It is imperative
> for our own healing that "we" release the
> past and forgive everyone.

> "I forgive you for not being the way I
> wanted you to be. I forgive you and I set
> you free." This affirmation sets us free.
> Self-approval and self-acceptance in
> the now are the main keys to positive
> changes in every area of our lives.[4]

I feel that these analyses are valid and many of the definitions of the sources of dis-ease have merit. Yet I have some problem with people's reactions to this information. It is often used to blame women for their dis-ease and pain. I feel this information does not go deeply enough into the traumas of women's lives, either this life or past incarnations. Nor is any sort of political awareness included in these germinal works.

I like to use the dis-ease definitions as information. They may give a woman ideas or directional clues to the source of her pain. I use them as questions in healing: "It is possible that your back pain comes from lack of support in your relationship?" The woman may say yes or no. If yes, I ask her what is needed to solve the problem. She will know, and I give her what caring and encouragement I can. If she says no, I ask her what she perceives the source to be. If she says there is no emotional source at all, I drop the subject. When she is ready to look for a source, the idea is there.

I also believe in the power of forgiveness, but I feel that for most women, much damage needs to be healed before forgiveness becomes possible. In the beginning meditations earlier in this book, women who worked with difficult emotions may not have been ready or able to release them yet. This is fine to begin with; just doing the meditation is a preparation for it. When asking her to send love or to forgive, she may not be ready, but, again, doing the practice is a very good start. Forgiving oneself is always the hardest of all.

———————— : : ————————

Try this exercise again. Go to your meditation space, ground and center, do full body relaxation, run energy, and invite your guides and angels to join you. Ask to see where there are emotional obstructions to your energy flow or to see the blockages at each chakra. Pick the first of these and ask what emotion, trauma, or person is its source. Meditate on the response. First, send love to the emotion or situation and then send love to yourself. Fill yourself with love and let it run through you. Try sending forgiveness next, to the emotion, to the trauma, and to yourself. Run the energy of forgiveness through you and through all that you can forgive at this time. The energy can be in any visualization form: light, color, sound, sensation, fragrance.

Now look at the person involved. If you are unable to send your love, send the Goddess' universal love. If you are unable to forgive the other person, send forgiveness to yourself, whether you think you need forgiveness or not. Go to the emotion again, if it is still there. Ask your spirit guide, angel, or the Goddess to take the painful emotion away and replace it with something positive for your growth. Let the emotion go, give it up. Do this next with the trauma or situation; see what comes in its place. Ask next to let go of all negative influence or damage in your life from the person and replace it with something positive as well. Ask to let go of the person if you feel ready. When this is done, fill yourself with forgiveness, self-forgiveness, or love again. Thank your guides and come back to now.

———————— : : ————————

Repeat the meditation about once a week. If an emotion, person, or situation just won't give, try a different one and come back to it later. Take the healing slowly. If you are unable to forgive the situation or the person, send forgiveness to yourself; if you are unable to forgive yourself, send love. The emotions will shift over time as the healing happens. Ask your guides, angels, and the Goddess to help. For up to three days after a major releasing you may feel more old emotions and memories come up in daily life. Look at them as pain that is releasing and leaving. Watch them like a movie and let them go.

If the emotions feel intense, allow yourself space and time to cry or get angry or feel them fully in another fashion. Don't refuse them or stuff them back, let them come, feel them, and watch them leave. Take sea salt into the shower and rub it over your chakras (not vagina or eyes), then rinse it off. Do this three times during the shower to clear

releasing toxins from your aura quickly. When everything is released, pat apple cider vinegar over your chakras after the shower and let it dry or rinse it off. This reseals your aura and feels wonderful; the vinegar odor fades when it dries. Releasing painful emotions can take time, don't try to do it all at once. Nurture yourself in the process or praise for all you are healing. You will be aware of the changes in your life and health.

Says Stephen Levine in *Healing Into Life and Death:*

> Letting go of our suffering is the hardest work we will ever do. It is also the most fruitful. To heal means to meet ourselves in a new way—in the newness of each moment where all is possible and nothing is limited to the old, our holdings released, our grasping seen with little surprise or judgment. The vastness of our being meeting each moment wholeheartedly whether it holds pleasure or pain. Then the healing goes deeper than we ever imagined, deeper than we ever dreamed.[5]

While forgiving may take time and readiness, removing the ongoing variety of negative influences from your life can be much easier. This is a chakra housecleaning that I like to do every few months. It involves removing anyone's energy that may be draining you or holding you back in any way. Deep-seated emotional stuff releases, if you do it thoroughly and fully, but so do a lot a minor and petty disturbances from people unimportant to your life. If anyone is pulling on your energy, this process removes their influence, and it also uncovers deliberate or unconscious psychic attacks. Though other people are involved, the focus here is in freeing your energy and letting go of them. It harms none, but someone draining you may be angry to be cut off.

The process is called uncording. It is a traditional psychic and Wiccan energy clearing technique that I take to its deepest levels and find extremely valuable for emotional release and healing. People we are holding onto emotionally in a negative way or those who are negatively holding onto us are separated from our auras and energy systems by it. You may be surprised to discover who these people are. There may be a great detoxification after doing this meditation; have the sea salt and the cider vinegar handy.

Be careful not to do too much too quickly. Take one chakra in a session to work deeply on or clear several centers more lightly at one time. It may take a number of nightly uncordings to clear all of your Kundalini chakras, and after a space of time you will look again to find more. When using this for healing emotional trauma, as I do, the process can take months. In the releasing, your emotions or detoxification reactions may become intense or uncomfortable. If so, go more slowly with healing space between the sessions. Every level and cord cleared is progress toward healing, but do it at your own comfortable pace.

——————— : : ———————

Enter the meditative state, ground and center, do full body relaxation, and invite in your spirit guides, angels, and the Goddess. Place protection around yourself; this is important for each session. Look within and ask your guides to show you the first layer of *negative* chakra cords to be removed. Look at your solar plexus center first. You will see coming from that center one or more of what look like electric cords plugged into it. They will seem ugly, dark, or moldy looking, and of various sizes and thicknesses.

Pick one to focus upon and ask whom it is connected to. You will see, feel, or know the person. If it feels right, ask to cut the cord; if it doesn't feel right, there will be another time cutting the cord does not harm the other person in any way, it just frees your energy from that person. To cut the cord, visualize scissors or light doing the job, or ask your guides to cut it or unplug it like a lamp. The cord will snap back to the person it came from; if it doesn't or there is a root of it left, ask your guides to take it away. Send light to the person who has been released, if you can, then fill yourself with healing light where the plug came out to heal the chakra.

Go to the next cord in the same chakra. Ask your guides if you don't immediately see the cord. Repeat the procedure until all the negative cords are gone. If there are any you are not sure you wish to release, you can always

invite them back again later if you wish. If the cord is shown to be negative for you, however, I recommend cutting it now. You have asked to see only negative cords. Think seriously before allowing it to return. Some of the people connected to these cords will surprise you. They may be people you haven't seen in years, people you barely know. It may even be a store clerk you may have recently had words with. The first layer is usually superficial, but it is a start, and it teaches you the process.

Repeat this at all the chakras. After the solar plexus do the centers either above or below it next. It may take more than one meditating session. Don't forget the third eye and crown; these can and do hold negative cords. After clearing the first layer, ask to go deeper, to the next layer, and then the next. Continue until all the Kundalini Line chakras are fully cleared on every layer and level. This may take several weeks. As the layers get deeper the people will become more significant. It may require your sending them forgiveness or universal love to release them and their cords. Cords in the crown chakra are especially deep and may represent very difficult life issues. You may also ask to see and remove any negative cords (or hooks and Hara Line hooks later) that come from a specific person.

When you have done enough for one session, stop and run healing energy through all of your chakras. Ask your guides to heal any damage and remove any toxins left by the cords and people. Place protection around yourself again, thank your guides and angels, and come back to now. Move slowly until you are fully present. Take a shower with sea salt to help complete the releasing, as there may be more of this releasing and old pictures for a few days longer. After the releasing ends, complete the process by patting cider vinegar on all your chakras to reseal your aura, and notice how your energy feels. After deep or difficult sessions you may need a few days of quiet healing space, nurturing, or increased sleep. You will feel your life change as these releases rearrange your aura and heal your emotional body, and your physical dis-eases will improve or heal. This is very profound emotional healing.

——————— : : ———————

When you feel that your chakras have been cleared of all negative cords in their deepest levels, ask in another meditation if there are any negative hooks in them. Hooks are similar to cords but they go much deeper. Visually, mine resembled fishhooks, some with double prongs and barbed points. They are from people you have shared karma with from past lifetimes and who have returned to Earth with you again. You will not see hooks from anyone you don't know in this life. These are major emotional and relationship issues that need release and healing; your rapist, batterer, or incest perpetrator will probably be among them. There is rarely more than one hook to each chakra, but there can be more.

Make sure of protection and invite the help of guides and angels to remove these. Do not pull them out or rip them away—I tried it and was very sick for a week after. Instead, as you see each hook and learn its source, ask your guides to remove it from you in the easiest and gentlest way. They may surround it with light and ease it out, dissolve it, or remove it as you would a fishhook, by cutting off the straight end and pulling it back through. Let them do it and ask that they do it gently. Watch or feel it happen. Ask them to heal all damage and remove all toxins from every aura level. Run energy and reinforce your protection at the end of each session; make sure your shields are two-way so the pain can fully release. Repeat the meditation until all hooks are cleared; it may take several sessions with healing time in between them. Work slowly.

Give yourself a week or a month's rest after this, then look again. Ask to see if there are more negative chakra cords; there probably will be. Clear them. Ask again to see if there are more hooks and clear them also. There will be far fewer hooks but probably some deep ones remain to be cleared. Repeat this in another week. Ask to heal all remaining damage on all aura levels. Fill yourself with light and run energy. Remember to thank your guides.

New cords and hooks will probably surface from time to time for a while at deep levels, as you are ready and strong enough to clear them. New superficial cords come from daily life. When you use your energy protection bubble and chakra shields, they are reduced or eliminated from coming in and attaching to your energy. When all the cords and

hooks seemed cleared, go to the Hara Line chakras. There will be no negative cords here, but the negative hooks at this level are from people whose influence is obstructing your life purpose (or who have done so in the past). These are always karmic relationships, and they may or may not repeat some of the deep cords and hooks from the Kundalini Line.

Clear these one at a time as you did the other hooks, but only one to a session. They will look like bigger construction-type hooks, not fishhooks this time. Take these very slowly as the detoxification reactions to removing them may be extremely intense. You are getting down to bedrock at last. As they are released you may enter a very emotional state for a few weeks or even a month. You may see floods of old pictures going back as far as infancy and even past lifetimes. There may be anger, fear, grief, or simply great relief. Watch the movies, feel the emotions, and let them go. You may feel highly toxic energy releasing from your aura for a long time also. The first three days are the strongest. Fill yourself repeatedly with light and ask your guides to clear you and heal the damage. Remember the salt and vinegar. Wear an amber necklace if you have one, as it protects and reseals the aura, but it is important to clear the amber frequently.

By the time you have finished this process, which may take several months, and undergone the initiation that results, you have changed your life. You will feel definitely lighter in every way and the things that held you back in your growth and healing will now be mostly gone. You may find some of the people around you dropping away and new ones coming in as your energy level no longer matches their vibrations. The damage to your emotional life from past traumas or sexual abuse will be greatly or fully released, changed, and healed.

Your emotions will be freer and more positive and your thought forms healthier. You will feel very vulnerable for a while, but once the process is done and the clearing is completed, stronger than ever before. Take the work slowly and gently, nurture yourself, and appreciate your growth and transformation. Have as much loving support around you at this time as possible, but keep people who are negative about your process away from you during the time you are releasing your cords. Uncording at deep levels is a direct route to profound emotional healing, physical healing, and life change. I have been through every step of this uncording and I promise that the procedure works. This work is usually done alone in meditation, but may be guided by another healer if you wish. The healer will have to tune herself fully to your needs.

The next exercises, for healing the hurt inner child and reprogramming traumas, can also be done by yourself, but the help of another healer is recommended. It is sometimes very difficult to direct and experience these processes at the same time. I feel it is important to have a clear idea of the trauma to be released before you begin. This is essential later for karmic reprogramming and release as well. The day a woman uncovers the memory of her incest for the first time is too soon. Instead, these healings work best for the woman who has examined her situation, felt and explored her hurt and anger, understands the damage that was done to her, and is now ready to let the trauma leave her life. The previous uncording work is a good preliminary step.

Healing the inner child can be done at any time, even at the beginning of the healing process. Yet I found inner child work the most difficult aspect of my own healing until I was almost finished with it. I was terrified of the child that was my early self. I shrank back from her and from all children (whom I have always loved) for a long time. I couldn't talk to my child self or hold her, or any child. I even found forgiving my abuser easier to do. I have presented the exercises in this chapter in the order that they worked for me. You may be different; follow what you know you need.

———————— : : ————————

To begin this with two participants, the healer starts hands on healing and only begins taking the receiver to her inner child when she reaches the heart center. Do this in a very quiet healing session where there has been no other intense happening or emotion. The healer's hands do the positions

quietly at the heart, solar plexus and particularly belly chakra as the work is happening. In doing this as a self-healing, enter the meditative state as usual, get fully relaxed, and run love energy before beginning. For both methods, call in your guides, angels, and the Goddess, and place protection at the start. Avoid uncording, forgiveness, or other processes for this healing session. If you or the healer has Reiki II, use the Sei-He-Ki and Hon-Sha-Ze-Sho-Nen symbols. These heal the emotions and transcend time and karma.

When you are ready, the healer asks you to visualize yourself as a child just before your incest or trauma took place. Then go to the child as your adult self. Hold your inner child, cuddle her, and tell her you will be there to help her when she needs you. Give the child a gift: a crystal, necklace, magick key, or golden horn that she can use to call you when she needs your help. Show her how to use it. The healer leads the receiver through the visualization, as the adult receiver makes friends with her inner child.

Now move slightly ahead in time, going to your child self just after the first incest or trauma. No one is there but the child, and she has used her gift to call for help. The adult woman goes to her inner child to protect, heal, and nurture her. Fill her with comfort and love. Tell her she will survive and be strong and whole. Ask her what she needs as her adult self and give it, using visualization and metaphor to do so. Remind the child of your gift and that you are there to go with her through the pain and the healing. Ask her for a gift for you; it may be an object or a hug. Do as much healing as you can, as much as she will accept. Leave the child comforted, knowing she will be okay, that she is good, loved, and not alone. The healer directs the receiver to return to now, and continues and completes the healing session.

———————— : : ————————

This is usually quite enough for one healing. The receiver will experience memories and emotions. She may have a new view of who she was when her traumas occurred. These may continue for some time, but a sense of healing and greater peace come with her recollection. The receiver of this healing, whether she has done it alone or with another healer, may need a few quiet days alone to finish the process and releasing. She may need a lot of sleep for a few days. The healer needs to check in on her during this period and support her. The receiver of the healing needs to know that she is loved and that she is not alone, and that she has someone to talk to if she wants to. She may go to her child self again if she chooses to, at any time.

——————— : : ———————

Here is a variation or additional session for women whose parents have not been positive. The adult again goes to her child self, but this time she goes as the inner child's fairy Goddess Mother, wand and all. You may go to your child dressed as Glenda the Good Witch, Cinderella's Fairy Goddess Mother, or the great Mother. This magickal adult self asks her inner child to describe her ideal parent or parents, replacing her real parents with perfect ones. As the child adds each detail, the adult self incorporates it into a growing positive image that forms in the room. Use as many of your senses in the visualization as possible. If the child wants parents who look different, have her pick storybook ones. When she has fully designed her new family, the adult Goddess self brings the new images to life.

The inner child meets them and gets to know them. Change anything she wants changed, and help the parents and child get to know each other. Everything the child wants is in these new parents. Now teach these ideal parents what children need and how to raise a child with compassion, respect, and love. Ask the new parents and child if anything more is needed. Give them what they need. Watch the child growing up and then finally grown with her new family. See how she is different from the way the receiver of the healing is in the present. Bring the healed child with her perfect parents into the magickal adult's heart. Ask to bring the healed inner child into your adult life to heal your adult self. Bring the healing into now and the received awareness to the present. Finish the healing.

——————— : : ———————

After the receiver feels finished with the two previous healings, at least a week later, take the process further. Reiki healers again use the Sei-He-Ki and Hon-Sha-Ze-Sho-Nen. Healer and receiver begin the session as previously. Make sure to invite in both healer's and receiver's guides and angels. Start by having the receiver visualize herself as a child just before her incest or trauma began. The child is more healed this time, as a result of the previous sessions, and is stronger for what is to come. The adult is also stronger, having benefited from the experience and grown. Time does not exist in psychic healing and age regression for healing the past heals the whole Be-ing at all times of her life. It is this idea that is central for this session.

The receiver as her child self before her trauma began describes her life in positive terms. She may show the healer and her adult self her room, what she is doing in school, her new dress, and what is happening right now. Keep it positive, make it up if necessary. Suppose that her incest was to happen that evening, but this time in a new version of reality it does not occur. Have the child describe that evening in a new form, without trauma or incest. Again make the picture fully positive and ordinary. If the receiver/child can't think of what the evening would have been like, ask her to imagine it, create it, or to make it up.

The receiver/child describes an ordinary evening, perhaps homework, television, a bath, and bedtime. Her favorite doll or teddy bear is with her, and the child goes to sleep and dreams peacefully and safely. The healer directs the receiver to move to the next day and asks her, "Since the incest didn't happen, how is your life different?" Have her describe the next day briefly, again in ordinary terms. Throughout this visualization healing, it is extremely important that all images in it are completely positive. Remember that what you think you create, and visualization in the deep meditative state of healing is extremely powerful. The receiver/child briefly describes her day—school, the playground, an ice cream cone, then home to her favorite dinner and TV. Ask her to describe how she feels.

Now the healer guides the receiver as her child self to her next birthday. She asks her to describe her life since the incest hasn't happened. Ask her how she is different for this change in her life. Keep the descriptions from here on fairly brief; the point is to make them positive. Then the healer guides the receiver to a birthday five years later, asking her again to describe how her life has changed. Go to ten years later and do this again. The child is grown or nearly so now. She describes a life undamaged by incest or trauma, and creates a positive, hopeful scene.

The healer allows the receiver to rest with the new images and new life for a short while, then directs her to bring her healed reality to the present. Ask her how her life is different and what has changed to positive well-being. Direct the receiver to return to the present, bringing the changes with her. Tell her to bring the healing into body, emotions, mind, and spirit on every level. Finish the hands on healing and allow her to rest and reintegrate. She may need a longer time than usual, and she may be spacy for a longer time after the session. These feelings may continue for several days.

———————— : : ————————

The receiver may say at this point, "But it did happen. I can't just pretend that it didn't." Of course it did and nothing can change that fact. Ask her, however, "Which version of this lifetime would you rather have for yourself and your future?" The woman will choose the positive new one. Tell her to bring the healing into now and accept the new reality and new memories with it. Her acceptance and choosing will make the new vision real. None of this is to deny the woman's earlier suffering. It is a way of reprogramming her mind to heal the emotional damage of the past.

The mind that creates our template reality is easily confused. It accepts a vision or thought form of reality as fully as an actual event. Since the mind can't tell the difference, give it the positive choice of a carefully created new life. Every image in it must be positive. By doing this, the mind is confused as to which set of memories is real. Even knowing that the trauma is real, the new memories confuse the mind enough to dilute the old thought form. This releases and heals the damage held in the mental and emotional bodies. When the woman looks at her memories, the real events are still there, but the emotions are diffused. The technique is used in hypnosis and in neurolinguistic programming (NLP) and it can be spectacularly effective.

For a period of about the next week or ten days, the receiver will feel her body's energy shifting and realigning. For me it felt as if my molecules were rearranging and I was becoming freed of a great weight. My face changed and softened as the muscles relaxed, and my back began to straighten. My

skin and eyes looked clearer. I felt calm. My depression was gone and a new sense of being present on the planet began for the first time. I felt the need to sleep almost straight through the next three days, and when I awakened I felt good, but too spacy to do much. The sensations were wholly pleasant. The healing changed my life in ways I could not have believed possible.

This reprogramming is the last step in a long process. The woman must have full knowledge of her past before doing it and have gone through and healed her emotions beyond the period of rage. She needs to be ready to forgive at least herself. Forgiveness is last in the process and reprogramming requires an almost last stage readiness. If the woman has not been able to forgive before the reprogramming, she will probably be ready to do so after it. She must be able to become her inner child, and be able to envision a better life. The process of uncording is a crucial preparation, as are the inner child healings described before the reprogramming. For the woman who enters this healing with readiness, it can be a complete transformation. The technique can also be used for past lives.

The key to all emotional release healing is the willingness to let go. Forgiveness may come later but is not as strong an issue, letting go is the key. This is extremely hard to learn for women who have had no control of their lives and are struggling to find empowerment. Once they are able to trust the Goddess and their own competence in their present life, however, it suddenly becomes easy. When pain becomes too much, admit you can't control it, that it can't be controlled. Give it to the Goddess, your spirit guides or angels, or give it to the Earth. Give it up and let it go; Spirit will take care of it. Let the Goddess take it away and turn it into something positive and useful, into something that is healed.

Letting go does not mean fighting and resisting, it means accepting and going on. It does not mean losing control but rejecting the need for control. There is no need, nothing is needed. A memory or emotion that triggers no resistance has no power:

In each moment of letting go we enter our birth and ease our death.

In each moment of letting go, we let things be as they are without the least force or need to be otherwise . . .

In each moment of letting go, healing passes through the mind/body.[6]

After years of struggling, letting go was a sudden peace for me, an "aha" experience. (Why didn't I get it sooner?) It took long-term helpless despair to push me to the brink of surrender and accept it; this despair is unnecessary. All healing begins from the moment of giving up control. All healing starts and ends with letting go.

Women doing deep emotional release work also need to know about chakra scars. These start from the wounds of repeated abused trust, betrayal, fear, hurt, or lack of love. Just as a child who is traumatized may bury the conscious memory until she is old enough and strong enough to deal with it, she may also store deep emotional wounds in her aura. These are always connected to a specific trauma, situation, or incident and are usually held in the energy of the belly chakra or heart. The suppressed traumas remain unhealed and affect the grown woman's emotional life, though she may not consciously remember the incidents. Such wounds become karmic if not healed in this lifetime.

When women begin deep release of negative incidents and emotions, the chakra scars surface for clearing. This is ultimately very positive but may not seem so at the time. It can happen after an old memory or painful emotion is accessed and then released; the scar is reopened later, usually with explosive force. When the wound is at the belly chakra, its opening brings an intensive, agonizing flood of flashbacks, anger, and fear, resentment, and self-hate. The sheer, shaking force of these emotions, often when the woman has thought herself past feeling them, can be totally unnerving and upsetting. The suffering may be intense but the clearing is also rapid; it is usually over within an hour.

When the scar is at the heart center, something similar occurs. In my case these were accompanied by overwhelming emotional and physical pain, a pain I felt in my whole body but was focused at my heart. I clearly knew the source to be emotional. I experienced explosions of despair, grief, and wishing for death. The intensity of the breakthrough reflected the literally breathtaking agony. These releases usually happened upon waking and always seemed to come when I could stay in bed and wait them out. Within an hour or so they were gone. My heart chakra felt blown apart, and I was shaky and weak for the day, but the intense pain was over. Major shifts in emotional outlook always followed, along with a sense of accomplishment and great relief.

When this experience happened several times, I came to dread but to understand the pattern. I describe it here not to frighten you, but to tell you that you can go through it without fear. It is painful and intense, but also quick and positive in the long-term. It is sometimes preceded by a day or two of uneasiness or anxiety. The way to best handle this process is simply to let it happen and let go. Look at the pictures in your mind without holding on to them or resisting them, and they will pass quietly. Feel the emotions but don't fear or hold on to them, and let them go as well. When the siege ends, head for the shower and the sea salt to complete the clearing. Later when it's all over, use apple cider vinegar, patting it on your chakras to reseal and heal your aura. Rest and nurture yourself for at least a few days.

The process of emotional release is seldom easy but it can be done quickly and effectively step by step. I have presented it in stages that have worked for me and for others that I've taught. The process can be done alone the way I did it, but I strongly recommend working with another healer if possible. When the going gets rough it is good to have support and human guidance. A healer must be fully compassionate to be of help in this work. Don't forget to ask for guidance from your guides at every step.

Healing for women is emotional release. It is the only real way to clear, heal, and end the pain, and go forward after sexual or other abuse. This is women's initiation and trial by fire. Along with healing your life and the lifetimes to come, it will train you as a healer to help others through the process. The Earth changes are happening in women's bodies and emotional release is the central clearing. By healing ourselves, we heal the Goddess and the Earth.

The next chapter discusses crystals and gemstones as tools for healers and women's healing.

Notes

1 C. Norman Shealy MD, Ph.D., and Carolyn M. Myss, MA, *The Creation of Health*, pp. 66–67.

2 Alice Steadman, *Who's the Matter With Me* (Washington, DC, ESPress, 1966), p. 9 and 15.

3 Louise Hay, *You Can Heal Your Life* (Santa Monica, CA, Hay House, 1984), pp. 12–13.

4 *Ibid.*, pp. 14–15.

5 Stephen Levine, *Healing Into Life and Death*, p. 55.

6 *Ibid.*, p. 216.

CHAPTER EIGHT

Crystal Healing

Gemstones and crystals are some of my favorite things. I always have bulging pockets full, and women tease me, telling me that I clank when I walk. I always wear several necklaces and gemstone rings and earrings. According to some of my friends, gemstones are the only things that hold me to the Earth. Some women refuse to go shopping with me; my pendulum checks over everything from cucumbers to clothes to other crystals (and on some days likes to buy everything and on others will not buy anything). Yet there is a method to the madness: all the gem energies are chosen carefully for what I need in healing and are chosen to coordinate energetically with each other.

I use gemstones and crystals in virtually all healing and in every part of my life. They heal me and heal others. If I am not using them directly on someone's chakras, I am using the pendulum to channel information, or the gemstones on my hands and body to help me access guides and transmit crystal frequencies. When my erratic psychic vision or psychic hearing senses give no clues, the pendulum run by a spirit guide tells me what I need or the receiver needs to know. I also give "readings" of psychic information for myself and others with it.

When used directly in a healing session, whether under the massage table or placed in the hands of the receiver, on her energy centers, or over a blockage area, the results are always positive. The crystals focus the session on what the receiver needs to accomplish at that time. Crystals and gemstones placed in the room also are active in the healing. They help with protection, clearing, moving out negative energy, and reestablishing energy flows. I have used them to scoop out pain from the chakras and aura bodies, to repair damaged chakras and aura energy, and even to do psychic surgery. They do much in the way of emotional healing and reprogramming. While crystals and gemstones are not required for psychic healing, they are powerful and beautiful tools that enhance the effectiveness of the healings in every way. Moreover, they bring great beauty into a healer's work and life.

The composition of the Earth is fully one-third quartz crystal, and the silica and water that crystal is composed of are also major components of the physical body. Quartz is fossilized water and our bodies are 98% water. Crystals' piezoelectric effects, their energy fields, match our human energy and electrical frequency. The Earth's magnetic field is crystal vibration energy and so is the magnetic field of the human aura. A cleared and tuned crystal clears and tunes human energy. It matches women's energy to the vibrational frequency of the planet and therefore heals it. A cleared crystal is tuned (programmed), and the planet is tuned, to vibrate the frequency of good health on all levels and to bring it into Be-ing.

A network of crystal energy intersects the Earth. At ground level these are the ley lines, the planet's acupuncture map. Beyond the Earth's body, and mirrored at the level of the human mental body aura, is the universal grid. This is formed by crystal energy radiating from the planet and the galaxy, and also is incorporated into human energy. The Wiccan adage for this is, "As above, so below." The grid contains our individual minds and the collective Mind of society, as well as access to the Universal Mind of Goddess or the Void. It is the interface between our auras and the auras of Earth and universe. The crystal grid is the energy transmitted of the Nonvoid, the way in which mind creates matter from the Void.

Connecting Earth's ley lines to Her mental aura energy grid is a series of giant tuning crystals, most of them underground or underwater. These physically exist on the planet, scattered around the globe in key places. Many of them are sacred sites to local people who still practice ancient ways. Some of these crystals are unknown or forgotten. They have been dormant or nearly dormant for thousands of years. They were deactivated at the time that human DNA was unplugged, as they are a major part of the information network that is our heritage.

Like human energy, this network of connecting crystal transmitters is now waking up. I have watched the crystals awakening. In 1992, my friend Jill made a trip to the sacred sites of Mexico with a New Age group. Ritual was done there to activate a crystal known to be in the ocean off the Mexican coast. When I looked psychically at the crystal later, I saw it was indeed opening but also that it needed clearing badly. With my guides and other nonphysical healers, as well as two human friends, I worked on clearing it, as I felt it would do more harm than good

the way it was. I was shown at the time the full crystal network, or as much of it as the planetary healers wanted known to me at the time.

I had the idea, or the guides gave it to me, that if this first crystal could be cleared and tuned, it could also be programmed to awaken, clear, and tune the rest of the network. My Earth healing guides approved, as did the deva of the giant crystal. Crystals are healers and they want to work. The crystal agreed to open the next transmitter and clear it, also programming it to go next in line. As each crystal opened, cleared, and healed, it went on to heal the next. As the full grid awakened, the next job was to heal the smaller crystals on the planet, also programming them to open the next smaller ones yet.

The ultimate goal was to awaken, clear, and heal all the crystals of Earth, from the energy grid giants down to the tiny ones in computer chips and jewelry, and every size of crystal in between. When all the crystals were healed, the energy frequency of the planet would be healed. In healing Earth's planetary crystal energy, all human energy is also activated, tuned, expanded, and healed. Doing this planetary work in psychic healing seemed very simple at the time, with its implications only revealed to us later. All I and two healer friends knew then was that we were brightening up some big crystals that needed clearing. I watched in meditation each night as the opening giant crystals awakened, brightened, and cleared, and more of the stones were visible to join the network each evening. I was shown a map of the planet, with new bright lights that located each stone.

The process of awakening the first giants took a month and six months more for them to fully clear. I saw thirteen of them in all. Earth's energy became very heavy with their releasing for a while, a dark pall around the planet that is still clearing. People's energy is clearing now in the same way, and the remaining crystals of the Earth are still opening. I feel that the clearing of the crystals and their programming for healing the Earth and people are major factors in the Earth changes. It has also made even the little crystals and gemstones more powerful for healing on the planet. Not all of the giant grid crystals are clear quartz, though many of them are. I was also aware of amethyst, smoky quartz, pink tourmaline and aquamarine crystals among the giants, and I'm sure there were other kinds of crystals.

Crystals are a major factor for healing women and the Earth. As the crystals are opening and healing, their healed frequencies also heal people by opening, tuning, and programming human auras. The giants are a connecting link between the ley line system and the universal grid. Their activation also connects the human aura into the universal grid as well as into our own Bodies of Light. We are intrinsic in the universal Goddess plan, our minds are part of Mind. Galactic and solar system energy now can reach us through the grid, plus the help of healers from other planets.

The extension and connection of the grid to individuals has made it possible for the Jupiter college, Pleiadian, and other positive healers and planetary protectors to affect and help us and the Earth. For the first time, the healers are receiving help and healing; we are no longer doing it all alone. Those little crystals and colored gemstones in our pockets and jewelry do more for us than we know, and their energy is due to increase as time goes on.

My favorite healing tool is the pendulum, which I make at home and use primarily in order to talk with spirit guides. Lately I've attempted to hear the information directly rather than using the tool, but I still use a pendulum for many things including writing and healing. A pendulum can be made of anything that can be dangled from a string or thin chain, but I prefer them made of a very clear quartz crystal for the swinging end and a gemstone to hold onto at the other. The chain in between should be a pure metal (silver, copper or gold) if it is metal at all, as pot metal alloys block energy transmission and reduce accuracy. Use stones of a comfortable size and weight, and the chain of a comfortable length for the woman holding it. My own pendulum chains at this time are about five to seven inches long, and the stones about the size of marbles.

Probably the central requirement for an effective pendulum is that its energy should be kept fully cleared at all times. Stones attract and hold negative energy and then they release it cleared. However, while in use, they may gather it too fast to clear quickly enough. Heavy use also builds up a frequency overload that the stones collect and hold. This overload is a form of electrical static that, as on the radio, can interfere with clear transmission. A pendulum used to channel spiritual energy or, as they are usually used by advanced healers, to bypass the conscious mind and reach the grid of Universal Mind, needs to be kept completely clear of negative energy and static. If it is not clear, the light/information moving through it is distorted and cannot be accurate.

Pendulums in metaphysics are generally used to bypass the conscious mind and reach the intuitive or higher mind. The information gained this way broadens daily life but is not as yet Goddess or universal energy. By linking your psychic abilities to the crystal and programming/tuning it to reach the grid, much greater information is accessed. By programming the pendulum to work with a spirit guide who has indicated willingness to speak through it, even higher level information and healing can be gained. The tool itself, the pendulum's gemstones, must be kept energy-cleared and you must make certain that only the highest level of positive energy and spirit guides are to work through it.

Crystals and gemstones can be cleared in a variety of ways for pendulums or any other use. Sea salt or sea salt water are what most women use. Soaking the stones overnight or longer is highly effective. Salt tarnishes silver mountings, however, and rots the cords that beads are strung with. Clear running water, even tap water, may be used, but cannot clear very overloaded stones. Some women smudge with sage or cedar smoke, a very effective method; you can smudge yourself and your home to clear them as well. Placing the stones under a pyramid overnight or longer is another way. I use this method. Even a pyramid made of cardboard works, if the dimensions are correct. A small pyramid, however, sometimes has difficulty in clearing large quantities of overloaded crystals and gemstones.

If you are a Reiki healer, the Reiki II and III symbols clear and program stones beautifully. I hold the stone in my hand or place my hands on a larger one, and visualize the symbols entering it. Do the Dai-Ko-Myo first to open the stone's aura, then the Sei-He-Ki for clearing. Next use the Cho-Ku-Rei while you silently state the intended purpose of the stone: "I dedicate this crystal/gemstone/pendulum to the Goddess for healing me and others." For healing stones I add the Hon-Sha-Ze-Sho-Nen, then finish with the Dai-Ko-Myo again, asking the stone to be self-clearing. In effect you have given the crystal a Reiki attunement and though it still needs clearing, it will need it far less often in the future.

You may also ask your guides and angels to clear and program/tune stones for you. Hold the stone in your hand, and ask your guides and the deva of the gemstone or crystal to come in. First ask them to clear the stone, then dedicate it to the Goddess or the purpose (healing, protection, etc.). Tune it to the energy of the person who will use it by stating who it is for. Ask the deva of the stone if it agrees with your intent once the stone is cleared and before programming. If the deva has other work for that particular gemstone or crystal she will tell you so. Crystals work with specific people and purposes, while gemstones may have more generalized energies. Do this clearing and programming for all new stones, and clear them frequently thereafter. Though your guides work with you to clear your gemstones, also use physical methods like sea salt or pyramids often. Gemstones or crystals need reprogramming only if you decide to change their purpose.

Using a pendulum, ask it to tune itself to the universal grid, or simply program it for "the clearly and highest possible truth and information." Then ask if any of your guides or angels is willing to operate the pendulum for you so that it will be an accurate healing tool. By doing so you make your pendulum much more effective and you will eliminate much frustration. It took me a few years to learn this. If none of your present guides wishes to do this

work, ask if a guide or angel "out there" might like to join you for the purpose. Specify that only energies of truth, wisdom, light, and Goddess are permitted to enter.

Next, learn to work with your pendulum and its guide. Hold the gemstone loosely in the thumb and first finger of your dominant hand with the crystal dangling. Ask your pendulum guide to join you. Then ask to see the pendulum swing that represents a "yes" answer. This may be different from a "yes" for someone else. Focus your mind thinking "yes" or "show me a yes" while looking at the crystal. The Hara Line vision chakras run pendulums tuned to the grid. Watch the response, asking for "yes" a few times. Then do the same asking to see the swing for "no," watching the pendulum and focusing your mind on the "no." This is very similar to the earlier exercise of bending the candle flame and moving a hanging bead. Ask to see the swing for a "maybe" or "undetermined" answer.

Once you are familiar with the responses, ask some questions that you already know the answers to. Keep your mind neutral, not thinking yes or no, but focus on the swinging end of the pendulum. Your only possible pendulum answers are "yes," "no," or "maybe/undetermined," so the questions need careful phrasing. If your name is Pat, a question phrased "Am I Pat or Sandy?" won't get a reasonable or accurate answer. Ask instead two questions: "Am I Pat?" and "Am I Sandy?" The simpler the question, the more useful the response, so information may take a number of questions to resolve. Ask questions in the beginning that you already have answers to in order to teach you what the pendulum can and cannot do. You have to learn how you and your pendulum spirit guide can work together.

I find pendulums of great value in healing work. They pick a vitamin or homeopathic remedy for myself or others, and determine the dosage and frequency of use. Ask, "Is twenty-five milligrams enough?" (no); "is seventy-five?" (yes); "is seventy-five too much?" (no). The dosage is seventy-five milligrams. "Is once a day enough at seventy-five milligrams?" (no); "twice a day?" (no); "three times a day?" (yes). Ask which chakra or emotion needs work to heal a dis-ease. "Is it the belly chakra?" (yes); "solar plexus?" (no); "heart chakra" (yes). The energy is stuck at belly chakra and heart. On through all the chakras, asking about each one. "Is the emotion that is the problem grief, anger, fear, rage, blame?" Ask at each chakra whether there are cords to clear here. "How many? Have I cleared them all? Are there hooks?" Each part of this is a separate yes/no question. The possibilities are limitless.

The more you work with a pendulum, the more fully you will learn its benefits, uses, and limits. It is definitely not infallible, but the accuracy of a tuned, cleared pendulum for an experienced user who can access grid and guides can be as high as 90% or higher. The user must have an information base for the pendulum to choose its answers from. Where the questions have an emotional weight for the user, the accuracy is not as high, as our conscious mind and desires will influence the responses and can override spirit guidance. If you want it to say "yes," it will honor your desire. Keep your mind as neutral as possible and ask questions in an emotionally neutral way for best results.

A pendulum that is not kept completely energy-cleared cannot be accurate. The response may be "no" to everything, or may swing in senseless circles. I have made several pendulums for myself, and one clears under the pyramid while I use another. I interchange them and have learned to feel when a pendulum is getting "full" by the weight and sluggishness.

Gem and crystal jewelry and pocket stones need to be cleared nightly, and stones used in healing require complete energy cleansing before and after each use. Uncleared stones can actually make the receiver of their energy in a healing feel sick. Likewise, the uncleared crystal giants reflected the sickness of the Earth, and clearing them releases that sickness from the planet.

Using crystals and gemstones on the receiver's body for healing is called the laying on of stones. It is a powerful method of releasing negative energy, clearing and balancing the chakras, effecting emotional release, and bringing light and healing into all the aura bodies. The cleared and tuned stones move the receiver's vibration into alignment with the planet and the universal grid. This results in a freeing of life force energy in the chakras and the aura, a healing of the Body of Light, and a transformation of negative or dis-ease energy into health. Aligning the receiver's energy with the grid enhances the ability of her mind to clear the mirror of emotions and accept positive change and growth. Laying on of stones also affects the chakras on both Kundalini and Hara Line levels.

This process may be done for oneself or as part of a hands on healing. It may be done with clear quartz crystals only, colored gemstones only, or a combination of both. I prefer to do laying on of stones as part of a Reiki/hands on session, using crystals and gemstones together. I have done crystal-only sessions, gemstone-only sessions, and sessions using only one type of gemstone geared to the receiver's needs. All of these variations are positive and valuable.

Energy in this type of crystal healing needs to move in one direction through the body, either Earth to sky or sky to Earth. Determine the direction at the beginning and stay with it; this is something a pendulum can discover. If the energy is Earth to sky, all of the crystals or gemstones that have points are placed with the points turned toward the receiver's crown. If the direction is from sky to Earth, it is the opposite, with the crystals pointing toward her feet. Though other hands on healing begins at the head and moves toward the feet, in laying on of stones it is the opposite. Begin placing the stones at or below the feet and move upward on the body to above the receiver's crown.

The sky to Earth direction in a gemstone layout is used to ground the receiver and bring her into her body. It moves spirituality/Goddess life force energy in through her crown and out her feet, rooting her into the Earth. This is a good direction for someone who has been abused and needs to be in her physical body more. It is also good for women who spend too much time at spiritual work, are spacy and ungrounded, or have difficulty with Earthplane functioning. Placing the stones Earth to sky brings Mother Earth energy into and through a woman, moving the receiver's energy to a higher vibration or more spiritual level. It connects a very Earth-based receiver to her spiritual and psychic abilities. It is often used in a healing where psychic or spiritual information is needed to resolve a physical dis-ease. It accesses the grid and galaxy and intergalactic healing guides.

When a hands on healing is done along with laying on of stones, the stones are placed upon the receiver's body first, from feet to head. The healer then begins her hands on session as usual, starting at the head and moving toward the feet. She places her hands on top of the crystals and gemstones to do the hand positions. Most laying on of stones is done on the front of the body only. If the healer wishes to continue on the receiver's back she may do so, but she will remove the stones before the receiver turns over. If she wishes to place more stones or crystals on the back, she may. As with other forms of healing, allow your guides and your intuition to direct the session.

A laying on of stones healing can be quite intense. More frequent emotional releases, past life and this life trauma opening, and transformative events happen when gemstones and crystals are used than would occur without them. This is as effective with a few stones as with a full body layout, if the few stones are chosen carefully. A layout of only rose quartz or kunzite, or a combination of pink stones, can clear heart scars positively and intensely. The changes will continue happening for three days to a week after the session. A layout of clear crystals can bring about a strong physical and emotional detoxification that will continue happening for up to a week. The changes are always positive and are usually gentle.

There are a number of patterns that can be used for placing crystals and gemstones on the body. Following the line of the central channels is basic and all that is actually required. When using different colored gemstones, place the stone color that matches each chakra on that center. Use the Kundalini Line colors and stones, or those of the Hara Line, or both. There may be some color alternatives, as a choice of black or red for root chakra. One stone per chakra and color may be used or many. The manner of arranging them when there are many stones can be artistic or not. Gemstones are always beautiful.

When using clear quartz layouts, the pattern again follows the line of the central channels. Place a crystal below the feet or between them and on each Kundalini chakra, with one above the crown. I like to put a large crystal in each of the receiver's hands as well. The crystals, or most of them in laying on of stones, should be larger ones of at least three inches in length for optimal healing results. Use the clearest ones possible for any healing work, including the ones for pendulums, with unbroken points wherever possible.

The colored gemstones used in laying on of stones can be in any form—cut and faceted, raw with or without matrix, tumbled, eggs, cabochons, as pieces of jewelry, or as strings of beads or chips. The forms can be mixed with some of each, whatever you have available. I use a laying on of stones set for traveling with very fine, quarter-inch to one inch, gemstones. They work well and powerfully for healing, but are hard to keep track of, and I lose too many of them. I prefer stones measuring one inch to three inches. I also use some necklaces of stones. Stones move around in a healing and drop off the receiver's body. When doing gemstone healings outdoors, place the receiver on the center of a large blanket or the stones will disappear in the grass.

When using crystals and gemstones together, I like to place the gemstones on the chakras. I put clear crystals in the receiver's hands, above her crown, below her feet, and in a circle around her body a few inches away. Place the points either toward Earth or sky along the vertical length of the central chakra channel. Crystals around the body point toward the receiver. Clear crystals can also be used at each chakra, surrounded by the colored gemstones. They can be placed between the Kundalini chakras so that they are over the Hara chakras and activate the Hara Line.

---- : : ----

Begin a laying on of stones healing in the same way as a hands on healing session. The receiver lies on her back on a padded floor or massage table, with pillows under head and legs for comfort. The healer may use a chair or stand beside a massage table, but needs to be able to move freely. The space should be quiet, comfortable, warm, and private. Since the stones need to be cleared before using them, either do this before the receiver arrives or smudge the stones, receiver, room, and yourself with sage as a beginning of the session. Be sure the receiver can tolerate the smoke before doing this. Have a safe place to put the sage or smudge stick when you are finished with it. I use only stones for body lay-outs that have been dedicated to the Goddess and pro-grammed for healing. Invite both women's guides and angels into the session, and I usually invite any other high level nonphysical healers who wish to participate.

Start by placing the crystals below the receiver's feet, in her hands, and above her head. Then go chakra by chakra moving from feet to crown. Spread the stones where you can reach them and select what goes on each center. There may be stones you do not use for a particular person, and stones that are drawn to a chakra where their colors don't logically match. Let yourself be guided, there are no real rules. A stone whose energy is not needed for the session or inappropriate for the receiver's energy will roll right off, or roll to a place where it is better utilized. Allow this to occur. If you "forget" to place a stone, it is because its energy is not useful for that person or that healing. If the receiver says a stone feels uncomfortable, take it off; the energy isn't right for her needs.

When the stones are all in place, the healer has two options. She can go behind the receiver's head and begin a hands on healing. She must place her hands carefully not to scatter the stones. Her other choice is to sit quietly beside the receiver and simply wait, allowing the stones and guides to do the healing. As the receiver's chakras and aura absorb and are balanced by the crystal and gem energies, the stones begin to roll off one by one. The woman may say that something now feels uncomfortable or feels finished; move that stone from her body. Sometimes all the stones seem to jump off at once, though the receiver is lying perfectly still. It can startle and is often funny when this happens. Do not replace them.

When all the stones are off, or you or the receiver feel finished though some stones remain, the healing is over. Allow the receiver to lie quietly for a while without the stones. While she is doing this, the healer can gather them up from the table and floor and clear them again before putting them away. (I keep mine in a pouch that protects them.) There is often a major energy shift or emotional release during a gemstone layout healing.

---- : : ----

It is harder to do a full body gemstone layout for oneself, but it can be done. Place the surrounding crystals on the floor then lie down in the center of the arrangement. Have the stones for each chakra separated by color into piles beside you, using a pendulum before starting to determine which stones to include. Keep it simple. Use only a few stones. An all crystal layout is the easiest to use for one's own healing. Invite your guides into the session before you begin. Make sure the crystals have been cleared. With the stones in place on your body, meditate and rest in the energy and feel your guides and nonphysical healers work-ing through the stones do the healing.

---- : : ----

An even simpler form of gemstone self-healing is to hold two stones, one in each hand while you sleep. Pick the two stones for energies you especially need. Though at first you will not hold onto them all night, they still remain close enough to affect and heal you. After a while you will get used to holding them and wake up with them still in your hands. You can also take a gemstone or crystal in each hand and, lying on your back in bed, place one over your heart and the other somewhere else that it is needed. Put the stones down when finished or sleep with them all night. Let them roll off your body or away from you when their energy and healing are done.

---- : : ----

Most women who work with gemstones use them for the Kundalini chakras and channels. There are many books about gemstones for this purpose. I will briefly describe a few stones not generally discussed that I have found especially positive for healing. Everyone who uses gemstones has her own favorites that other healers may not know about. I find most of my stones at local gemshows, held every year. The prices are cheapest there. I learn their uses by sleeping with them and asking my guides to show me what they do. I will list some unfamiliar stones for the Kundalini chakras before describing gemstones that activate the Hara Line centers.

The first of these gemstones for the Kundalini root chakra is *black tourmaline*. I most often use black grounding energy at this center though its primary color is red. I like all of the tourmalines for their ability to cast a protective aura. This tourmaline in particular absorbs and transmutes negative energy and negative thought forms from oneself and others. It heals fear and panic, and gives a sense of safety and protected security. Black tourmaline aids and activates one's ability to ground and center, and to feel present and welcome on the Earthplane. It helps those who resist being in their bodies.

Tektite is another black root center gemstone. Its origin is not of this planet, as tektites are meteorite material. The stone helps the user to expand, align, and clear all the chakras and the full Kundalini channel. It is also an energy protector and grounds the recipient into Earth reality, safety, and security, as well as bringing her into the fullness of the galaxy. It draws positive help from non-Earth sources.[1] Tibetan tektite is considered to be the most powerful, but it is expensive and rare. American tektites can be found at a cheaper price at gemshows.

For the belly chakra, two useful gem energies are red phantom quartz and orange Pecos quartz. A phantom is a clear crystal that looks as if another crystal is inside it. In a red phantom, the inner gemstone is an orange-red color; it looks as if a thumb is embedded in the clear stone. Phantoms open memories, feelings, and pictures, and they release this life's negative emotions. They are particularly useful placed at the belly chakra for healing anger by opening the memories of the anger's source. Take this energy in small doses, putting the stone down before you get too much feeling to assimilate.

Pecos quartz is a nontranslucent gem in a deep orange color. Like red phantom quartz, it comes in small points, usually around an inch in length. This stone transmutes anger rather than opening it, changing this life and past life anger and rage to understanding, compassion, and forgiveness. It also helps to protect clairsentient healers who take in too much of others' pain, or match their own pain experience to the receiver's, by releasing it through compassion. Pecos quartz is an important stone for healing women's past sexual abuse, rape, and battering, and for releasing the karmic patterns of abuse from the aura. It is less intense than red phantom quartz and may be worn as a necklace or carried daily in a pocket. There is no danger of overload.

The following two stones for the solar plexus are more generally known. The first is *natural citrine*, as opposed to the heat-treated amethyst that turns golden and is usually sold as citrine. It is found in light yellow single points or in clusters. The natural form is a cleanser and detoxifier for the whole Kundalini Line, a tissue regenerator and spinal balancer, and helps to clear, expand, and align the energy of the aura bodies. Citrine is a great help for women with cystitis (bladder infections) or other urinary, kidney, or digestive dis-eases.

Golden or champagne *topaz* is often overlooked. It focuses major energy for the solar plexus. Its primary use is in stabilizing and facilitating life changes from birth to death, healing the etheric double, and balancing the central nervous system. It balances the body's energy, mind, and emotions on all levels, and clears and heals the Body of Light. For those women who are experiencing reincarnations while in the body, or any strong healing, releasing, or detoxification, this stone is a valuable protector and stabilizer of the process.

The heart center is next with two of my favorite stones, kunzite (pink) and dioptase (green). *Kunzite* provides a sense of calm, balance, stability, self-confidence, peace, and compassion. It aids in both openness and protection. Its energy is similar to pink tourmaline. Kunzite heals the negativity that comes from oneself and others, due to fear and insecurity. This gentle Kwan Yin energy connects and clears the heart, throat, third eye, and crown. It aids psychic intuition and makes working with guides easier for healing and self-healing.

Dioptase heals the inner child, and releases this life and past life traumas. It calms and relieves pain and is the gentlest method I know for opening and healing heart scars. The energy of this gemstone is happy, playful, and childlike. It heals the physical body through heart healing, releasing past abuse and promoting karmic understanding. This sparkly, deep green stone is both expensive and fragile, and can sacrifice itself in a healing. I wore a small pendant during some heart release work and watched the stone disintegrate in the process.

Two light blue throat chakra energies are angelite and kyanite. *Angelite* is an emotional and physical stabilizer and calmative. I find it so useful that, like kunzite, I carry it in my pocket. It enhances creativity and speaking ability, particularly when these qualities are combined with channeling. This soft, robin's egg blue stone helps in awareness of and connecting with spirit guides and angels. It draws angelic protection to one's self and one's home. Melody in *Love Is In the Earth* (Earth-Love Publishing, 1991) also credits angelite with aiding telepathy and empathy, astral travel, rebirthing, and dispelling anger.[2]

Kyanite is a silver blue stone that connects the energies of the Kundalini and Hara Line chakras and channels, and balances, aligns, opens, expands, and heals the energies of both systems. It is also a stone specifically for the third eye and for the Hara Line thymus and causal body chakras. This energy removes and heals blockages and burnout from all the aura bodies. It heals any dis-ease of the throat, aids communication including psychic communication with guides and animals, calms, promotes manifesting, and stabilizes the immune system. I consider it an important all-healing gemstone energy.

For the third eye chakra, I have chosen blue aventurine and azurite, both deep blue/indigo stones. *Azurite* is the third eye counterpart to dioptase and resembles it in form. It offers an intense transformation and transcendence energy. It can be used only in small doses and will probably keep you awake if you take it to bed. I use it for healing at times when I feel as though the process is stuck and I need to go to the other side for new teaching. It actively connects the user to her Light Body and the universal mind grid, to the Nonvoid and Void, to spirit guides and Goddess. It is essential for women who do Earth healing or deep level meditation. When buying this stone, pick a deep colored, good quality specimen with shiny facet crystals and active electrical energy.

Blue aventurine as another indigo electrical gemstone. This one is more focused on teaching and regeneration than azurite. It takes the wounded inner child from the belly chakra and heals her into the heart. Use it for inner child work and every aspect of emotional and mental/psychic inner healing. Blue aventurine heals the emotions via the mind and universal Goddess Mind, and is another access to the Goddess-within, the Body of Light, and the Earth grid. It accesses guides to teach and help in healing, and aids in releasing space junk and negative entities from the chakras and aura bodies.

Some crown center gemstones are rutile amethyst, sugilite, and violet tourmaline. *Rutile amethyst* is amethyst containing metallic hairs or strands. These have the usual qualities of amethyst but raise them to more advanced levels. Instead of healing only the crown, this amethyst aligns and raises the energy of the entire Kundalini channel. It clears energy and emotional blockages from Ida, Pingala, and Sushumna, rather than from the individual chakras. It balances and clears the Ki/energy flows to the brain, central and autonomic nervous systems, lymphatic channels, and the acupuncture meridians. Rutile amethyst also helps in understanding and healing personal karma.

Sugilite is another crown center energy that opens and balances the whole Kundalini channel, this time including all the chakra centers. Melody describes it as connecting mind and body for the healing of disease in both. It helps the user to live in the present, cushions the harshness of living on the Earthplane, and heals and releases despair, hostility, and discouragement.[3] Sugilite tunes one's energy to Earth's vibration and the universal grid, Goddess-within, and the Nonvoid, and balances the left and right hemispheres of the brain. It is helpful with dis-eases like dyslexia and strokes.

Violet tourmaline offers protection of spiritual energies by preventing and clearing spirit attachments, negative entities, low level spirits, and negative alien interference. This is not the pink tourmaline or rubellite of the causal body chakra (see below) but a tourmaline actually violet or purple in color that I found at a cheap price at a gemshow. The stone clears the human energy system, emotional and mental aura levels, and Body of Light negative vibrations incurred in this lifetime only; it will not heal those brought in from past lives. It brings light and cleansing through the Kundalini channels and the Ki/energy flows.

Gemstones for the Hara Line chakras include old standards and some newly noticed gem energies. The information from my guides on these follow the chakra colors and positions less predictably than for the Kundalini centers. Tourmalines of all colors seem important for both Kundalini and Hara Line growth. I will begin with the Earth chakra and move upward to the transpersonal point.

Stones for the Earth chakra (black) include black velvet tourmaline and boji stones. *Black velvet tourmaline* has a shiny but rough, almost furred texture, and a vibrating energy that has to be felt to be believed. I couple it with a similar looking white (not clear) quartz phantom for the transpersonal point, placing them below the feet (black) and above the crown (white) to open and balance the entire Hara Line immediately and electrically. The pair connect individual energy to Earth Ki and Heavenly Ki, filling the Hara channels and chakras between with transforming light. Though these stones are each only about an inch long, they are a direct entrance to the Void and Nonvoid. It is interesting to me that I was guided to use black gemstones for both Earth chakra and Kundalini root center; the Kundalini root chakra is usually given as red.

For grounding one's celestial beginnings into an aware Earth incarnation, try *boji stones*. Like tektites, these are off planet energies that clear and stabilize the whole aura system, but this time from the emotional body Hara level. They heal the emotional body of negative feelings, emotional patterns, and old pain, translating the changes into physical level healings. Bojis used singly heal chronic pain on all levels; in pairs they open the aura and release blockages from the human electrical system and acupuncture meridians. For best results keep one in your pocket every day, clearing it at night, as bojis work very slowly and absorb what they clear.

Elestial quartz is a gemstone for the Hara grounding chakras at the soles of the feet (brown). The energy of these stones is transformative. I was surprised that my spirit guides placed these crystals at this position. Apparently the deep releasing and life change these gemstones catalyze is in the focus of grounding women into their life paths. Sleeping with them for a few nights opens a whole new way of viewing one's life and shows you where you are going. Their energy can be sudden and drastic.

A gemstone for the dark green movement chakras behind the knees is *moldavite*. Again, I was surprised to find this stone in this position. Moldavite is another off planet energy. Its main use for me has been in connecting to positive Pleiadian help for protection, healing, and self-healing. This work includes the removal of past life negative implants and spirit attachments. The stone also gives one a sense of being free to move among dimensions and galaxies while still living safe on Earth. It is a distinct psychic opener and enhancer with a very strong yet gentle vibration.

Stones for the maroon perineum chakra were hard to discover. Rubellite seemed natural to me here, but my guides rejected it and chose red *spinel* instead. This stone is a major detoxifier that also aligns the etheric and emotional bodies, thereby clearing and connecting the Hara and Kundalini channels. Melody calls it the "stone of immortality," and an aid to rejuvenation and regeneration. It replenishes spent energy, enhances physical vitality, and offers encouragement for difficult tasks.[4] These definitions fit with the perineum chakra as the Asian "gateway of life and death," the energy pump for the

Hara chakra system. Contracting and closing the physical perineum muscles also connects Hara and Kundalini Line energy flows.

Amber is the energy for gold-brown Hara chakra. Though as fossilized pine resin it is not technically a stone at all, amber stabilizes the entire Hara system, offering calming, certainty of one's path and choices, mental and emotional strength, energy balancing and cleansing, and all-aura healing. Where the aura has been torn by too rapid emotional release, karmic release, psychic attack removal, anesthetics, or other negative agents, amber heals, refills, protects, and repairs the tear. It is also a shield against absorbing others' pain during healing work and protects against energy intrusion, psychic attack, and psychic draining by others.

Two gemstones for detoxifying the lime green diaphragm center are green tourmaline and emerald. *Green tourmaline* opens and drains the toxins of this chakra and is a purgative to release negative emotions from one's life purpose. I have never found it to be a gentle energy, but nothing at the diaphragm chakra seems gentle. Like other tourmalines, this one places an aura of protection around the user, allowing her to go through the diaphragm purging process safely and with trust in the Goddess and the outcome. The stone does its job as quickly as possible and with ultimately positive results.

Once the diaphragm is opened and released, *emerald* heals and repairs the damage and reprograms the chakra and Hara Line/emotional body. It transforms and detoxifies negative into positive emotional energy and is stabilizing and deeply soothing. The stone creates a sense of security, harmony, and closeness to Goddess Source. It connects one to Goddess-within and provides a vision of oneself and one's life purpose in relation to the Earth and universal plan. Melody says of emerald:

> It can be used to eliminate negativity from one's life and to bring forth the positive actions required to assist one in remaining centered in the practicality of one's lifework.[5]

Blue tourmaline and aquamarine are the gemstones for the aqua Hara Line thymus chakra. Again the tourmaline is transformative and the aquamarine (which is an emerald of a different color) is regenerative. *Blue tourmaline* opens and clears the thymus chakra and connects the emotional body Hara Line to the etheric double Kundalini channel. It cleanses and stabilizes the Hara Line and Hara chakras. The stone transforms emotional healing into the healing of physical dis-ease and translates spiritual energy and purpose into service for the Earth and all people. Blue tourmaline brings the individual a sense of desire and dedication to her life purpose and protects her in accomplishing that purpose.

Aquamarine fills the Hara Line with healing light that carries over to the Kundalini through the thymus. It calms and supports the individual through periods of intense physical, emotional, or karmic release and cleansing, and aids a life path of service. The stone shields and protects, and as a representative of ocean energy, reminds us of the constant presence and love of Goddess in one's life and life purpose. Communication with spirit guides and angels is enhanced by aquamarine, as is spiritual and psychic awareness, and connection with one's oversoul. This is powerful and gentle gem energy that also heals deeply on all levels.

Two stones for the mystical causal body chakra are blue sapphire and pink tourmaline. *Sapphire* is a transformative electrical energy that radiates spiritual light and life force through the Hara Line. It steps up one's connection and communication with guides, angels, Light Body, oversoul, the universal mind grid, and the Goddess. Sapphire helps to activate and manifest one's life purpose successfully and bring it into Earthplane consciousness and intent. This is an energy radiating joy, prosperity, peace, and beauty. Though considered a precious stone, raw pieces are available at a cheap price; only a very small chip is needed to make use of this powerful energy.

Pink tourmaline or rubellite is the other causal body chakra stone, the red violet color of rosé wine. This gemstone offers the recipient a comforting love energy that opens and heals the entire emotional body by radiating its effects from this chakra. It brings one's life purpose awareness into all the Hara Line chakras and into Earthplane consciousness for a compassionate life of service. Rubellite balances the energy flows of both Hara and Kundalini Line and all of the chakras on both levels. It transforms and removes blockages and negativity from the entire Be-ing, and fills chakras and channels with light, peace, joy, and universal love.

Gemstones for the silver vision chakras include danburite and labradorite. *Danburite* is a silver white gemstone that intensifies and purifies any other energy it is used with and it does so very gently. It opens the new potential galactic chakras described by Barbara Marciniak and opens the individual's awareness of other realms and dimensions. This nurturing energy does its transformative work at the user's own pace, without force or stress. Danburite connects women with their angels and enhances creativity, psychic ability, and awareness of mind.[6] I use it to strengthen my homemade flower essences. It also enhances the Reiki attunement process.

Silver iridescent *labradorite* connects one's emotional and mental bodies to physical purpose and action. The stone also intensively protects the aura, clears blockages, and activates the Hara Line. It opens the eyes/vision chakras for use as lasers in healing and for working with pendulums. Melody credits labradorite with the ability to give the individual a conscious awareness of her life purpose, and to connect the user to interplanetary Be-ings and galactic healing levels. She says that the stone is of extraterrestrial origin.[7]

Transpersonal point clear gemstones include Herkimer diamonds and phenacite. *Phenacite* is relatively new on the gemstone scene but is so expensive that I have only been able to hold it in metaphysical shops, never to buy it. The energy activates the Hara Line, bringing Heavenly Ki/Goddess energy into the Hara and Kundalini chakras and all the channels and meridians. It has a flowing, gently cleansing, comforting, and balancing energy. When you hold it, it enhances your sense of yourself as a part of a greater Goddess plan on both the Earth and in the universe.

Herkimer diamonds are another of my favorite gemstones, though I find only the large and very clear ones interesting. These are expensive, but I've had some beautiful ones come to me through bargains, bartering, and Goddess' good luck. The energy of these stones is both gentle and transformative; they are pure love and pure information/light. Herkimers carry the vibration of harmony, fine tuning, expansion, clarity, abundance, and fulfillment—the art of living in the present peacefully. They connect the other dimensions and stars to and with the Earth and one's life purpose, and connect the individual to the universal grid, her Body of Light, and oversoul.

These are just a few of the hundreds of gemstone energies available for healing. I have chosen only a few of my favorites. Every healer who works with stones has her own selection of common and less common ones. You can find rare gemstones at Heaven and Earth, P.O. Box 249, 956 Rt. 14 S., E. Montpelier, VT 05651, phone 802-476-4775. Their *Heaven and Earth Network News* offers valuable information on and the availability of healing stones, both new stones and old stones.

One further energy needs to be discussed in this chapter, though it is a manufactured rather than natural gemstone. This is the Tachyon energy bead, tiny white iridescent cabochons that look like opals. These were designed by Japanese physicists. Made of silica ceramic Optimum Resonant Materials, they have the property of increasing energy flow through the body and aura bodies. The company literature says they are anti-entropic (they work against decay and wear). They increase blood circulation, endurance and Ki in the body, and create order out of chaos.

My spirit guides state that these Tachyon beads work positively on the Hara level to open, expand, and clear the Hara Line and Hara chakra energy. The beads increase the physical body's ability to recover and heal itself, to generate energy without depletion and exhaustion, and to regenerate spent energy more quickly. One woman told me that for her the beads increase all positive energy on all levels, while another feels that they stimulate transformative positive change. One woman said they straightened her own spinal curvature over a three-week period, wearing the Tachyon belt.

I generally am not attracted to human-made gems, but when I saw these in a New Age catalog, my spirit guides pestered me with them until I had to try them. I ordered only two tiny beads as they are quite expensive, but they are so tiny that I lost them almost immediately. Then my guides insisted that I order a Tachyon pendant, a hollow silver castle that contains ten beads. When I finally did, I first felt that the vibration was making me sick. I was told to make friends with the pendant and dedicate it to the Goddess, and upon doing so it calmed down and now feels wonderful. Other women tell me they like to hold it because it feels almost alive. They say that its energy upsets them and feels "weird." It seems to have tuned itself to my specific aura energy.

In the six months of wearing the pendant, I feel that it is expanding my Hara energy and opening the series of Hara Line chakras to bring them to my understanding and awareness. It has also stimulated an intense, almost overwhelming process of detoxification and releasing on all chakras and aura levels, including the higher energy bodies and etheric template. My ability to channel and to find meanings

and use of such things as flowers for flower essences and healing gemstones has increased considerably. It has helped me connect with angels and other-dimensional positive Be-ings.

The beads come singly, but they are really too small to handle, or in the pendant, wristbands, headbands, belts, charged water, and a body lotion. Look for these on the Internet. Though really expensive, they are useful self-healing tools for the women who are drawn to them. They can also be used in the laying on of stones for healing with others.

Crystal healing is a complex art that I have barely begun to cover in this chapter. The next chapter teaches distance healing: what is generally known as psychic healing or healing with the mind.

Notes

1 "Tibetan Tektites," in *The Heaven and Earth Network News*, Issue 9, Winter, 1993–1994, pp. 5–6. And "Tibetan Tektite Update," Issue 10, Spring–Summer, 1994, pp. 9–10.

2 Melody, *Love Is In the Earth: A Kaleidoscope of Crystals* (Richland, WA, Earth-Love Publishing House, 1991), pp. 54–55.

3 *Ibid.*, pp. 418–419.

4 *Ibid.*, pp. 409–410.

5 *Ibid.*, p. 153.

6 "Danburite," in *The Heaven and Earth Network News*, Issue 10, Spring–Summer, 1994, pp. 8–9.

7 Melody, *Love Is In the Earth*, p. 232.

CHAPTER NINE

Distance Healing

W hen most people speak of psychic healing, they are referring to distance healing. This technique carries healing across time and space into past and future lifetimes and the between life states after death. It is also used in hands on healing and self-healing to access deeper levels. This healing is virtually limitless in range and scope. Psychic/distance healing works on oneself and on others, animals, nations, the Earth, and beyond the planet. The healer does not need to know those she helps. It heals all the aura bodies and the physical body, reaching even into soul body levels. It works on the Kundalini and Hara Line chakras and channels, reaching the Light Body and the universal grid, and enters the levels of the Goddess-Void.

Distance healing is a process of using the mind and Goddess Mind to draw change, creation, and transformation from the Nonvoid through the Void. The mind is the all-creative power that makes and changes realities. Conscious use of mind in the meditative state has the ability to direct and change realities of every type and level. Particularly when the negative emotions that cloud the mind-mirror have been released, the aware mind has the power to choose, create, and manifest positive transformation. It can change dis-ease to health in every way.

All the healing tools I've written about in this book have been preparation to make this psychic use of mind for healing possible. Distance/psychic healing is basically done by visualization in the meditative state. The depth of trance or meditation is deeper than what is needed for hands on healing. Therefore, skill in meditation is the first essential. Very deep altered states are required, even to the theta level, to effect and sustain deep change and especially to reach the outer aura layers beyond the body, etheric double, and emotions. It requires the concentration and control of mind.

Visualization is the medium by which the mental body/mind effects change. It is only the conscious mental body level that is able to accept information/light/energy in words. Words (the technology level) are the only method modern science has learned to access, and the only method of information in this time that is commonly taught. Modern medicine (technology) is therefore trapped in the conscious mind dense physical and is not fully effective even there. All the other aura body levels reject words—words can't reach or affect them.

Visualization through the senses is the medium that the aura energy bodies perceive and respond to. The more fully and clearly a healer learns to use visual and other sensory images, the greater her control, range, and access to effect change on all levels in healing.

Images, symbols, feelings, sounds, emotions, and to a lesser extend fragrances are the media for creating and directing change on every level except the rational technological mind. The mind can make few changes using words, but many with the other senses. A sensory picture of what needs to happen in the body can be used by the creative mind to cause it to happen. Likewise, feeling negative emotions and releasing them from the emotional body by fully accepting and experiencing them removes the obstructions to mental clarity. Releasing negative pictures along with the emotions accompanying them, old flashbacks of hidden pain, also removes the obstructions to a clear mind. The clear, creative mind, the unclouded Buddhist mirror, is freed by visualization. It can then be reprogrammed to more positive visions of healing as a new reality.

Along with deep meditation, visualization as a directing medium, and emotional release as a way to uncover truth, working with spirit guides is essential in psychic healing. This is the primary factor which can only be achieved through expertise in the other skills. Where visualization and emotional release access the Nonvoid, meditation and spirit guidance access the greater Mind of Goddess and Goddess-within, the Void.

Every Be-ing is a part of the oneness of Goddess, though the clouded mirror prevents her from knowing this and creates separation of self from Source. The Goddess-within (or Buddha nature) is intrinsically perfect; it needs no change, growth, or healing. But all the blockages, illusions, misperceptions, and pain of ego/separation hide this from us. Psychic/distance healing, aided by spirit Be-ings who know our real Goddess selves, helps to uncover the Goddess-within selves we don't readily perceive. Spirit guides are perceived in the mind and are a bridge from the individual mind to the Goddess/Void/Universal Mind.

Working with spirit guides, angels, and nonphysical healers is central to psychic healing. They bring the perspective of the Goddess Mind into the session. These guides understand and access both the healer's and receiver's Goddess-within wisdom. The healer is given information in the session she could not otherwise obtain, and the receiver is healed at a level beyond her ordinary reach or the healer's. In hands on healing, spirit guides work through the healer's hands. In psychic/distance healing, they work through her higher mind.

Psychic healing is done from the spiritual body levels, brought into physical consciousness and manifestation through the throat, brow, crown, and heart (higher mind) chakras. The throat is the energy center of the first spiritual body aura level, the level of the etheric template. It is the most complex of the seven chakras that access the physical body and can be used for conscious direction. The throat is the center of empathy and telepathy (receiving and sending thought), communication, and expression on physical and psychic levels, psychic sound and hearing, and creation and self-creation on the Earthplane and beyond.

The throat chakra, the fifth center, accesses this first of three spiritual body aura layers. Barbara Ann Brennan defines this level as holding the template or life blueprint for the first chakra (root), the physical body/etheric double aura. She calls the throat chakra the level of divine will, that brings the individual into oneness with the All:

> Divine will is a template or pattern for the great evolutionary plan of humanity and the universe. This template is alive, pulsating and constantly unfolding. It has a powerful, almost inexorable feeling of will and purpose. To experience it is to experience perfect order. It is a world of precision and a level of precise tones. This is the level of symbols.[1]

In healing terms, the throat chakra is the stepped-down spiritual energy of the first creation level of the human electrical field. It can access the spiritual/

DIAGRAM 13

The Aura Body Levels[2]

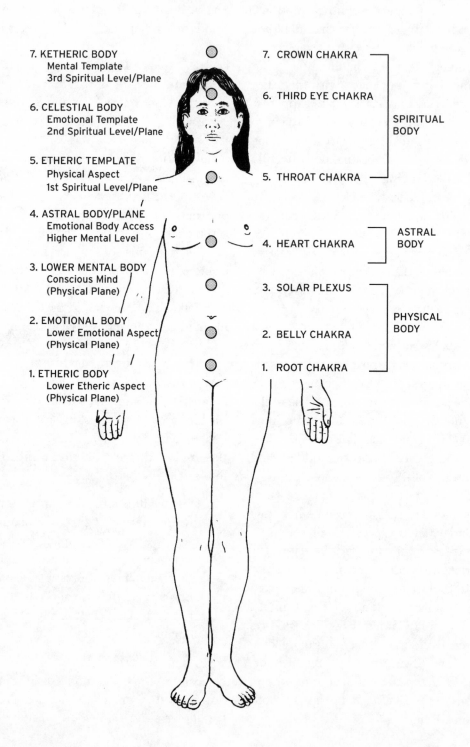

7. KETHERIC BODY
   Mental Template
   3rd Spiritual Level/Plane

6. CELESTIAL BODY
   Emotional Template
   2nd Spiritual Level/Plane

5. ETHERIC TEMPLATE
   Physical Aspect
   1st Spiritual Level/Plane

4. ASTRAL BODY/PLANE
   Emotional Body Access
   Higher Mental Level

3. LOWER MENTAL BODY
   Conscious Mind
   (Physical Plane)

2. EMOTIONAL BODY
   Lower Emotional Aspect
   (Physical Plane)

1. ETHERIC BODY
   Lower Etheric Aspect
   (Physical Plane)

7. CROWN CHAKRA

6. THIRD EYE CHAKRA

SPIRITUAL
BODY

5. THROAT CHAKRA

4. HEART CHAKRA

ASTRAL
BODY

3. SOLAR PLEXUS

PHYSICAL
BODY

2. BELLY CHAKRA

1. ROOT CHAKRA

etheric template level of the Void to effect change and manifest it in the dense body. This is the place where individual ego discovers the oneness of her Goddess-within or Buddha nature. To psychics able to see this aura layer, the structures in it look like photographic negatives with light and dark in reverse. Healers viewing my own throat chakra and etheric template level describe it as having many rooms with opening and closing doors.

Healing and psychic perception at this level are especially conducive to sound. Buddhists say that the sound of chanting the Om (Om Mani Padme Hum) is the vibration that created the universe. This is the place from which healers hear guided information and receive healing information in symbols, and the place of speaking and communicating with one's spirit guides and of channeling. Brennan describes the throat and etheric template level as "alive, pulsating and constantly unfolding." It manifests Goddess' will, and the human awareness that each woman's life has a spiritual reason for Be-ing.

The next level of the spiritual body aura used in psychic healing is the celestial body, with its stepped-down energy anchored at the third eye or brow chakra, the sixth chakra. This is the level of psychic awareness and psychic knowing that is purely analytical and of the mind. Yet it contains the energy template blueprint for the emotional body and the belly chakra. The third eye/celestial aura level is where we perceive and can create a myriad of realities and truths. It is the unclouded mirror or the Goddess-within mind that is freed of negative emotions. Where the previous level contained divine will, this one experiences and reflects divine love into all the other levels and chakras.

Barbara Ann Brennan visually describes the celestial body level as radiating rays of light in all colors of the rainbow. She defines it:

This is the level of feelings within the world of our spirit; it is the level of our divine love.... It is experienced as spiritual love, as joy, elation, and bliss. We reach this level laboratory silencing the noisy mind and listening. We reach it through meditation . . . chanting or reverie. We commune . . . with all the beings of the spiritual world of various heavens as well as of humanity, plants, and animals of the Earth.[3]

Our ability to work with spirit guides and follow their directions is at this third eye/celestial template energy layer. Guides, angels, and other nonphysical healers come to us from a place of great love, and offer their help in that light. Their help is accessed through the unclouded, illuminated mind that is free of distractions and negative emotions and is able to focus in a one-pointed meditative concentration. As in the throat center, there is access to the Void at this level, but to a deeper place in the Void. Healing that creates and forms healthier realities is sent from the celestial template/middle spiritual body level through the clairvoyance (clear perception, psychic sight) of the third eye.

The third spiritual body level, anchored into the Kundalini system at the crown (seventh chakra), is called the ketheric aura body. It holds the energy template for the solar plexus, the lower mental body or rational, technological, conscious mind. At this aura level, this is the divine mind, Goddess, and the Buddhist Void, the place all creation is drawn from. Brennan describes this level as a gold grid whose interweaving strands form all the attributes of the physical body. This grid is surrounded by a golden egg of protecting light. It is an entrance to the Light body, to the universal grid of collective mind, and to the universal Goddess Mind grid.

The crown chakra, where the stepped-down energy of the ketheric aura body reaches the etheric double, is the place of spirituality. It is the thousand petaled lotus, the myriad lives and possibilities of life and the universe, with the jewel in the center. Often pictured as the center jewel is the Buddha or the bodhisattva/Goddess Kwan Yin. This center of all planes of reality, mind, and existence is Enlightenment, the mind that is free of all illusion, Goddess/Goddess-within or Buddha nature. The crown is the place of women's knowing that they are the perfection of Goddess, the place of total oneness, and of understanding how one's life and service operate a part of Her greater plan. Thought is the nature and creation of all reality including physical reality, and it is from this Mind of Goddess through the individual mind that all healing comes.

Says Barbara Ann Brennan about this level:

> The seventh level golden threads of light also exist throughout and around everything, whether they be the cells of an organ, a body, a group of people, or the whole world....
>
> We experience divine mind within us and enter into the world of the universal divine mind field.... Here we know perfection within our imperfections.[4]

One further and perhaps most important chakra and aura level used in distance/psychic healing is that of the heart. This fourth chakra is the transformer for the higher mental body level on the physical plane and the bridge to the astral body and the Hara Line. The heart and higher mind are the place of compassion and of feeling for oneself and others. All healing comes from this place of experiencing and giving love which brings creation energy into the emotional body from the spiritual levels (the spiritual body chakras and aura layers). Before mind energy can reach the etheric double and dense physical body it has to pass through the emotional/astral body layer. In other words, for healing to be effective it must be transmitted with love.

The higher mental aura body at the heart center is the access place to the astral. This is where we go when we go out of body and into other than Earthplane awareness. It is where our guides meet us to work with us when we invite them into a healing or meditation. The astral is where we reach through to do healing with a receiver who is not physically present in a distance healing. It is the emotional/astral body of the receiver (or oneself) that accepts the energy of psychic healing done as distance healing.

Barbara Ann Brennan describes healing or any other interaction between two people:

> Whenever two people interact, either overtly or covertly, great streams of colored fluidlike bioplasma reach out from each to touch the other's field. The nature of the interaction corresponds with the nature of the energy-consciousness of these energy streams.[5]

It is this interaction between the auras of healer and receiver that transmits healing, either hands on, or as psychic/distant healing. It works at any distance through the astral. The help of guides, angels, and nonphysical healers in a healing situation enters the healer's aura through her spiritual body. It is then transmitted to the receiver through the healer's heart/higher mental/astral body. The energy is taken in through the receiver's astral body as well, then distributed to her chakras and physical body level.

———————— : : ————————

With all this theory in mind, and the skills of meditation, visualization, and spirit guide contact, begin a simple psychic healing. To start, enter meditative space, ground and center, and do full body relaxation. Invite your guides and angels to join you. By this time you may be able to enter a meditative state simply by shifting into it. A healer experienced in psychic work learns to do this and can do distance healing at any time and in almost any place. Her concentration and one-pointed focus become complete or nearly so. It is not something ever to do while driving, however, or when your total Earthplane attention is essential. It can't be shared by any activity. What may seem like a moment's change to the astral altered healing state can be much longer than a moment; it can even extend beyond an hour. Time does not exist at this level, though time passes by on Earth.

When in the meditative space, remember the earlier exercise of visualizing a rose or other flower. This time give the rose your name and ask it to represent your state of vitality. If you are bright and healthy, the rose will appear bright and healthy. If you are tired, its leaves may droop, and if very tired the flower itself may droop. If you are nicely grounded and rooted, the rose will show this, perhaps by appearing to look planted in a lovely garden. Don't expect the rose to look a certain way or attempt to create it that way, just give it your name and ask it to mirror your health.

The rose may appear in any color. Remember that color is symbolic. Look at the image and read the energy assessment it offers you.

Now send healing to the rose.[6] Try sending it first as healing light of an unspecified color; the color will become what you need. Send it as a sound, again asking only for the sound that has the most to offer you at this time. How does the rose respond to light and sound? Do the same with a variety of positive emotions, asking again for what you need. The emotions may be joy, love, fulfillment, comfort, admiration. Notice what emotion/s you require. Bring in an image of the sun over the rose, sunlight filling it with healing and wellness in its golden rays. With each step, notice how the rose responds and how your body feels.

Now dissolve the rose and see standing in its place an image of yourself. This image or picture will probably not be clear or detailed. It may only be a shadowy or fuzzy outline, or a haze of color. Whatever you see is fine; ask to see your state of health. Send the same images to this image of yourself as you sent to the rose. Send them one by one, noticing what you are directed to send each time. Notice how each energy form you send may change the image of yourself. Are the forms the same as what you sent the rose? Notice any sensations in your body each time. Notice the colors and emotions. Ask if there is anything else your guides and angels want you to do, see, send, or be aware of. Make one more image, this one of yourself in full health, vitality, and joy; make it the self you wish to be. Give yourself the time you need to do this. Thank your guides and come back to now.

Return to present awareness slowly and notice how you feel in your body, emotions, and mind. What did you learn about yourself and your needs from this psychic healing? Did you receive any instructions from your guides or angels to carry through on the Earthplane? They may have told you to do things such as to get more rest, drink water, go to the beach, or take a walk in the wilderness. How much of the healing you sent to the rose with your name on it was what you needed?

———————— : : ————————

In another session make another rose, this time giving it someone else's name that you know needs and will accept healing from you. This should be someone who has given you permission to do so. (How to ask for permission astrally is described below.) Do the same thing with the rose for someone else that you did with your own rose. How is the rose different from your rose? How are the images that your guides direct you to send for this other person different? Are there guides or angels present in this healing that weren't there before? Do they give you information of what to do or send, or information to tell the other person? Watch the rose respond and notice what images this rose responds to most readily.

As in the previous healing, dissolve the rose and see standing before you the person it represented. Again, the image will probably not be clear, but only something that tells you who the person is. If you do not recognize what you are shown, ask the woman in your mind, "Is it ____?" You will perceive a reply in some way. She may say "yes," smile, wave, or show herself more clearly. Clear visualization of self and others in psychic healing increases with practice. This skill is like a muscle, it grows strong with frequent use.

Ask the receiver of your healing what she might need, or need more of, for her healing. You have already sent much healing to her in the rose image; she may or may not need more. Let her or her guides, or your guides, show you what she requires and visualize it or send it to her. As in the previous healing meditation, see the woman healed, happy, and healthy before you dissolve the image and return to the present. Don't forget to thank your guides.

———————— : : ————————

If you feel ready to talk about this healing to the receiver, do so. Since she has given permission, she is probably someone open to hearing your impressions. She will probably have perceptions and confirmations of her own to offer. Hearing them helps your self-confidence, especially for healers who are just beginning psychic work. When I first began distance healing, it felt so easy that I thought I was making it all up, especially as I was not deeply in trance at the time. No one could have been more surprised that I when a woman over two hundred miles away wanted to know if I was sending her gold light on Thursday around 10 p.m. I was. She had asked me in a letter to send her energy.

Once you are experienced at doing healings with roses and then turning the roses into people, drop the roses and simply visualize the people from the start. More information will begin to come to you as you gain experience. Ask to see the area of the receiver's pain and send your healing directly to that area in light, color, sound, or symbol. All of these methods are not needed for most healings—only one or two of them. Some healers prefer sending light, while others like to use sound as their dominant modality.

Sometimes dis-ease is not what it seems to be. The area where the dis-ease appears may not match what you have been told by the woman before the healing. However, she will usually confirm what you see afterwards. A woman's headache may show up in the healing as pain in her lower abdomen, and since many headaches are intestinal in origin, this makes sense. If a woman's stomachache is from fear held in her throat chakra, you may see the pain at either or both places. Sometimes unexpected pains may show up. Ask the receiver what's going on in that chakra or part of her body.

Another way of doing psychic healing is to ask to see the receiver's chakras. Areas where energy is stuck or blocked will appear different, less attractive than the healthy areas. A healthy chakra is a bright and even color, with no dark spots, cracks, or muddy places. It is aligned on the body with the other centers, in a vertical straight line. Send the healthy color of the chakra to such areas to clear and heal them. Send light blue to a red spot in the throat center, for example, or green (or pink) to a cloudy heart chakra. Again, you can use sound or other sensory images, if you prefer.

There are probably as many ways to do distance healing as there are women doing it. Another method—I call it Tinker Woman healing—is simply to go in and fix a pain area when you see it. A knowledge of anatomy and what needs to happen for the healing will work, but there are other ways to do it. The mind can work in symbols and metaphors. If a bone is broken or there is a wound, use Goddess Tape to repair it. If a red throat needs soothing, try blue or green Goddess paint on a paintbrush or a roller, or visualize ice cooling it. Where there is a cut or hole to repair, use a Goddess sewing needle and healing thread. If there is a fever, lower it with a Goddess firewoman's hose and cool water, or again visualize ice on the pain. Ask for spirit guidance and always visualize the receiver in full joyous health at the end of the session.

As a Reiki healer, I incorporate the Reiki II and III symbols into every healing, hands on or distance. I also am very aware that healing is to be done only by permission of the receiver. Since not everyone who needs healing has specifically asked for it— women often call and ask me to do healing for someone else or a pet—I use the method before to gain permission telepathically on the astral level. Below is basically the practice I follow, though as times goes on I am given more and more guided information and suggestions of what to do in my healings.

——————— : : ———————

Begin with the meditative state as always and invite your guides and angels to be there with you. Take a few deep breaths to center yourself, then visualize/imagine the person you wish to help. I usually see her clearly enough to recognize her. Next ask her, "Do you want healing from me?" or "Can I offer you some healing?" You will receive some answer. It may be her voice saying, "yes" or "no," or she may turn toward you (yes) or away from you (no). You will know and are ethic-bound to respect her choice. Often someone who refuses, or you think might refuse on the physical level will welcome healing when she is asked in this way on the astral plane. Use this method with someone in a coma and also with pets or infants, those who cannot give physical level permission. If the receiver agrees to your request, you may proceed. If not, withdraw quietly with love and end the session.

If you are not sure of the answer, send the healing with the clear intent that the recipient has the free will to accept or reject it. If the person refuses the energy, it can go instead toward healing the Earth, healing Bosnia or the Arabs/Israelis, or healing someone else who wants it. Unwanted healing energy may be recycled in this way for positive use, while still not violating anyone's free will. To force unwanted healing on anyone is totally against healers' ethics. People and animals have the right to hold onto their dis-ease if they choose to do so, and sometimes they will choose to refuse healing.

If permission to continue is granted, send the woman light. Do not designate a color, but let the light become whatever color is needed. All the colors are positive, as long as they are bright and beautiful. Black is positive in healing, the velvet black of a night sky with stars, or the black of Mother Earth's fertile ground. When black designates something negative, you will know it. There are many reasons why someone might need black, and black sent with love and healing intent is comforting and grounding. The color, or no-color, to use less of is white. It is far more effective to send a color that focuses on the receiver's needs than to send white light as a catchall for everything.

Many of the colors that appear in distance/psychic healing are not Earthplane colors. They are hard to describe in words, and as far as I know have no names. They are incredibly beautiful and positive. These are the previously discussed Hara Line astral colors that are complementary to each of the Earthplane's basic Kundalini/etheric double chakra colors. They very often appear in distance healing; they are the main reason not to designate color when you are sending light. Naming Earth colors limits what can appear, including preventing the appearance of the astral complements. By your not specifying a color, the woman receiving the healing, her higher self, her guides, or your healing guides, can choose the color/s most useful for her needs.

Let the colors fill the woman's aura, and then if you have Reiki, send the Reiki symbols. Rather than drawing them, send them whole, simply by willing their appearance. They seem to fly through space to scribe themselves down the length of the receiver's body. Start with the Dai-Ko-Myo to open the aura. The Hon-Sha-Ze-Sho-Nen is the symbol that transmits Reiki across space and time; use it with every distance healing. The Cho-Ku-Rei increases the power of the healing energy, and the Sei-He-Ki treats the emotional components of the dis-ease. I generally send all of the symbols in most absentee healings, and finish with the Dai-Ko-Myo again at the end. The symbols also take on color, often the Hara Line astral colors, and become what is best for that healing. Once you have sent the symbols, you may hear a message from your guides or the person receiving the energy with directions to do something more. "Fill her aura with gold light," might be one such message. Guided messages are always positive and life-affirming, refuse anything else. When this is finished, visualize the woman recovered and well, and going about her daily life. You might hear her say she feels fine. Then withdraw the meditation (dissolve the rose), thank your guides and angels, and return to present awareness. Doing the distance healing process takes seconds, far shorter than the time it takes to explain it.

———————— : : ————————

Asking permission is so very important that I ask before I begin any healing meditation, even if permission has already been given on the physical level. It is just as important to ask permission from infants, children, pets, and others who are unable to tell you directly as it is for conscious and aware adults. Animals and babies know exactly what they want and need, and will tell you so in the meditation. Ask them also what is wrong with them and what you can do to help them. They will often give you information you would not otherwise have had.

You can do a distance healing seated next to or across the room from the human or animal receiver, where a hands on healing is inappropriate or there isn't time for a full body session. Use it when touch would cause pain, as in a burn patient, or risk infection to either receiver or healer. Use it in hospitals where touch may not be allowed or may be uncomfortable. Do it for sleeping pets when the animal won't otherwise cooperate with hands on work, but still indicates she wants help. Likewise with infants. This is a good method for use with animals in the wild or in pain, and with farm animals that are not pets. The same techniques can also be used for healing yourself—instead of visualizing someone else, visualize yourself in the meditation, as you did when you used the rose.

A student asked me once to do distance healing for her mother in order to see if I could get the mother's permission (my student could not). I visualized the mother, whom I never met, and offered her healing. Her response turned out to be the same as my student received: "No, honey, let me go; it's my time." When I assured her astrally that the healing would not hold her back if she chose to pass over, but would ease her process, she accepted it gratefully. I told her to use it to ease her pain and for any other purpose she chose. She asked for it to help her die in peace. My student continued to do as her mother wished, giving the woman free choice. She died quietly in her sleep with a smile on her face a few weeks later.

Never work to prevent a death when the receiver does not wish it, or when it is against her will or best interests. Sometimes death is the only possible healing. Send energy in such a way that the receiver can choose how to use it for what she needs. Ask your guides to help you define what this is. When I send healing light, I send it to the whole person, not just to her dis-ease. I send the light with the affirmation "according to free will."

This simple process of imagining or concentrating on the person, sending her light and/or Reiki symbols, seeing her well, and returning to now has profound effect. Healing done in this way can actually be more effective than a hands on session, and takes seconds instead of more than an hour. The more fluent you become working with your guides, the more complex these healings can become as to what you perceive and may be guided to do in them. You will learn to work within the receiver's life force energy field, her chakras at both Kundalini and Hara Line levels, and in her aura bodies. I have done self-healing as far into my own aura as the mind grid and Body of Light, and into the etheric template of others and further. Use the psychic healing techniques while doing hands on healing as well, for the best possible results in any session.

The person receiving absentee healing, whether she knows about it consciously or not, is likely to feel it happening. If she is very open to energy and psychically aware, she may know exactly what you did and at what time. She may not have full consciousness, but may be thinking of the sender during the healing. She may suddenly feel peace, or color, or start feeling better. Pain (physical, emotional or mental) may stop at the time of the healing, and it may not return. When most healers first begin doing distance sessions, they think they are "just imagining it" or "making it all up" as I did. A few confirmations from receivers will quickly change the healers' doubts and they will thereby gain respect for the process.

When a healing meditation is done, return to the present and forget about it. Dwelling on the healing keeps the energy with the healer instead of releasing it through the astral to go to the receiver. As with hands on sessions, judge the frequency of doing psychic healing by the seriousness of the situation. For something as simple as a headache or menstrual cramps, one healing meditation may be enough. For more serious dis-eases, repeat the healing as often as every few minutes, but between sessions let the energy go. Once or twice a day is usually enough for most non-critical conditions. When spirit guides and angels become involved, one session may be everything that is needed for even very serious problems. I ask my guides if more is needed and when before repeating distance healing.

Time does not exist on the nonphysical body levels and this can be used to great advantage in distance and psychic healing. I have already described how an adult can heal her child self—those healings were psychic healings. In emotional trauma, go to the source of the trauma to heal it. Ask your guides to show you the receiver at the time and place the trauma happened. Once the healing at the source is done, ask your guides to bring the healing and the receiver into the present. Do not be surprised if the original source happened in early childhood or in another lifetime; just access the situation with your guides and do the healing. (There is more information on karma and past lives in the next chapter.)

Reiki II healers are taught to use the Hon-Sha-Ze-Sho-Nen symbol when healing outside of time. It can be used to program a healing to repeat at given intervals (hourly, twice a day, etc.) when needed. Always designate a limit to the repetitions—usually for "as long as she needs the help"—so that no unwanted energy is left free to bounce around the astral plane. For healers without Reiki training this still works but less effectively; you will need to repeat the healing sessions at least daily, or more often.

There are four Reiki distance healing techniques, focusing methods that work well for any psychic healer. Use them in the meditative state as with other distance methods. The four methods are:

1. Imagine being there and do a hands on session.

2. Imagine the person shrunk small and hold them in your hands for healing.

3. Use your left knee and thigh to represent the front of the person's body, and your right knee and thigh for the back. Do a hands on healing.

4. Use a teddy bear, pillow, doll, or photograph as a surrogate. Do the healing on the surrogate; give the bear, doll, or pillow the receiver's name.

———————— : : ————————

In method one, imagine that you are there with the receiving, doing a hands on session. This sounds simple enough, but is actually the most difficult of the four methods. It takes a long time to do the hands on positions, and therefore the healer must hold the meditation and visualization for a very long time. Most distance healing takes a matter of seconds, and unless you are very experienced, an extended visualization of this sort is extremely hard to do. It is good training in concentration and one-pointed focus, however. An option that helps might be to visualize yourself with extra pairs of arms, like those on a statue of Kwan Yin or Tara. This shortens the time considerably, but it still takes major effort. Yet, the times I have done psychic healing in this way have been very loving experiences and highly effective.

———————— : : ————————

The second method is to imagine the person, or even the planet shrunk down small. Hold it in your hands between your cupped palms. Psychic healing can be done for the Earth and I frequently do healing that way, as with the crystal grid work of the last chapter. The Earth needs all the healing we can send Her. An alternative to this for Earth healing is to take a small globe, the kind they sell as marbles or key-rings, and hold it in your hands while visualizing sending the planet light. With the image or visualization in your hands, send the color, light, sound, or symbols of the healing into it. This is probably the easiest of the four methods.

———————— : : ————————

The next two techniques use a focusing object, rather than a visualization. In the first of these, sit in a straight chair and imagine that your knee and upper leg are the receiver's body. The roundness of your knee becomes the person's head, your thigh is her torso, and your hip represents her legs and feet. Do the healing as if your hands were actually on her body, holding her image in your mind while doing an imagined hands on session. Use your left knee to represent the woman's front, and your right knee for her back.

———————— : : ————————

The fourth method is my favorite. Use a teddy bear, doll, pillow, or photograph of the woman as a surrogate or focus. The key-ring globe for Earth healing above is an example of this. Do the healing on the bear, then imagine giving the healed bear to the person receiving the distance treatment. Tell her, "Take what you can use from the bear." This method is particularly good when in asking permission the response is "I'm not sure" or "What do you want to do?" Show the receiver the healing done on the bear, then astrally give it to her. Give the bear the receiver's name for the time of the session.

———————— : : ————————

All of these are done in the meditative state and with the assistance of spirit guides and angels. Remember to ask them to come in at the beginning of any healing session, as they cannot work with you unless they are invited. Remember also to thank them at the end of the session. Work with guides cooperatively in every step of the process; they will show you what to do and how to do it.

Some of the most satisfying and demanding psychic healing is Earth healing, and though always a challenge, I ask women who are healers to make Earth work a regular healing meditation practice. This can be done very simply by visualizing the planet, or visualizing holding Her in your hands, and sending Her light and energy as if you were healing a person. Visualize Earth as bright, healed, and healthy. It can also be done in more complex ways.

Your spirit guides will lead you in this work if you are willing to do it as service to the Earth.

Some possibilities for this work: Ask to see a place on the planet where your energy and love can help. These might include an earthquake fault line, endangered species, polluted bay or river, devastated forest, or an area that has leaking radiation (there are far too many of these). Ask your guides for direction every step of the way in these healings. If in doubt, send light and love without visualizing changing any circumstance or doing anything else. Your spirit guides and angels will usually tell you what to do quite clearly, however. When doing any type of planetary healing, it is extremely important to place full protection around yourself, and to run replenishment energy at the end. If something needs to be done that seems dangerous to you, ask your guides or angels if they will do it or protect you in it. Be very careful to work for very short periods of time—you may be amazed at how intensive and exhausting Earth healing work can be.

About a year ago, a friend and I were told in a channeling she did that the Russian nuclear power plants are leaking enough radiation to cause cancer and Earth damage for hundreds of years to come. The Russian government either does not have the technology, the organization, or the awareness to stop it. We both do Earth healing and were asked to help. For a couple of weeks we each asked in our meditations to go where we were needed and compared notes later of what we saw. Our visions were amazingly alike.

When I first did this, I saw what looked like a huge, dark red, flickering fire that I was told was in southern Russia or one of the satellite countries. I was shown a map but don't know enough geography to accurately place it. I asked what to do and was shown a black box, presumably of lead shielding, that had to be set over the fire and then closed from underneath it, underground. I attempted to do this, but though I moved the box into place, the red fire still seemed to come through and I could not close the box. The visualization lasted for probably no more than two or three minutes but I was very sick

the next day and for the following week. My friend Jane in her meditation in her own home was able to close the box, but even then we still saw fire leaking through it. She also felt quite sick afterwards.

It took a few days before we could try again, and this time we tried it together by linking psychically over the telephone. Our guides asked for a second lead box to be placed around the first one. As we moved it into place, I asked if they could protect us from getting sick this time. They set the box on the ground and went into conference, then told us to move back and watch. A troop of angels came in, put the box in place and closed it.

We were taken to this same site once more for yet another insulating box, then to other sites, a couple of sessions at each power plant. We asked the angels to do what we were told needed to be done. I didn't get sick again, but still got very tired after each session. The angels and guides said that the radiation could not hurt them, but it could hurt us. There were a total of nine sites, and though much healing happened in the weeks we worked on them, more still needs to be done. There are toxic places like this all over the planet. Proceed very carefully not to cause further harm to others or to yourself. Put full protection around all participants, and do only a little at any one session.

I asked the guides and angels why they needed human psychics for this work, when we are really not strong enough to do it. I was told that Earth is a human physical planet, and nonphysical or nonhuman help can only be accessed by invitation. It is our planet, and we must join them in the work and in the intent. Spirit guides and angels cannot do anything until we ask them to, and telling them to "just heal everything that needs healing" is not something they are permitted to do. The request has to be specific and precise, with Earth Be-ings seeing what needs to be done and directing it. We can be given information about danger areas, then we must ask for the help and participate in the work of the healing. Obviously, lots of Earth healers are desperately needed for this.

There are also times when the healers know what needs to be done but are not permitted to interfere. Hurricane Andrew is a case in point. When I first felt that something very bad was coming into Florida, I tried as I usually do to push the hurricane out of the path of the land and the people. Often it works and the hurricane bypasses land or downgrades safely. Many healers, especially on the coast, do this work. I was told with this hurricane, however, "Don't touch, this has to be." A number of other Earth healers I talked with during the hurricane and afterwards told me they had gotten the same message. I was told this again about the slaughter in Rwanda. On healing for Bosnia, I was told, "This one's not your job, others are working here." We are all part of a greater plan, and some of the Earth changes are not to be alleviated. It is always welcome and good, however, to send healing collectively or individually to those affected.

When an oil spill from a tanker collision happened near my home in Tampa Bay, three of us got together to move the spill into the Gulf of Mexico where it wouldn't defile the bay and beaches. We saw the oil moving out to sea in the way the scientists on the newscasts said it would do the least harm. Other Earth healers along the Florida Gulf Coast were doing the same, I'm sure. The healing went so well that as the oil moved out we stopped checking on it, but we stopped too soon. A line of thunderstorms turned it back again several days later, and the oil reached land after all.

We were embarrassed and appalled. We next used guided healing to support the cleanup and prevent as much damage as possible. The potentially much worse spill, which consisted of balls of tarry goo coming up on the white sand beaches with the surf, was cleaned up in only two days. Despite this happening in midweek, over six hundred volunteers shoveled it from the sand and coastline, and many dozens more rescued, fed, and washed the affected seabirds.

When asking to heal nations at war and conflict, be very careful to work with spirit guides' permission. Many of these situations are karma playing itself finally out with the Earth changes after hundreds or even thousands of years of struggle. However bad what is happening may be, letting it happen now may finish the karma once and for all, preventing continuous wars in the ongoing future. If your spirit guides and angels give permission, do the work, but work closely with them and only do as they direct. If guidance says "no" to something you propose to do, be sure to listen to it and obey. Violation here can have serious karmic consequences for the healer and the planet, as well as for the situation involved. Always remember we are each part of a greater Goddess plan.

Distance healing for people and the Earth has so many possibilities that it is impossible to describe them all. Your only limits are your ability to enter a deep trance state and your ability at gaining psychic information, usually through visualization and spirit guidance. Time and distance dissolve in psychic healing and are no longer limits. What may be impossible on the Earthplane level happens readily in a distance healing session, and the healing changes the physical body of both people and the planet.

All realities are created by the mind and thought to be brought through the Nonvoid from the Void. Thought is an energy force that effects change in matter, and all matter including the Earth and our bodies is created from this energy. Energy is what we are and were and what we will become, and energy is Goddess, which can neither be created nor destroyed. Psychic/distance healing uses the energy of thought to create and transform realities on every level, from the human body to the Earth Herself. It is the creative life force of the Goddess, and its use by healers presents us with great gifts and greater responsibilities.

In this time of Earth changes, people, animals, and the planet need healing. Psychic healing is a way to do this, and many healers are needed now, more than ever before. For those women on the Goddess/bodhisattva path, healing and Earth healing are a way of giving service in the suffering of our time. Use the skills wisely and always with respect, reverence, compassion, and love.

Notes

1 Barbara Ann Brennan, *Light Emerging: The Journey of Personal Healing Through the Human Energy Field* (New York, NY, Bantam Books, 1993), p. 24.

2 Barbara Ann Brennan, *Hands of Light: A Guide to Healing Through the Human Energy Field* (New York, NY, Bantam Books, 1987), p. 47.

3 Barbara Ann Brennan, *Light Emerging*, p. 25.

4 *Ibid.*, p. 26.

5 *Ibid.*, p. 23.

6 Based on an exercise by Amy Wallace and Bill Henkin, *The Psychic Healing Book* (Berkeley, CA, The Wingbow Press, 1978), pp. 99–101.

CHAPTER TEN

Karma

Much of who we are in this lifetime and in the spiritual growth of our Be-ing is an accumulation of past lives on this and other planets. We are simply not here long enough in any single life to learn

what we need to about who we are in the Goddess' universal plan. From a cosmic viewpoint, we have returned so many times that each incarnation is like a single day at school. Some days seem harder or easier than others, and though we are made to forget the details of each incarnation, the learning comes together as a whole in who we essentially are. Just as no one comes to Earth alone, we come far more than once. The evidence for it is overwhelming.

While witches accept a variety of ideas in the Goddess Craft, two beliefs are central. One is in the Goddess Herself as an immanent Be-ing, and the other is in the concept of karma and reincarnation. The immanence of Goddess means that She is a part of everything that lives and exists in every Be-ing. A tree, dog, bird, crystal, and ocean wave are all Goddess, and so is every person and everything that every person creates. She is a part of us, and we are a part of Her. All that lives is one.

The other central Wiccan belief is in reincarnation. We have been here before and will be here again; there is no beginning and no ending to life or our lives. Many women have sought for confirmation of

this in their own experience and have readily found it. Just ask for it in meditation. Healers find it again and again when in healing work they ask to see the source of a dis-ease or problem and find themselves in another place and time. The place may not even be on Earth, and the time can be somewhere far more technologically (and humanely) advanced than now.

Every religion, including Judaism, Christianity, and Islam, once held a belief in reincarnation. The Western religions dropped the concept by the fifth century in order to gain more governmental control over their followers. By declaring this the only life and inventing a reward and punishment system in the afterlife, Western religions made their followers dependent upon their god as both a religious and political power. Each Be-ing became separate, alone, and unworthy. The political powers grew to co-opt people, countries, and continents. In the East, where reincarnation is accepted by everyone, religion and spiritual growth come from within the self. These people live in spiritual freedom.

Buddhism defines reincarnation, the Wheel of Rebirth, as ordained, but when a person reaches

Enlightenment the wheel stops turning. Buddhist faith requires acceptance of two ideas: compassion for all Be-ings and the understanding that all life is one. Earthplane reality must be understood as illusion created by mind; all that appears to be real, including one's life, is only the mind's creation. True reality is the emptiness of the Void, which is bliss, attained by freeing the mind from separation, illusion, and the negative mind creations that bind one to return.

Mahayana and Tantric (Vajrayana) Buddhism affirm the Enlightenment can be gained in this lifetime by spiritual practice, compassionate service, and awareness of mind's truth. Everyone can be enlightened and free. In the Buddhist world view, existence (life) is seen as intrinsically unhappy and filled with suffering. The suffering comes from selfishness (separateness, ego) and desire (craving), which can never be fulfilled by their very nature. By making emotional attachments, holding onto things, places, and people on the Earthplane, Be-ings are thereby bound to repeat their existence in different bodies. When they die, their souls are drawn back into incarnation by these emotional connections and attachments. By letting go of selfish craving and accepting that the ego is illusion and that all life is one, the spirit at death is freed from its necessity to return and suffer again. Full understanding of these concepts is knowledge of how the universe works, and how to end incarnation and suffering for everyone.

Buddhism bases its concept of rebirth on the continuity of consciousness/mind. The quote below is from His Holiness, the Dalai Lama:

> All the elements in our present universe, even down to a microscopic level, can be traced back, we believe, to an origin, an initial point where all the elements of the material world are condensed into what are technically known as "space particles." These particles, in turn, are the state which is the result of the disintegration of a previous universe. So there is a constant cycle, in which the universe evolves and disintegrates, and then come back into being again.
>
> Mind is very similar. . . . If you trace our present mind or consciousness back, then you will find that you are tracing the origin of the continuity of mind, just like the origin of the material universe, into an infinite dimension; it is, as you will see, beginningless.
>
> Therefore there must be successive rebirths that allow that continuum of mind to be there.[1]

Once again, the language of modern physics is catching up to ancient wisdom. The mechanism which turns desire and holding on into rebirth is karma. Karma is defined simply as the action of mind. In Wicca the similar concept is, "What you send out returns to you." Every action has a reaction. By living a life of negative action that requires redress to release, the soul is forced back into rebirth. Negative action, however, does not necessarily or only mean wrongdoing. Any holding on to life results in karma and rebirth as well. Karma is engaged by painful emotions or events retained in the aura that have not been healed before death in that lifetime.

Therefore, to give an example, a rapist incurs negative karma by his action against a woman. It is an action of separateness and ego not healed in the original lifetime. He must redress the action in some way, perhaps by a next lifetime in service to women, or as a woman who may experience rape or other abuse. He also has a karmic debt to the woman he harmed. By learning compassion for women and understanding the wrongs he committed, and perhaps by doing good for that woman in other lives, he is freed of that piece of karmic attachment.

The woman he rapes also collects karma, though she is not blamed for the experience. In her case, it is the damage to her mind and emotions with which she must reincarnate in order to heal that damage. When the healing has occurred, she no longer carries the negative emotional or mental pattern in her aura forward to future lifetimes. Such karmic patterns recur until they are healed, let go of, and released from the aura and the woman's karma, though it may take any number of lifetimes to do so. While the goal is to be freed from the Wheel of Incarnation, karma is accrued by action while in body, and it can only be healed in the body. Both Wiccans and Buddhists see the human body as a precious gift, for the healing of karma (in both the woman and her rapist) can only be done while incarnated in a body.

Likewise, any action or relationship creates emotions to hold onto that result in karma and rebirth. When you love someone, but hold onto them with ego attachment rather than oneness and letting go, you are forced to reincarnate again and again to be with the partner until the relationship becomes healthy and compassionate. When it does, the two of you may still choose to stay together, beyond the need to work things out. If there are wrongs to redress in the relationship, karmic patterns occur to cause them to be resolved. If a woman is jealous of her partner, for example, the situation recurs in various ways until the jealousy is healed and is no longer a problem. By the same universal laws, positive deeds and relationships heal karma, bringing benefits and life gifts, and move the souls of both partners toward freedom from rebirth.

Karma is not a punishment but a learning process aimed at spiritual growth and development for the soul. It is magnificently complex and the ultimate expression of free will. We are who we are because of what we do and how we treat other people. When we have learned the lessons of compassion, right action, pure thought, service to humanity, and nonattachment, we become free from rebirth and suffering:

> According to this doctrine, we ourselves
> are responsible for our lives, for our
> circumstances, our pain and joy, our
> opportunities and limitations, even our
> character traits, talents, neuroses and
> personality blockages. . . .
> All the thoughts, motives, emotions
> which we generated in the past have gone

into the complex strains that make us what we are today.[2]

Karma in the individual may be seen as an independent study program. The lessons are designed for the specific person's needs, the things she has chosen in the pre-life state to work on in this lifetime. There will be joyful and harsh lessons. The lessons become harsh only when the woman refuses easier learning. There will be positive gifts and abilities, like skill in painting or the ability to repair machinery, and things more difficult to learn. Everyone comes here with a life purpose and a set of learning goals. There will also be a group of important people to do the learning with. Every significant relationship and probably many that are less significant, are karmic relationships. An individual's karma includes family members and lovers she has incarnated with again and again. It also includes and is part of the karma of her planet, country, gender, and race.

I have been aware of past lives as a gay Roman soldier; as a male witch; blacksmith, and animal healer burned at the stake in sixteenth century Britain; as a female witch drowned in the Italian women's walk to the sea; and drowned again as a female witch in colonial New England. I was a priestess and healer in ancient Crete, a Pueblo midwife and shaman at Mesa Verde in New Mexico, and a woman weaver who worked on the Bayeaux Tapestries in France. In another male lifetime I was a New York State shopkeeper who emigrated by flatboat and wagon train to California. I was a Jewish lesbian who died at Buchenwald around 1940. These may be only a few of many more incarnations that I know nothing about.

I am aware of a woman I now love deeply being present with me in many of these lifetimes as my mate. We have been male and female couples of alternating gender, gay men and lesbians together in many different countries. In one lifetime on another planet, she was my brother and we were both male. I am aware of knowing several friends from other lives, without always having clear knowledge of our past relationships. When I meet someone I've known before, the relationship feels intimate quickly, and when I look for the source I usually discover past relationships.

Souls live in families between lifetimes and reincarnate together. An oversoul is comprised of essence selves or souls. The oversoul may release up to four essence lives to incarnate at one time, though essence selves rarely meet in body. Each essence self, however, divides into countless incarnations or individual lifetimes. Each soul/essence self belongs to a family of other essence selves from several oversouls. These selves incarnate together again and again, and come home to each other in the between life state. The inner circle cluster group of up to twenty-five souls reincarnates together through eternity and are central to each other's growth and learning. Circles moving away from the inner circle soul group are less intense relationships.3

Past lives are important for this life healing. In these Earth change times, much past life and this life healing acts also as karmic healing. At times of millennium we see a karmic clearing of the slate in which the soul's karma for that millennium is purged before the new age begins. We are in such a period of opportunity. Karmic healing of past life situations with regard to people, emotions, and dis-eases is happening in an accelerated way in this lifetime. Emotional, mental, and behavioral patterns from the past are rising once more for us to clear and release. Negative attachments held in the aura over lifetimes are being healed. By the time we leave our present incarnations, we will have evolved and grown in every way.

Such healing means learning about who we are as souls and reading the relevant parts of our Akashic Records. The Akashic Record is the book or record of each soul's incarnations, and the major events of each lifetime. We are usually permitted to know about only those past life situations that are important for clearing a present life issue, or for accomplishing our purpose in this incarnation. Past lives often come up in healings as the source of a current situation or negative pattern, particularly those that seem to have no understandable root in this life.

Once we are given the Akashic information, it is a sign that the trouble can now be released and finished. Sometimes only knowing what happened in the past life that has been repeated in this life is enough. Sometimes the knowledge opens a flood of emotions which, once felt, are released. In one of my own experiences, knowing where I had erred in a past incarnation freed a pattern in the present one.

Karma is a construct of mind, as is all reality, and the mind can also be reprogrammed. The age regression incest healing in the chapter on emotional release is highly effective for reprogramming the karma of a past life. Once the situation is known, it usually can be healed, and, with the knowledge, healing is usually permitted by the Lords and Healers of Karma—if the receiver chooses to accept it. The ability of the healer to move beyond time is a primary factor in this work. Buddhism (and physics) describe time, space, and even karma as illusions created and directed by mind. Understanding that these limits are self-created transcends and removes them and makes the limits mutable.

Try the following meditation for discovering a past life. There are very formal meditations for this, but I find them to be unnecessary. A very good one can be found in Brian Weiss, *Through Time Into Healing* (Fireside Books, 1992), and in many other sources. Hypnotists and psychotherapists who use age regression for healing phobias and negative habits often find their clients describing situations from other lifetimes. When they do, the phobias or situations they uncover are usually cleared quickly. Healers also see this phenomenon frequently and can use it for self-healing. In the beginning meditation below, ask only to see your own past life, thus becoming familiar with the process before directing it for a specific healing. For most women, their first access to a past life happens spontaneously—it comes without either recipient or healer asking for it, in meditation or when asking to release a dis-ease.

——————— : : ———————

Enter the meditative state at a time and place where you will not be disturbed. Go through the process of grounding

DIAGRAM 14

Reincarnations[4]

The Oversoul releases up to four strands to incarnation at one time, called Essence Selves. Each Essence Self (incarnated Be-ing) has multiple lifetimes or reincarnations. Essence Selves rarely meet while in body.

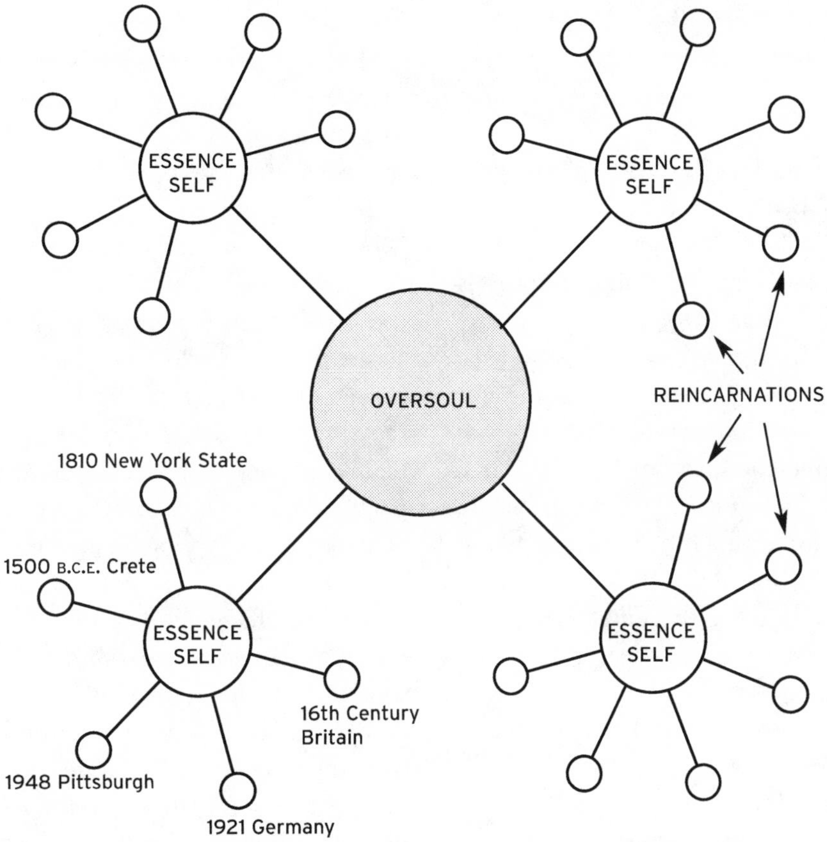

and centering, full body relaxation repeated twice, and running energy to fill your aura bodies and chakras with light. Do these processes even if you can now shift to meditation without them, as a deeper trance state is required. Place protection as a bubble of light around you and invite your guides and angels to come in. Tell them, "I would like to see a past lifetime that has relevance for me in this life," and ask them to take you there.

See yourself in a dark tunnel, going down a staircase, or crossing a bridge or stream. Follow the light at the bottom or end and go through a bright doorway into another time. Look down and see your feet; are they male or female? What is the color of your skin, and what kind of shoes are you wearing, if any? Look at your clothes, and

then your surroundings. Where are you, and when? Ask your guides for answers if you don't already know. Who are you? What is happening at this time? Is anyone else involved in the experience? Who is the person to you in that lifetime; do you know her now? Watch the scene unfold. If the scene fades, ask for another scene from that life.

If the scene involves pain or trauma, ask to "watch it like a movie" without being affected by it, experiencing pain or fear. If you are to observe your death, birth, or giving birth in that life, do the same. When your spirit guides have shown you what you need to see and the pictures fade, ask them how the past lifetime is important for you now. You may already know. When you feel that the pictures and learning are finished, come back to now.

: :

You may do this meditation as often as daily for a while to get a fuller understanding of who you are. Often just seeing something from the past that has relevance for the present releases a present difficulty. Sometimes deeper or more specific work is needed. Sometimes much more knowledge must accumulate before the whole pattern, or full healing, becomes clear. When a situation or lifetime has been especially traumatic, you may be given it in small doses over a period of time.

It may also be necessary to go through the negative and painful emotions once more to release them. These can feel as if they are happening right now and be very intense. After past life meditations you may start to get flashbacks of scenes you have witnessed and others from that past life. Watch the scenes passively. Let them go, neither resisting nor holding on to the information or the pain.

Now try the same meditation, but this time ask for the past life *source* of a pattern, situation, relationship, or trauma in this life that you wish to heal. For best results, do this with a situation in which you have already done the emotional work in this lifetime. You may find another layer from another incarnation, especially if the completed work in this life has not resolved the problem. When you have seen the past life source, ask if other lifetimes are involved. Several lives together may be operative in a karmic pattern. Try to be aware as to which past life is the source of the problem. Don't try to change anything just yet. A full overview is needed first.

Where the situation involves another person or persons, there are ethical considerations, especially if you recognize who they are in their present incarnation. First of all, someone who has done a wrong to you in the past, even a great wrong, is not a criminal in this lifetime. The focus here is on healing, not vengeance; leave karmic retribution to the person's own Akashic Records, her spirit guides, and the Goddess. To violate this may have severe consequences for you. Your only responsibility—and it is responsibility without blame or self-blame—is in healing the situation for yourself. When you are

healed, the other person may also be healed. Be very careful not to manipulate any other person's karma unless that person agrees and fully participates with you in the process.

Secondly, everyone has lived different kinds of lifetimes. Intentionally or not, others have wronged you, and you have wronged others. The point is to heal the problem for the present and the future. Everyone has done wrong things in other lifetimes as well as this one. If you observe yourself doing wrong to another, your responsibility is to feel shame in knowing what you did, and to learn the lesson from it fully so you will not repeat the wrong. Ask your guides for help with this. If someone has done these things to you, they are not to be confronted about it now. To do so is pointless. Remember you are not exempt. Judge this life relationships for what they are now. Heal today by letting go of the past. Blaming others or yourself will not heal you or them. Such blame is ego-driven. Be in a neutral space, with compassion for yourself and everyone involved.

Again, knowing the situation may be all that is needed to change and resolve it and to release disease or pain from your life. Give the information time to settle in. You will understand it more fully as you think about it later. Several days of flashbacks granting you new information may be forthcoming. Give the process time to unfold without rushing it or holding back. Allow emotions to go through you, allow them to come. They usually happen just before you fall asleep or just after waking up when you are the most relaxed. Gain a full overview and understanding of the situation before going any further. If there is a series of past lives involved in a situation, you need to know them all, or as many as your spirit guides feel the need to show you. If you find yourself forgetting information, you will be given it once more when and if you need it. Don't hold on to anything, watch it and let it go.

———————— : : ————————

Now do the next step, a past life regression meditation to heal the karma of the situation. Go into the meditative state with full relaxation, running energy, and protection. Ask your spirits guides to take you to the lifetime where the problem started, the source of the dis-ease or karma. Ask your guides to reprogram and heal the source. This time when you get to the source lifetime, change the movie. Before the decisive action, rewrite it so it does not occur, or solve the problem in a positive way.

If someone murdered or raped you in that lifetime, in the new script they won't show up for the date with destiny. If bankruptcy caused a suicide, as it did in one past life healing I did with a woman, a lot of money comes (by magick, if no other way) and the suicide no longer happens. If an argument in the past is causing relationship difficulties now, settle the argument in the past life with full forgiveness. It doesn't matter who was right or wrong, just forgive them. Create solutions that are fully positive for everyone, but the changes must occur in yourself. Remember that any evil can be overcome with love.

When the situation is healed, ask to see your life in the incarnation the day after the corrected trauma. Do this in the same way as the emotional release in the incest healing. Then go to the next year and look at your life at that time with the negative karma changed. Move ahead five years, ten, and then observe without pain or discomfort your death in that lifetime. Ask your guides what else is needed at each step. After the death, ask them to bring the healing forward through all your lifetimes and aura levels to change your present life and future in a positive way. Thank your guides and angels, and come back to now.

———————— : : ————————

You may need a week of quiet, nurturing, and extra sleep to assimilate the changes of this healing. Give yourself as much space as possible to do so. Drink lots of pure water. If you feel ill or are releasing toxins heavily, take sea salt into the shower, rubbing it on your chakras and then rinsing it off. If you feel like a "gutted fish," where your aura feels exposed, ripped, or bleeding, pat apple cider vinegar on your chakras after a shower, or put a cup of it in a bathtub full of hot water and soak yourself for twenty minutes to half an hour. Wearing amber at this time helps to protect you and to heal your aura.

———————— : : ————————

When the feelings have cleared and you feel strong again, do one more meditation. This time when you ask to see your past life again, you'll be amazed at the changes. The trauma or source situation is gone. Then ask to see the next past life that was a part of the trauma pattern. Change it as you did the source lifetime; it will move very quickly. Ask for the next lifetime in the pattern and do the same. Continue this until all of the lifetimes that are part of the negative karmic pattern are released. When your guides indicate that there are no more to show you because the situation is totally cleared, ask them to bring the healing into your present life and future on all levels. Thank them and come back to now. There may be another few days of integration, but the pattern will be healed and the karma will be at an end, completed. Because the mind is able to create new realities, you will have rewritten your Akashic Record for this situation or trauma, and the karmic pattern will be changed.

———————— : : ————————

I recommend this process for any incested or abused woman as a completion to her healing. All of this life work should be finished before going into the past life source. The method is also useful in troubled personal relationships to understand and heal the pattern and source of conflict. Major relationships may have much karma to clear, where less major ones may clear very quickly and easily. If the problem lies only in this incarnation, you will be told so. In clearing problems in your present life where others are involved, remember that the changes can only be in you. Ask your guides each step of the way as to what solutions may or may not be permitted or acceptable. The goal is for the highest good of all. Be neutral in your assessment. Use compassion, love, and be without a judgmental attitude. Be aware that important life changes happen in these karmic healings. Take them very seriously and responsibly.

The technique can also be used quite effectively in healing with others. The healer leads the receiver through the process, guided by the receiver's descriptions of what she sees. The healer may be able to link psychically with her and watch it unfold. If you have Reiki, the symbol to use is the Hon-Sha-Ze-Sho-Nen throughout, both in self-healing and with others.

If a healer is available who works well with you, do accept her help rather than attempt to do the karmic reprogramming alone. With someone to lead you, you can go deeper into the lifetime and the meditative state. When you don't have to be simultaneously aware of the process itself and the next step, it is easier. Either alone or with help, you will experience profound life changes. If you are not ready yet or the reprogramming is not permitted, you will know. It may be time later, after you receive other healings or get further information.

I have done a number of these karmic reprogrammings alone and with other women. In one case, two women had an obsessive relationship and one wanted to heal it. Another healer worked with me and in the meditation I saw the receiver murdered by the other woman, who in that past lifetime was male. The receiver sat under a tree, as a young, obese woman in a white summer dress, waiting. A tall, thin man came from the forest and stabbed her violently again and again until she lost a great deal of blood and died. I recognized the man as the other woman, though his form was very different then. The other healer saw energy forms rather than the event itself. She described clear light fouled terribly with a spreading blackness. The receiver told me later that she has a recurring dream of dying, bleeding in the other woman's lap. Such violence is actually infrequent in these sessions.

There is a further karmic release process, that I use only in extremely serious past life cases. This is not to be taken lightly. I described it to one amazed woman who commented that it was like "going to god and asking him to change the Ten Commandments." I use it mostly for life-threatening dis-eases, and for life situations with serious consequence. Do this life emotional release, and the full karmic meditations, and reprogramming before even considering it, and then do it only if nothing else has worked in any way.

The process is called karmic release and involves two nonphysical healing groups, the Lords of Karma and the Healers of Karma. The Lords of Karma—

they seem to be male (this was the name I was given for them)—are the Be-ings with whom one designs an incarnation's learnings in the pre-life state. They are the writers and guardians of the Akashic Records, and the administrators of personal and group karma. In the few bits of information I have located on these Be-ings, I have found that they are also called the *Lipika*, a Hindu word, or the Recording Angels:

> We find in the Hindu religion, that the *Lipika* (Lords of Karma) have become the personal karmic administrators in the same way that Jehovah, the God of the Jews, Gentiles, and Moslems, has been personalized as a just but stern God.[5]

or

> There is a tradition of certain agencies known as the *Lipika* or Recording Angels. They do far more than keep ledgers of our acts. They are constantly being programmed with new information which added to the materials stored in their "memory" feeds back on this and alters the resulting impact from moment to moment. This result is in perfect dynamic balance from instant to instant. There is perfect justice throughout the whole universe.[6]

——————— : : ———————

I have gone to the Lords of Karma on several occasions for healing, and when the healing is granted it begins a major clearing and releasing process that is transformational. Again, please make very sure first that all other avenues have been exhausted. Go to these Be-ings with great seriousness, respect, and reverence. These are not folks you want to be angry with you. If they refuse your request, let it be. You don't want your next lifetime to be even harder than this one.

To do this, in deep meditation ask to speak with the Lords of Karma. Your guides and angels should be with you. You will see, hear, or feel these Be-ings' presence very strongly. They are positive and loving although awesome and stern. State your situation and ask to know the specifics of the karmic contract. Once you know why something is and understand it, you may also know the need for letting it remain unchanged.

If you still wish to revise it, ask if it is permitted to do so, and if it is possible. You will hear a "yes" or "no," or you will be asked how you wish to make the changes. Re-word the contract extremely carefully, after consulting with your spirit guides and angels. Be careful what you ask for, as you will have to live with the consequences, even into other lifetimes. You probably won't be allowed to make another change. If you want healing for a dis-ease, state that you want full and complete healing on every level, and a dis-ease free life through this lifetime. You will not usually be permitted to go beyond this incarnation, but changes in this life will affect future ones. Freedom from a life-threatening dis-ease could also be accomplished by death, so be careful to state *how* you want that freedom, though not the specific healing mechanism. Be careful to state when the healing should begin. You don't want it to start *after* this lifetime ends. Leave nothing open to misinterpretation. Be clear. Don't be ambiguous.

When you have chosen your specific request and you and your guides approve the wording, state it to the Lords of Karma. Ask for their approval of the wording, too. Ask them if they can grant it at this time, or what you need to know for it to be possible. You will hear a "no" or "granted," and then they are gone. They will not discuss it. They may show you a past life situation than needs to be cleared before your request can be approved. Ask them if the release is permitted for that source lifetime. If it is, and you choose to, request it. You may or may not see changes in the scene, but again will hear a "no" or "granted." You may need to do karmic reprogramming for that situation. Thank them and the meditation is over; it may have taken only seconds.

———————— : : ————————

From the moment you hear the word "granted," every aspect of your life may shift radically. You may be in an altered state for days, see visions and past lives, see light and rainbows in unimaginable colors. You may go through a period of intense emotional or physical releasing. This period can last as long as a month. You may feel very sick, spacy, or out of control. You are undergoing radical change and complete transformation, and must honor the process by gratitude, rest, quiet, and nurturing. Trust the Goddess and the changes.

Later, if you need help with the reintegration or with processing and implementing the changes in your life, there is a second group of healers to call upon. These are the Healers of Karma (rather than the Lords of Karma). They are less severe but only slightly more personal. They will work with you through the life changes following karmic release. You can also call upon them if the process seems to stall or is incomplete. However, give it time enough before calling on them. You can call on the Healers of Karma for healing animals' karma as well. In many cases of karmic release, you will be directed to them rather than going to the Karmic Lords/Lipika. Ask your guides and angels for advice.

I have asked the Lords of Karma to heal the constant and sometimes overwhelming fear that has been with me throughout this incarnation. I lived with fear throughout my childhood, but have done much in my present life and past life work to heal it. Yet the fear remained, often coming up for no discernible reason, and usually with a force beyond any sense when the reason was apparent. Because it has hurt my life in so many ways, I decided to go to the Lords of Karma for help.

The first time I asked them to release the unjustified fear from my life, I was refused. When I asked my guides and angels what to do, they indicated past lives. When I requested to know the source of my overwhelming fear, I was taken to the concentration camp. Knowing this to be the source didn't change or heal the fear. A few days later when I came up with another idea, I went back to the Lords of Karma. This time I asked if it was permitted to release and heal from all my levels, core soul, and aura bodies the damage done to me in the concentration camp lifetime. The release was granted.

That was not the end of it. As soon as the release was given I felt an incredible sense of joy, peace, calmness and release. Then a sudden sensation of pain began running through my body and into the Earth. It felt like pouring water going through my body and it was wonderful. By the next day, however, I was extremely sick, and the pouring came from my throat and heart chakras. It felt like heavy and toxic dark smoke coming from my throat. I had heart palpitations and felt so weak I could hardly walk. The sickness and extreme weakness continued. I went through a second week of extreme terror wondering what the guides had done to me, and why they couldn't or wouldn't repair the damage. I seriously thought that I was dying. Brede sat beside my bed all night each night—I wasn't sleeping either—and she talked to me, but couldn't seem to help.

After the fear subsided, I remained sick and very weak for about another month. Since that time, all my fear is gone, and several dis-eases in my body that I thought were permanent have healed. These included difficulties with my bowels, uterus, eyes, and nerves. After the two months of initial intense release, a healer appeared and helped me. Apparently I experienced the concentration camp horrors one more time in a condensed way, and thereby completed and released it. I had no flashbacks, for which I was grateful, but only sensations and emotions. It was healing that badly needed to happen, but it was possibly the hardest process I have ever gone through. The karma from that lifetime, however, will no longer blight my present or my future. It is no longer in my aura, life, or soul.

This is not a form of healing to take lightly, but it can be life-changing and life-affirming when used as a last resort. In a case where I used it with another woman, she had none of the frightening reactions that I had. This was a graduate student with a blood dis-ease of the spleen that was seriously damaging her immune system. I found her information on immune support and naturopathy, suggested a heavy metal detoxification remedy, and a low-phosphorus (no sodas) diet. And I did a hands on healing.

When I asked for karmic release for her, the Lords of Karma first showed her a past life incident. In it she was a boy, imprisoned for throwing stones at a horse that was part of an army invading her town. She recognized the man who imprisoned her as her father in this lifetime. There have been difficulties in their relationship. I asked her if she could forgive him now and in that lifetime, and she did so. We got no clear verdict from the Lords of Karma and were shown no more. The woman's blood condition, as defined by medical testing, has considerably improved.

In another instance, a woman with breast cancer didn't state a real request to the Lords of Karma and was only shown visions of herself floating through a desert canyon. I had asked the Lords of Karma for her, but she had to choose the release herself and didn't do so. Nonphysical helpers, even (or especially) those at the highest levels, will not violate free will. To be healed by them you must work with them. You must take responsibility. It is a cooperative process, and not everyone chooses to heal.

During one of these sessions, in which another healer helped me, we were granted karmic release for the receiver, but we had to coach her on what to ask for. Like many women, she didn't know what asking for a new life meant, or what she could ask for in the way of a positive life change. We had to prompt her: "Do you want joy in your life?" "A good relationship?" "Do you want to be healthy?" "Do you want to heal your diabetes?" "Do you want abundance?"

We healers became extravagant in our wishing good things for her, and the three of us laughed and laughed. Every good thing we suggested she accepted but couldn't think of any for herself. The woman chose what she did and didn't want for her newly designed life, and the Lords of Karma agreed. The changes are beginning to manifest, though not without some setbacks. Her body, which was not the major focus of the session, is noticeably healing, and her insulin needs are decreasing. The emotional work that was the focus of the healing is slowly being accomplished. This was the same woman I mentioned before who had sought help for the obsessive relationship and change is happening there as well.

I believe that such karmic release and healing would not have been possible thirty years ago, and perhaps not even five or ten years ago. The stress and pain of having chosen to live on Earth as a healer through the Earth changes is bringing this reward. Our increasing psychic opening, and our learning how to use our abilities for healing is also granting us these benefits. I no longer feel that any situation is hopeless, no matter what it looks like at first. I have seen so many things healed that should not have been possible that I feel anything can change, if it is in the receiver's best good to change it, and if she will only ask for it to happen.

I become increasingly angry and dismayed, however, when I hear of healers using karma as an excuse to blame others for their pain, or approaching karma with ego judgment and lack of compassion. Everyone has experienced negative situations, emotions, and relationships, and has perpetrated them. We all do the best we can with the understanding we have at the time. We must take the responsibility of learning from the past so the past can be healed. This is so both for this life and for past incarnations. No one is exempt from dying and no one is exempt from karma.

Buddhist philosophy says that the only way to heal karma is to go on the Path to Enlightenment, and to achieve it not for yourself but for others. If you are successful in becoming aware that mind creates reality and that all reality is illusion, you will not need to be reborn. All karma will end. Yet there is also great joy and great love in being in a body on a planet as beautiful as Earth. Being reborn is not all bad.

Many healers are here on the Bodhisattva path of compassion, returning from their own Enlightenment to teach others the way. They reincarnate vol

untarily to do this. Mahayana Buddhism says that when we leave the Wheel of Incarnation, we will all go together, so that no one has to reincarnate at all. Perhaps from that point, in body or as Light Be-ings, there will be no further suffering, but only the love that is also our birthright as souls that are part of Goddess.

If you are interested in working with karmic release, there are now easier and more comfortable methods. See my books: *We Are the Angels, Essential Energy Balancing, Reliance on the Light, Essential Energy Balancing II,* and (forthcoming) *Essential Energy Balancing III,* all published by the Crossing Press. Everyone who chooses to do so can now release and be healed of karma—all their karma on all levels—and achieve Enlightenment/ ascension in body in this lifetime.

Notes

1 Sogyal Rinpoche, *The Tibetan Book of Living and Dying* (San Francisco, CA, HarperSanFrancisco, 1993), pp. 89–90.

2 Shirley Nicholson, "Karma As Organic Process," in V. Hansen, R. Stewart, and S. Nicholson, *Karma: Rhythmic Return to Harmony* (Wheaton, IL, Quest Books, 1975, 1990), p. 24.

3 Michael Newton, Ph.D., *Journey of Souls,* p. 88.

4 Laeh Maggie Garfield, *How the Universe Works: Pathways to Enlightenment* (Berkeley, CA, Celestial Arts, 1991), p. 28.

5 Clarence R. Pedersen, "The Source of Becauses," in V. Hansen, R. Stewart, and S. Nicholson, *Karma: Rhythmic Return to Harmony,* p. 54.

6 Laurence J. Bendit, "Karma and Cosmos," in V. Hansen, R. Stewart, and S. Nicholson, *Karma: Rhythmic Return to Harmony,* p. 281.

CHAPTER ELEVEN

Soul Retrieval

Soul retrieval is considered a part of shamanism, but I use it in a psychic healing context. Shamanism is of European, Australian, Tibetan, Native American, and African origins; it is a form of psychic healing known to tribal peoples worldwide. In the way that I use it, I draw upon no particular tradition, but from the intent of all traditions. I gauge any healing technique by its results, how well and easily it works, and how well it helps to heal. I frequently combine, synthesize, and rewrite methods, and I have done so with this one. Soul retrieval, as I use it, is an effective method for repairing core soul damage and helping women to find new wholeness. I have seen spectacular changes in myself and others with this method.

The primary value of soul retrieval is its ability to do healing through the planes of existence. This is different from working through the chakras and aura body levels in that healing the planes of existence means healing the core soul or essence self. The planes of existence are accessed through the astral, mental, and spiritual body auras, and they also include a physical body plane. See the diagram on page 124.

The physical plane is the level of the root, belly, and solar plexus chakras and the aura bands that transmit energy into them. They are physical exis-tence, but not the core soul/essence self. The astral plane is accessed through the heart chakra and its aura body. It is the spirit twin of the emotional body, plus the universal world of out of body travel, the spirit world. To access the mental plane means the connection may be made through the mind grid to the Body of Light, the interface between one's own mind, the universal Mind of Goddess Earth, and the interface between Earth, other planets and the galaxy. This access is made through the aura levels connected to the throat and third eye centers, but is beyond these centers' aura bodies.

The spiritual plane is accessed from the crown chakra and beyond the aura levels that transmit into it. It encompasses the etheric template, the celestial and ketheric bodies, then goes beyond them through the Body of Light, and into the oversoul. The core soul is comprised of the astral, mental, and spiritual planes, and the levels beyond them, and is the essence self in all of her many incarnations. It does not include the physical plane.

Kenneth Meadows in *Shamanic Experience* (Element Books, 1991) defines these planes in contemporary shamanic terms. The Energy Body and Hidden Self below are the astral plane; the Human Self is the mental plane, and the High Self in his description refers to the spiritual plane of existence.

> Thought provides the pattern from which the physical takes form. The Energy Body which surrounds and interpenetrates the physical body and is part of a human being's auric cocoon, is derived from the initial thought form of the immortal High Self. This is subsequently affected and modified by the thoughts, attitudes and beliefs of the Human Self which are sub-consciously projected into it. The Energy Body is primarily the vehicle of the Hidden Self, and is composed of constantly changing tones and hues of sound and color as it absorbs the thoughts and feelings of the Human Self. The Body Self operates primarily through the physical body; the Hidden Self through the Energy and Emotional Body; the Human Self through the Mental Body; and the High Self through the Soul Body.[1]

Healing at these levels is advanced work, with the potential for expanding, healing, and repairing the essence self/core soul. Why would the essence self need healing, and how can it be done by those of us in bodies, the lowest energy level of the chain? The essence self/core soul is subject to the wear and tear of the suffering of countless incarnations. While energy is indestructible, the essence self may not be, though it is amazingly resilient and self-healing, and is immortal. The oversoul is indestructible and immortal and is an actively conscious part of Goddess. An accumulation of lifetimes of extreme suffering without repair could conceivably destroy an essence self, but the lack of repair is not likely to be allowed to happen. Nothing can destroy the oversoul.

The essence self can also be damaged or even shattered, again by lifetimes of extreme suffering. When this is the case, there will be dis-ease on the physical level, as well as in the astral/emotional, mental and spiritual bodies. The astral twin can split off from the physical body that it maintains, with the silver cord that connects the bodies too loose to hold and unify them properly. Like a straw on a camel's back that is just one weight too much, seemingly small traumas in the soul's incarnation can result in damage or shattering, if the essence self has incarnated in an already damaged state.

Shamans term this damage as it manifests into the incarnation "soul loss." They describe it as occurring from a perceivable trauma but my feeling is that the perceivable trauma is only the tip of a very big iceberg. The trauma from this life is the last of many straws.

> Soul "loss" usually results from a trau-matic situation. Devastating news and deep shock, for instance, may cause the recipient to withdraw from conscious reality for a time.... She may feel "dead to the world," or "beside (her)self." An accident may leave a person feeling "spaced out" for several days, and a bad illness or a surgical operation may sometimes produce a sensation of being "dissociated" from the physical body—an uncomfortable wooly feeling. Bereavement, separation or divorce, loss of job, enforced retirement, rape, incest, child abuse—can all cause a feeling of prolonged numbness, a strange sensation that part of oneself is "missing." And, indeed, that is exactly what happened.[2]

Women will recognize themselves in the above description, particularly women who have suffered such severe traumas as incest, rape, battering, or abused childhoods. Such traumatized women have great difficulty staying in body and spend much of their time out of body on the astral plane. I know, as I am one of those many women. When women who have been traumatized in this lifetime begin to look into their past lives, they see a karmic pattern, not as punishment, but because the essence self/core soul is damaged. The pattern repeats, because the essence self is crying out for healing.

Remember that karma can only be healed while the soul has a body to operate through. This seems also to be the case with core soul damage and shattering that are an extreme working out of karma. A lifetime of trauma or abuse that has not been healed results in its being carried forward to the next incarnation. If it is not healed there by the soul's creating a repeat of similar trauma in an attempt to release it, the trauma will be carried forward to the next lifetime. When repeated without being healed, such lifetimes create a karmic pattern, which can lead ultimately first to core soul damage and then to shattering.

This is how and why such damage is possible to heal while incarnated in the body. It is the only place where it can be healed. The concept explains much in the way of women's suffering, why people who are good and harm none may inexplicably suffer so much. After death, the soul is given healing from the previous incarnation but the traumas, karmic patterns, and soul damage reincarnate with them again. Damage that has happened while incarnated has to heal while incarnated.

Every method of healing in this book so far has been directed at healing this damage, beginning from the physical plane and moving outward into the aura. Core soul healing begins with karmic release (Human or Mental Self) and continues with healing into High Self and spiritual plane by way of subpersonality integration and soul retrieval. It includes bringing the astral twin into proper relationship with the physical body to heal and operate the body in a healthy way.

Core soul damage can mean more than chronic spaciness and being out of body. It can result in parts of a person's psyche criticizing, hindering, and even sabotaging one's growth, even causing repeated "accidents." It can result in split or multiple personalities in a shattered essence self. A damaged core soul can bring a woman a lifetime weight of chronic pain on any or every body level, an inability to function successfully, and a sense of never belonging or even really living here on Earth or in her body.

Healing in this book began with meditation, visualization, and running energy, and has moved through the levels in a step-by-step way through this book. A woman who has followed the chapters and used the information and meditations from each of them in her healing (self-healing or facilitated with another healer) has moved through the levels and planes. I realize that this material is becoming increasingly complex. While I have made it as simple as possible to understand and work through, realize that it *is* complex information, each woman can only follow it at her own pace. If you have gone with me this far, you are ready to heal your astral twin and soul and to repair many incarnations' damage to your essence self. You have also become healed enough to be a healer and facilitator for many others. And you are needed desperately to do so.

Shamanism recognizes only two root causes of sickness: one is something in a person's energy field that should not be there. These intrusions, which I call spirit attachments (different from Buddhism's emotional attachment of holding on) are discussed in the next chapter. The process of their removal, called by shamans "extraction," is also discussed there. The other source of dis-ease is when something that should be a part of the energy field is missing. Shamans call this an "abstraction," and it results in a loss of life force energy and vitality. Abstraction is healed by the process of soul retrieval,[3] which I begin with astral twin and subpersonality healing. These techniques heal what is missing, damaged, or shattered, and returns it to proper place and functioning in the aura and existence planes. The result is wholeness, and a healing of the damaged essence self and all her incarnations.

To use my own experience and past life experience as an example: In my first past life awareness of extreme abuse, I was burned at the stake as a witch in Brittany. I was a male blacksmith and animal healer at that time, my wife and soul mate a healer for humans, and we were high priest and priestess of a well-established village coven. When the Inquisition came, she was repeatedly raped and we were both tortured, beaten, and then burned to death. Somewhere in that horror, severe damage and splitting off occurred for both of us.

In two subsequent female lifetimes I was again a witch. In one life in Italy, I walked with hundreds of other women into the sea to drown, rather than be taken by the Inquisition again. In a later one in New England, I was drowned in a ducking stool, though this time did not die of the experience. The damage was not healed, and the karmic pattern was repeated at least twice, increasing the damage each time in attempts to heal it. I have always both feared and loved water, and have never learned to swim.

In my most recent past lifetime, I was a Jewish lesbian, and incarnated again with my soul mate who was also female. As adolescent cousins living in the same household after my parents were taken away by the Nazis, we were repeatedly incested by a grandfather who lived with us. As older teenagers, we tried to escape Germany by train, were caught going through customs, and taken to Buchenwald, the German concentration camp. We took care of each other as best we could through the Holocaust. We were frequently raped and were subjected to medical reproductive experimentation for about a year, until we both died before the age of twenty. We reincarnated again very quickly, as often happens after a violent death.

The present lifetime has brought the pattern back again. As a child, I was physically beaten from infancy, emotionally, mentally and spiritually abused, and grew up with all the specific behavior patterns of incest (along with those of the other abuses). The incest did not surface in my healing process until I began viewing past lives, and the key piece of the grandfather in Germany was almost the last puzzle piece I saw. My body reflects the past and present life battering, and uterine dis-ease suggests the emotional aura body cause of rape and incest. Crossing a border, even to Canada, once brought anxiety to the point of terror and illness. Airport security checks did the same. This stopped once I understood the cause, the customs capture in Germany.

When I began core soul self-healing, I discovered fragmentation and subpersonalities, though the fragments were not yet developed or shattered enough to make me a multiple personality. My astral twin was so far away that I didn't know she existed. Subpersonalities included those whose negative thought forms obstructed my growth, whose constant inner voice's best message was, "You can't do that, can't have that, don't deserve that."

I had a behavior pattern that I desperately wanted to change, but no healing over years or a decade even began to change it, or to help me understand it. When I was even slightly threatened, I often became quarrelsome, belligerent, and angry, always with people I didn't know. Afterward, I always wondered what had happened, why I had done it, and couldn't control it. I felt extremely guilty, horrified, and upset. The negative inner voice had a field day with it, "You're just no good." I knew something was wrong, a lot was wrong, but even after fifteen years of spirituality and healing I didn't know what to do.

I also felt I didn't belong on Earth, to the point of wishing to leave and go home to wherever it was I belonged. (I am not suicidal in any way.) Here in this foreign place, I had great difficulty in managing a simple daily life. Machinery of any kind totally eluded me, and I just didn't like gadgets. I dropped and spilled things, and forgot about dinner until it usually burned. Crowds of people, other than women's or spirituality groups, frightened me. I could never look anyone directly in the eye. I spent so much time out of body that I often had no memory of where I'd been in a day, and I was always stressed, fearful, and absentminded.

Three things changed my life by healing all of the above aberrations. The first was bringing my astral twin back into connection with the physical plane and emotional body. Apparently core soul damage loosens the silver cord that connects the bodies, and the astral twin then operates too far out on the astral plane to maintain physical and emotional functioning. The second was healing the subpersonalities of the mental plane, and the third and most fascinating was the soul retrieval of fragments from the astral, mental, and spiritual planes of existence.

The astral twin operates on the astral plane of existence, and is the emotional Energy Self. Its job is to be a bridge between the emotional and astral planes, and the physical body level. It brings all the planes of existence together and unifies them so that the planes and aura bodies work as a whole. It brings the light/information of the mental grid, Light Body, spiritual plane, and oversoul into aura bodies and chakras, allowing for the fullest awareness and coordinated spiritual development on every level.

Bringing in one's astral twin is an extremely joyful healing, and I recommend that everyone try it. It's a simple meditation that needs to be done only once. In women of good intent, the astral twin is always a Be-ing of love and positivity. Some women see her as a Goddess or as an embodiment of Goddess-within. The astral twin is golden and beautiful.

——————— : : ———————

To do this, enter the full meditative state by grounding and centering, a deep body relaxation process, placing protection, and running energy. Always use protection when entering the astral plane. Ask your spirit guides and angels to be with you. With the affirmation that only positive energy may come to you, go out on the astral to find your astral twin. By thinking yourself there, you will go there. Ask to see your astral twin, talk with her, and invite her to come home. You will know her because she looks like you, or as you have always thought your best self would look. Her energy is bright and golden; she is rainbow light. She will not be damaged or need healing.

If your astral twin agrees, bring her into your heart. You will feel her golden energy radiate out through your aura and all your chakras as she takes up residence there. Feel your aura energy brighten considerably. Thank her and your guides, and come back to now, bringing your astral twin with you. After the healing, you may feel spacy in a golden, floaty way for several days. It is a joyful and very safe feeling, and you will feel more present and at home on the Earth and in your body afterwards. Your spiritual and psychic growth from this point will increase immeasurably, and your life will gain in positivity and newfound peace. The meditation only needs to be done once.

——————— : : ———————

When you have gotten used to your new Be-ing, begin working with those little nagging critical selves that still hold you back. When the astral twin self is a part of you on the astral plane, these subpersonalities are mind creations that are not you, but keep you from experiencing the Pure Mind of the grid. They block your ability to open and heal your Body of Light. As a woman develops spiritually, these subpersonalities become more and more demanding. They are old thought forms that no longer have a place in your evolution, thought forms you have outgrown, and that are now in conflict with your growth. Their distortions, criticisms, and worries harm your positivity and your life.

LaUna Huffines has worked with healing subpersonalities for many years and describes their structure:

> Subpersonalities are not real, but until you see that they are not you, they will seem real. Think of your subpersonalities as the displays in a holographic exhibit. A three-dimensional hologram of a dancer looks solid. It seems to move as you walk around it, but if you reach out to touch it, your hand goes right through it. . . . Subpersonalities—even those which feel most anxious or guilty—are no more solid than a hologram.[4]

To begin this healing, first become aware of all the negative voices. Some are nagging, others fearful or worried. They may be thoughts that are unjustifiably angry or jealous, or anything that hampers a positive self-image. Fighting them by yelling at them or telling them to leave does no good. They are not separate entities, and your angry resistance only feeds their fears, justifying their criticisms. It gives them energy and they just get louder and more insistent. This approach with mine left me increasingly frustrated, and the negative voices only mocked me and came back stronger.

The key to dealing with them is in understanding their intent. They are actually trying to help or protect you, though their way of doing so is something no longer positive or useful. You have outgrown their methods. They are like uneducated children that need discipline, security, and love. Think of them as your own inner child in her "terrible twos" stage of bullying and whining. They need a mother, someone to teach them the facts of your new life and who you really are.

LaUna Huffines suggests:

Here are some ways to merge your subpersonalities into your core self. Begin by getting to know the major ones. Listen to each of their needs and make an agreement with them that you can keep. Tell them your needs and vision and get their agreement to cooperate. Coach them in new ways to help you .... Let the light of love pour over and permeate them. The power of like—working together with the guidance of your mind ... will finally enable you to merge them and their energy into your central personality self.[5]

——————— :: ———————

Now try a meditation for meeting and healing these thought forms that seem to be oneself, but are mind creations. Enter the full meditative state with body relaxation, running energy, protection, and calling in your spirit guides. Ask to be taken to the mental plane to meet your subpersonalities. Sit in a grassy place, as your guides bring them to you one by one. Talk with each, find out her fears and how she wants to protect you. Give her a new job. If a subpersonality comes to you as a child, treat her as one; if an adult, treat her as an adult. Reason with an adult, but give a child an ice cream cone and tell her she is safe.

As you finish talking with each subpersonality, have her sit beside you in a circle on the grass. When everyone is there, invite your astral twin to teach them and fill them with light/information/education. When your astral twin is done, bring in the Goddess, asking Her to heal these thought forms so they will cooperate and help you on your spiritual path. They may fade into her light. This takes the healing through astral, mental, and spiritual planes. When your spirit guides indicate that the work is done, thank them, your astral twin, and the Goddess, and come back to now.

——————— :: ———————

You may find the thoughts in your mind to be suddenly and peacefully very quiet from here on, and some negative behaviors healed. The meditation may need to be repeated; do it whenever necessary, any time you feel a new negative thought form gaining strength. For further information and work with subpersonality healing, see LaUna Huffines' book *Bridge of Light* and Duane Packer and Sanaya Roman's audiotape study course, *Awakening Your Light Body*, Volume I. These subpersonalities are best cleared before beginning soul retrieval, as it is important to know what is a soul fragment that is a part of you, and what is a thought form that only seems to be. Unhealed subpersonalities can also block soul fragments from coming in for healing.

The above are only preliminaries to the spectacular soul retrieval process. In soul retrieval, the damaged or split off fragments of your core soul/essence self are healed. They are you. Bringing home your astral twin gives your essence self a greater stability and unity, and a readiness to do this. It also helps to distinguish your healthy astral twin from a fragment that needs to be returned and healed. The astral twin, once brought into contact and proper connection with the physical plane, also is an agent for helping with the soul retrieval.

I learned this process about two years ago from Sandra Ingerman's magnificent book *Soul Retrieval: Mending the Fragmented Self* (HarperSanFrancisco, 1991). I have used it successfully on myself, for my dog Kali, with a number of other women, and with a woman who is a multiple personality. I have used it during hands on healing, psychic/distance healing, and as a self-healing tool. Some of the stories follow the meditations and directions. Along the way I have redefined and changed the process considerably from a shamanic technique to karmic healing for essence self wholeness. I must credit Ingerman's book for teaching me the beginning work, and I recommended it to any healer using the technique.

This version of soul retrieval is done in several steps. I give it below as a self-healing. It works beautifully with a healer and receiver, especially when the receiver is able to participate cooperatively in it. I find these healings to be gentle and nontraumatic, a great relief after emotional reprogramming and karmic releases. They can be quite intense nonetheless. The process also works with pets; ask your guides if a particular animal needs it. A woman or pet with a herstory of trauma or past abuse will usually benefit from this type of healing. It may take several sessions to complete the job, and I've found in myself new soul parts long after I thought the process finished. Once each fragment comes in and merges with you, however, she is home for good.

If you are an incest or multiple personality survivor, soul retrieval may become the completion of your healing. For these women in particular, I find it important to do a Lords of Karma karmic release either previous to doing soul retrieval or as the first step in it. Ask for full healing now from both the abuse and its karmic pattern on all levels. All the other techniques of this book are preliminaries for soul retrieval, and their completion before doing this process makes for easy and spectacular results. This is an end stage healing process, not the beginning of recovery. Bringing the astral twin into the physical realm, and learning to work with her in the subpersonality meditation, is also important before starting.

When working with multiple personality women, one other technique should be done before beginning. This is a meditation to identify any Be-ings that may not be you (soul parts of the receiver), and return them to the Goddess or to where they may belong. To do this, go to the astral with your spirit guides, angels, and full protection. Ask to identify these Be-ings, and ask the Goddess to take them from you, to heal them, and to send them where they need to go. There is more on this type of entity healing in the next chapter.

Suspect that a fragment is not you if it doesn't seem to look like you at any age, has a nonhuman energy or appearance, or is negative (rather than wounded or angry) in intent. In any soul retrieval or any trip through the planes of existence, it is important to place full protection separately around the receiver and any participants of the healing. This is particularly so in working with multiple personalities. Make the affirmation for healer and receiver both that "only what is mine comes into me." *This is extremely important.*

———————— : : ————————

Now begin by entering as deep a meditative state as you can access. Do full body relaxation, run energy, create a strong golden bubble of protection, and ask your guides, angels, astral twin and the Goddess for help. I consider soul retrieval to be a celebration of self and Goddess; approach it seriously but with joy. The needed healing of many lifetimes is about to begin, resulting in a brand new wholeness and a better life. And, moreover, better lives to come.

Ask your guides and angels to take you to the astral plane, to your astral twin. She will meet you there and join you. Ask her with your guides' and angels' help if there are any parts of you that need to come home and might be present on this level. Your astral twin or guides will find one or more and bring them to you. They look like you, but can be you at any age. You may be told their story, when and why they fragmented; I usually don't ask. On the astral plane, the fragment selves are all from your current lifetime. Offer each soul part healing until it is golden and healthy looking, then ask each if she is ready to come home and be part of you again. If she says "no," assure her that your life is a good one now and it is safe to come back. Remember that she left at a time of trauma, but you don't want to leave her out there any longer.

When she says "yes," ask her if she has any sisters on this level and to bring them to you now. A few more may appear. Heal them also, and ask them the same questions: "Are you ready to come home? Are there any more?" Now invite the soul parts into your heart/thymus chakra. Bring them in and anchor them there with a band or web of light. Ask your guides and angels to help. Extend the web or band from the soul fragments in your heart and thymus, upward along your Hara Line to your transpersonal point above the crown. The light weaves like a delicate spider web that may take some time to build. This web is the most important part of the healing and absolutely essential for it.

Next ask your guides, angels, and astral twin to take you to the mental plane and repeat the process there. These fragments are from past lives and may have less form than those on the astral plane. They will probably still look like you, but less distinctly. Again, find them all and bring them in—I prefer not to ask what happened to them. Reassure them that they are safe and you are safe to be with. Heal them, and then bring them into your heart as before, extending the web of light. Let the web build before going on.

Now ask your guides, angels, and astral twin to take you to the spiritual plane and repeat the process. The fragments this time will look like forms of light, but you will still know they are you. They are from past lives and there will be fewer of them on this plane of existence; it is also possible that there won't be any on this level. Bring them in as before, extending the web of light. Now place a web or cocoon of light like a golden egg around your entire aura with all the soul fragments inside. Tell them, "Thank you," and "Welcome home."

Return through the planes of existence to your body. Move from spiritual to mental, mental to astral, and astral to physical plane. Thank your guides, angels, and astral twin, and ask them to continue and complete the soul parts' integration. You may be extremely relaxed and spacy at the end of this meditation. It may have taken a short or long time. I prefer to do soul retrieval at bedtime and sleep afterwards. You will feel very good, but may feel floaty and strange for several days.

———————— : : ————————

The full integration process takes about a month. During that time the soul fragments first go to sleep, then fade into light in your heart/thymus and emotional body aura. They will feel bliss, and you will feel bliss also. Check the heart to transpersonal point light web at least twice a day, making sure each soul part remains firmly anchored. If you feel fear or discomfort at any time in the first week, it may be because this web has slipped. You may find the soul fragment floating in your solar plexus, very scared. Put her back into your heart and secure the web.

After a week repeat the above meditation, checking to see if anyone else is still out there, ready to come home. You may or may not find more, but if

you do, bring them in as above. Allow them all to integrate for at least another week before going further. Be very gentle with yourself during the entire healing and integration process. Almost from the first you will feel your life shifting and changing into something new, and your aura molecules actually rearranging. However positive, such change can be stressful and even overwhelming, though with soul retrieval I have always found the healing gentle.

———————— : : ————————

Now do the rest of the soul retrieval process. Go into full meditation again, remembering your protection; call in your guides, angels, astral twin, and the Goddess. This time as you go to each plane, ask if anyone else may be holding a soul part that belongs to you. There may be a few or several, again of any age. The people holding them may have kept them because they didn't know how to send them back, or they may be holding them to control, manipulate, or harm you. They can also be held by people who genuinely love you and wish you well.

Go to each of the people and ask for the soul fragment. Some parts will need much healing once they are free; give it to them. The Goddess and angels may be much needed for their healing here. Ask the soul part if she is ready to come home, and bring her into your heart, anchoring the web of light as before. Make sure she is healed and bright before bringing her in. Do these one at a time or after the whole group is freed and healed. Knowing who has held these fragments can be upsetting to the receiver; take this slowly and easily.

If any part being held by someone else is not permitted to go free, offer a healing to the holder in exchange for the fragment. This usually works. If it doesn't, try offering the holder something else that is positive in exchange. Should even this fail, ask your guides, angels, or the Goddess to intervene and they will get the fragment back for you. Heal the soul part, and bring it into your heart with the others. Extend the web of light, running it from the soul part and your heart/thymus through the Hara Line to your transpersonal point.

Go to the astral, mental, and spiritual planes of existence to do this. It will happen much more quickly than the initial soul retrievals. On each plane as well, ask if *you* are holding any soul fragments that belong to others. Former lovers and even present mates are good candidates. Ask your guides, angels, astral twin, or the Goddess to return them to where they belong. Even if the part you are holding is from a loving and good relationship, still return it. The relationship will get closer, better, and healthier for doing so. Do this on all three planes, then come back to now. Check the light webs for at least a week, and give yourself time, space, and nurturing to complete the healing. Be aware that your life is changing into wholeness, making physical, emotional, mental, and spiritual level transformations. Take each step slowly, one at a time, and do them gently and with joy.

—————— : : ——————

Like all the healing methods in this book, I used the soul retrieval process on myself before using it on other women. Working alone, I sometimes missed locating soul fragments that turned up in later psychic or hands on sessions, alone or with other healers. I brought my soul parts in one or a couple at a time. The risk in working alone was that the webs would not hold. But that did not occur when doing the healing with others. In doing this with other healers, too, I found the process went faster. More fragments came in at a session, often all of them in a single focused healing where the receiver participates cooperatively with the healer.

In one soul retrieval done by telephone with a psychically aware woman, the only fragment we found on the astral plane was her astral twin. Once the astral twin came in, she took us to the other planes and found the soul parts. On the mental plane were four fragments: one a tiny embryo, and three others, two children and an almost grown-up teenager. On the spiritual plane was a light form with only a glowing face visible, who brought us two others when we asked if there were more. The receiver was holding only one fragment that belonged to someone else. It was anchored to her by a strong rope, which her spirit guides removed when asked to, and they carried the fragment away to its proper place. The full session took an hour to complete.

Another soul retrieval done as a psychic healing, was for a three-month-old infant whose grand-mother is my close friend. Since birth, the baby girl has had episodes where her breathing stopped and her heart rate soared as high as three hundred beats per minute (it is normally about eighty-eight in a baby). The situation was obviously life-threatening, and the baby was on a monitor that would ring if her heart or breathing accelerated or stopped, so she could be quickly resuscitated.

I did a psychic/distance healing to find out why these episodes were happening. I found the baby's vagus nerve, which runs from the brain to the chest and regulates the heart and respiration rates, to be just a fraction of an inch too short for proper functioning. There were breaks in the nerve, and I was told that it would heal and grow. I made contact with Amanda, the baby, to ask her what she needed, and she was quite willing, aware, and very adult. I could talk to her. It seems she was going out of body, too far out and for too long, to be with her soul mate Edward. He was also willing to talk with me, and I saw them both very clearly. They were supposed to have been in Amanda's body together, but when the birth came a month early, he didn't get there in time. They have shared a body before and want to again. He promised me he could heal the child, and that she would live and be physically and emotionally healthy for it.

I used soul retrieval to bring them together in the baby's body. Edward had to shrink his adult male image down to baby size. It worked like the astral twin merging, except that it happened by the two Be-ings joining together at all the chakras before Edward's energy merged into tiny Amanda's. Her heart and breathing episodes dropped from seven a day to two or less. I have done further healing to stabilize the silver cord that connects the aura bodies for both souls. The child is also being given homeopathy (homeopathic *Opium*) and flower essences (including the Perelandra Soul Ray series). Except during her frightening episodes, she seems happy and totally unconcerned, and my healing guides tell me she will stay on Earth and live.

One fragment of my own was discovered by a healer during the time of karmic release from fear I described earlier. We were shown an image of me at two or three years old, locked in a dark closet, terrified and screaming. I don't remember this happening, but it is in keeping with my childhood. When the soul fragment healed and came in, she felt like a rush of warm light and seemed delighted to be in my heart and be home.

It took about three days for the soul part to completely merge into me, leaving just a glow of pink light, and a week to disappear completely. The whole process felt wonderful and I'm told she was the last of my fragments to need outside help. The web of light the spirit guides placed around my full aura signaled an important completion. I feel very different than I did when the process of bringing in soul fragments started; I feel positive, whole, and truly healed. All of the problems mentioned earlier in this chapter are gone, though years of other types of healing hadn't helped them. I believe that the karmic pain pattern is now healing or healed, and that my core soul is approaching wholeness at last. I will continue to check for other fragments, however.

My favorite soul retrieval experience was with Kali. I'd never thought of trying this for a dog, but the suggestion came from my angel. Kali came to me quite injured and abused, and the idea made sense. I put my hands on the dog, called in Kali's astral twin, asked Ariel for help, and we all went to the astral plane. A fluffy half-grown Kali rushed into my arms, a silly puppy with wagging tail. The puppy led us through the planes of existence to find others, and a total of five golden Kali puppies merged into the grown dog. Instead of in the heart, which is not a highly developed chakra in most pets, the puppies were placed by Ariel and the guides into Kali's belly chakra, a major canine center.

The dog was totally pleased with the whole episode which probably took less than five minutes. For a few days she walked around with five puppies trailing her, and when she lay down she looked as if she were nursing them. She didn't allow Copper near her brood and wasn't nice to him at all. Then they faded into her as golden light and disappeared completely in about a week. One good human friend

of Kali's was holding a soul part and readily let it go back to her. Kali seems happier and more stable since the process. I was told that soul retrieval wasn't necessary for Copper (who insists that these things don't exist).

The most intensive soul retrieval I have participated in was for my friend Tracy, who is a multiple personality. The healing took three extremely long and very awesome sessions that ran several hours each. There was need to do it three nights in a row; that was all the time we had. Also, it had to happen rapidly, as I suspect that Tracy's fear might have caused her to halt the process if it were slow enough for her to really think about it.

The week before making the trip, I did a psychic distance healing to see if all the personalities were really parts of Tracy. I found two that weren't, and asked the Goddess Kwan Yin to come and heal them, and to take them where they needed to be. One was an infant, and the other a baby of perhaps a year old. Tracy had experienced incest and was severely abused all through childhood, and we were aware of traumatic and abused past lives. Though the healing was done psychically with her permission, she was as aware of what had occurred as if she had been there. I also asked her to make a list for me of the personalities she was aware of, with their names, ages, and characteristics. I wanted to know at least a bit of who was there. She told me later that it was the most revealing part of the healing for her.

When we were together, Tracy and I did the healings with other women she wished to be present. One was her therapist, who became an expert in psychic healing rapidly over the weekend. She was a joy to work with, though I had initially been apprehensive of a therapist being there. In the first session, I placed protection around everyone, called in guides, angels, Brede, and the Goddess Kwan Yin. I placed protection around everyone and had everyone including Tracy repeat, "Only what is mine comes into me."

We began by asking the Lords of Karma to heal Tracy completely and to give her a joyful and productive life. The Lipika showed her an incident in this lifetime that she needed to be aware of, and then granted the release. She had blocked who her perpetrator had been and was shown him. Wads of what looked like white cotton stuffing came out of her heart chakra, which we then filled with pink light. The heart space became a pink room for Tracy's "kids" to come home to.

Next we went to the planes of existence and Tracy's "kids" began coming home. Each came in pretty quickly, but there were a lot of them, over a dozen fully formed personalities with names and individual needs. The therapist, Tracy, and I negotiated with each of them, trying to meet their demands in Tracy's best interest and bring them into her heart space. The one fragment who was male, a four-year-old named Tommy, would only come home if he could bring his fire engine, dump truck, and a puppy. He said the room was too pink and let the puppy wet on the carpet.

One of the girls wanted a swimming pool, and another her alternative rock music; she reluctantly agreed to use a headphone. One soul part was a self-mutilator who finally promised to not do that anymore. She was difficult to convince to come in, and one of the last to do so. Another skeptical one had to have a lot of proof before agreeing to come home. It was a long night.

In the next session, we worked on other issues that were necessary for Tracy's healing, but that were not directly soul retrievals. We convinced her that it was healthy to be angry, something she hadn't allowed herself before. I also checked the webs of light from the previous night's healing and made sure that all the retrieved soul parts were comfortable and happy. One of them wanted an ice cream cone, and we gave ice cream to everyone astrally.

In the third session, I checked the webs again, then took everyone back to the soul planes. There were a few more fragments, unformed ones without names, and we brought them into Tracy's pink heart space. She was holding soul parts from others that were hard for her to send home, but she did so. Her incest perpetrator was also holding a child-sized fragment of Tracy that he didn't want to return.

After some negotiation, he finally accepted a crystal in exchange for it, and the soul fragment he had held needed much healing from the Goddess. She received it and came home to Tracy.

When we had checked all the planes and brought in everyone we found, only a rag doll remained. It puzzled me, as I thought it was a soul fragment, but it didn't move or seem alive. I didn't understand it until Tracy identified it for me. It had been her doll as a child, and her perpetrator had forced her to submit to him by threatening to rip it up if she refused him. Tracy didn't want it back and was disturbed by it, so I asked Kwan Yin to take it away and take care of it. After this, we were done, and I placed golden light around Tracy's full aura and ended the session.

In the days that followed, the soul parts went to sleep and began to merge into Tracy. She missed them, however, and chose to wake them up and continue being a multiple personality with co-consciousness. It had to be her choice, as every step of the healing had been. After a year, she chose to integrate fully and did so, and she is gaining in strength and wellness on every level now. Other events occurred in these several hour-long sessions, and they were the most intensive healing I have ever witnessed or participated in. I recommend spacing the healing sessions much further apart, with time for rest and integration between them. The changes are too intensive otherwise.

Nothing but experiencing it can describe how the soul retrieval healing process changes lives. This healing is totally transformational, with effects for change in this lifetime and in all the lifetimes to come. The work of this chapter is advanced healing, but if you have followed this book slowly, step by step, you are ready for it. The work can be done alone or with other healers. This process of soul retrieval is in shamanism called "abstraction." The next chapter discusses the other shamanic form of sickness, called "intrusion" or spirit attachment, and how to heal those also.

Notes

1 Kenneth Meadows, *Shamanic Experience: A Practical Guide to Contemporary Shamanism* (Rockport, MA, Element Books, 1991), pp. 164–165.

2 *Ibid.*, p. 165.

3 *Ibid.*, p. 166.

4 LaUna Huffines, *Bridge of Light: Tools of Light for Spiritual Transformation* (New York, NY, Fireside Books, 1989), p. 115.

5 *Ibid.*, p. 118.

CHAPTER TWELVE

Spirit Attachments

While most psychic energy is good energy, some is not, and what is not can come in many forms. As a healer develops psychically she needs to know how negative energy manifests and what to do when she finds it. In these cases, protection is essential but is not enough; wrong energy must be cleared and dissipated permanently. This is not only for the sake of the healer, but for the receiver of the healing session, for anyone else who enters the immediate environment, and for the safety of the Earth Herself.

Psychic attacks and evil exist, and they do real harm. Some seemingly negative energy is not evil but only out of place. It is necessary to move it to where it needs to be. Some entities from other planets and their intrusive devices on Earth are highly negative, while others are our protectors, helpers, and healers. It is important to know the difference and how to respond to a variety of situations safely.

In any discussion of entities and spirit attachments, the problem of evil in the world arises. It is a riddle or a koan as to how evil energy can exist when the Goddess creator of all Be-ing is so fully and absolutely positive. Some women refuse to accept the existence of evil, but this is denial, and an unsafe denial at that. One theory is that good cannot exist without evil to test itself against. As noon cannot exist without midnight, so good cannot exist

without its contrast. Humans on Earth are given the power of free will and unimpeded choice. Choice creates our lives and karma as actions of mind. Earth as a planet is an experiment in free choice, and a range of errors may arise from human choice and intent.

Evil can be defined as the ultimate result of ego and separation, selfish desire, and lack of compassion:

> It is evil when there is no thought of
> kinship or love, when we act in separation
> from others, when we assume authority
> over or control of others, or are indifferent
> to those who are our responsibility. It is
> evil to fail to regard those within our sphere
> of influence with compassion. Where there
> is no love, evil fills the vacuum.[1]

No soul is created wrong or is inherently evil, but souls are affected and can be corrupted in the body by a damaged physical brain chemistry or faulty genetics. An insane mass murderer, a child molester, a horse gone renegade, or a rottweiler that becomes a killer are examples. Emotional disorder that becomes karmic core soul damage can be another source of evil, as can drugs' destructiveness to the mind. Says between lives researcher Michael Newton:

> I have come to the conclusion that the five-sensory human can negatively act upon a soul's psyche. We express our eternal self through dominant biological needs and the pressures of environmental stimuli which are *temporary* to the incarnated soul. Although there is no hidden, sinister self within our human form, some souls are not fully assimilated. People not in harmony with their bodies feel detached from themselves in life. . . .
>
> The evolution of souls involves a transition from imperfection to perfection based upon overcoming many difficult body assignments . . . . However, all souls are held accountable for their conduct in the bodies they occupy.[2]

In another view, the angel Lucifer was chosen to serve the good by testing it with temptation and wrong. This requires people to continually reassess their commitments and choices. Constant positive choice made under pressure forges and reinforces human character. There is a natural tendency for choosing good in the world; we are made in the image of Goddess. By overcoming negative desires and choosing good, good is reinforced with repeated awareness. Tested metal is strong and indestructible. In his role, Lucifer's testing offers hope for the reinforcement of goodness.

Everyone makes both mistaken and positive choices, and learning good by understanding error builds character and causes the soul to evolve and grow. Likewise, women confronted with negativity learns to handle and transform it, thus building their abilities for good as healers. A healer is never harmed in her attempt to release or transform evil or turn it to good, or to banish it in a healing. Most of the negative energy she confronts is error and misplacement, rather than actual evil. Some negative energy can also be deliberate, however, and the threefold law is fully in effect in these cases. A sender of deliberate wrong will receive it back, and a healer of such wrongs also receives return for her positive actions in clearing from in herself or others.

The distinction must be made between evil and suffering. They are two entirely different things. Suffering is not evil. The reason for suffering in the world is for soul growth. Some is karmic indebtedness, where a person who has done harm in one lifetime agrees and chooses to experience it in another life. This is for the purpose of walking in the other person's shoes in order to learn compassion. Some suffering is chosen by the self in the between life agreement as a way of building karmic merit or achieving a particular learning quickly. Tragedies in life are not coincidence. They are chosen by the essential self, *not the conscious incarnation*, for a purpose in the soul's overall plan of development. Evil is different from this in that it is the choice and intent to do harm to others.

When found in a healing, negativity can either be mind-created evil or random energy gone wrong because it belongs somewhere else. There is a clear difference between removing a psychic attack and sending a lost spirit that does not know she has died to the other side. As a part of the Earth change process, the planet is increasing in vibration, as is everyone on it. We are moving from third dimensional awareness (the rational mind, solar plexus), to fourth dimensional (universal compassion, heart chakra) and fifth dimensional (psychic communication and psychic ability, throat chakra) vibration and consciousness. Along the way, as we and the planet are now passing through the lower astral realm, much displaced energy is making itself known.

Cleaning out the astral plane has become a job of almost every psychic healer. This means moving passed over spirits, that are either stuck or refusing to go, forward to where they need to be on the spiritual plane. Once an incarnation ends, souls are supposed to pass over, but some don't. Some of these haunt houses, while others attach themselves to people's bodies, where they can cause dis-ease and disturbance. Those that inhabit places are often frustrated and they seek attention in a need to find help. They are called discarnate entities or, popularly, "ghosts." Those that inhabit bodies usually have a job to do there—to manifest the karmic learning of their dis-ease, or to teach their inhabitant how to help and heal discarnate (without physical body) entities. These are usually called "spirit attachments," and their end goal is also to go home to the spiritual plane and the Goddess.

Neither of the above is evil, but psychic attacks most often are. These are random or deliberate psychic violence, negative energy sent to target a specific person with harm. They can be random in the sense that the sender may not know she is making an attack, but her negative emotions toward a person are still forceful enough to cause damage. An example of this happened when I moved from one rented house to a different, better one. The new house became a constant parade of broken appliances and intrusive, inept repairmen. I felt frustrated and stressed. When I sought the cause, I found an attack from my former landlady, who had shown signs of emotional disturbance and who hadn't wanted me to move. When I questioned her psychically, she was very angry with me; she didn't know what a psychic attack was. She nevertheless wished me harm in my new home, sufficient to cause trouble to manifest, and she continued to cause it until I found the source.

A deliberate psychic attack is deliberate evil. I shudder at modern witches who condone "hexing," though I think there are probably very few of them who do it. The threefold law is quite plain, as is the law of harming none. There are this life and karmic consequences to such actions. Karma is caused by holding on emotionally or mentally to a person or situation. Someone who hexes has attached herself to the receiver of the hex by very negative energy that will return to the sender again and again. The act also connects the two participants to each other until the wrongs are balanced.

I would not want to be attached to anyone in this way, and for me the excuse that the evil of a rapist calls for retribution doesn't work. Let Earthplane or universal law, the Goddess, or the Lords of Karma

deal with rapists. I would rather focus my energy on healing women who have been raped and need help. It is better to prevent the woman's trauma from becoming a karmic pattern than to interfere with the karma of her rapist. Psychic attacks from past lives can also show up in healing, as well as this life bad energy. Attacks from the past have usually come from people the receiver knows and has trouble with in this lifetime.

Another category of negative energy is something I call space junk. This is stuff in the psychic form of objects in the aura, artifacts left over from past lives on Earth and elsewhere. It can look like the sword from a traumatic death in the third century, or a teddy bear you loved in your last lifetime's childhood. It can be a necklace or ring from another lifetime that may have been past life power or healing tools. It can be a collection of unidentifiable junk, ropes, plumbing pipes, etc. The objects themselves may be harmless, but they can also cause a lot of difficulty. A formerly physical plane weapon that was the source of a past life death can be the source of a dis-ease or pain area in one's present body. Removing the artifact heals the pain in this lifetime.

My least favorite kind of spirit attachment energy is alien instruments of interference. I tangled with this in brave, stupid, and traumatic ways for about a year. It was a very intense period in my psychic training. As clearly as I understand it, the Earth's Pleiadian source planets have been at war with those from Orion since almost the beginning of Earth time and herstory. It was the Orions who disconnected human DNA and have continually sought to control this planet. They may be the original and ongoing source of all evil on Earth.

Earth is now at the brink of recovering its place in the universe, and at the brink of spiritual development that will result in the New Age and reconnection of our DNA. Orion is active here again. Their goal is to corrupt and enslave us, to keep us in ignorance and violence. They will not succeed, though sometimes they seem to. Their influence appears in human auras as implants aimed at control and at the generation of fear. Some of these were put there in distant past lives to reincarnate with us again and again. Information is provided in this chapter on how to remove these and the other forms of negativity described above.

Helping an entity to pass over to the spiritual plane is the basic process for releasing most attachments. You will know that there are one or more of these in a house or building in several ways. (They can also be present outdoors, often at sites of fatal accidents.) First, you may feel you are not alone through the place is empty of other people. The feeling may or may not seem negative. Second, you may experience "things that go bump in the night"—pictures falling off the walls, the sound of things breaking, voices, footsteps, etc., when no one is there. These usually seem to happen at night or when the house is very quiet, and they can be disturbing and upsetting. I get a general sense of nervous unease and sleeplessness when these things are present.

Third, animals are often aware of entities. They may intently watch an entity, bark at it, or avoid a room or place in a room or yard where one stays. Dogs, cats, and horses are quite aware of nonphysical astral activity. Sometimes they even have entity playmates, including animal friends that have died. Fourth, there may be a cold spot somewhere in the house. Summer or winter, the area never seems to warm up. It always feels colder than the rest of the room. It may be a place that you and your pets avoid without quite knowing why. Lastly, you may become aware of an entity because you psychically see it. I would rather be able to see it and know what I am dealing with than to guess.

A discarnate entity is a spirit that has died but has not passed over completely, and this may happen for a number of reasons. The most frequent one is that it is lost and doesn't know how or where to go. It may not know it is dead, or may refuse to accept that fact. Spirits that become lost in this way have usually died suddenly or traumatically, and are confused and disoriented. They may have sent away their spirit guides who come to take them over. These entities usually return to where they once lived. Some of them also remain in their homes sim-

ply because they have been overly attached to that place in life. They don't want to leave. They may not want to allow anyone else to live in "their" house, or they refuse to leave their money or former belongings.

Some discarnate "ghosts" remain on Earth because they are so attached they are addicted. Alcohol attracts alcoholic entities whose addiction previous to their deaths still holds them. Most psychics find drinking alcohol a very negative experience, as these entities can attach to them, following them from the party or bar to enter their homes. Once there, they can create a great disturbance until they are sent on. These are usually lower astral level spirits and not pleasant. Drugs likewise attract similar low level entities.

Most spirit entities are less attached and more positive; they just want to stay on Earth a while longer. One discarnate entity I found who had not passed over stayed because she loved her garden and wanted to be there. The woman knew she was dead and knew how to leave for the spirit plane, but she asked to stay. She was causing no harm and the house's living occupant was willing, so I let her be there, telling her to find me if she ever needed help. She never did, and the house's occupant told me that she left a few months later. Her garden seemed to suffer for her absence; it didn't grow as well after she left it.

Psychics attract entities, or they seem to move to houses that need entity clearing. This may be because we are aware of them when other tenants have no sense of them being there. They don't find us, we find them. Psychics attract discarnate spirits because the entities are in need and come to those who can perceive and therefore help them. Our spirit guides place us there to clear them, too. Most discarnate spirits are harmless, and even noisy ones are only trying to get your attention so you can send them home to the spirit world. It also seems to be part of a psychic's job to help clear the lower astral plane, thereby both helping lost spirits in need and aiding the Earth's vibrational growth.

One house I lived in seemed to have entity after entity. People came for healing or just to visit and left them there. The house was full of them when I moved in, and the more spirits I passed over the more seemed to come. I disliked the house intensely and it sometimes felt like the energy was bad because the house wanted me to leave. I got a lot of training in removing spirit attachments of every kind there. One of these was an old Native American woman who was extremely angry. The tribe had left her to die, as was their custom for someone terminally ill in a time of famine—the children had to eat. This woman had not been ready to leave and was angry about it. I discovered her and finally passed her over but she came back again. She was looking for her beaded dress. When she found it somewhere in the vicinity of the laundry room she left for good.

In my last house before the present one, about a month after moving in, I awoke one night to see an old woman in curlers and a white nightgown standing over me. She wanted to know what I was doing in her bed. I passed her over, and an old man with a wrench showed up about a week later. He was "fixing things," he said. I was getting very tired of repair men by this time and sent him to join his wife. A child entity came in a few weeks later—pictures started falling off the walls at night. The dogs watched her, but weren't upset. She was looking for someone who could see her to help her leave.

———————— : : ————————

The process for sending such discarnate entities to the spirit world is very simple. Enter the meditative state and place protection around yourself. If you can switch to meditation easily you can do this anywhere; it does not require a deep trance. Call in your guides and angels, then ask to see and talk with the entity. Tell the entity that it has died and no longer belongs in the house or on Earth. Offer to help it go to the light. Call in its guides, a relative, or its perception of Source to take it where it needs to go. I usually ask my own spirit helpers, "Who wants to take this one over?" Make sure the entity is completely gone before ending the session. See them entering a light filled doorway and then the door closing behind them. Thank your guides and angels and come back to now.

———————— : : ————————

These Be-ings are to be treated with respect; they are generally not evil or even negative. They have come to you for help in the same way that someone in body may come to you for healing. Once they know they are dead and that you will help them, they usually go easily and with relief. The Be-ings and spirit guides that come to help them pass over may be a wife or mother, Mary, a saint, an angel, whomever they can trust by their own belief systems. Occasionally one refuses to leave. Call in its guides and ask them to take it where it needs to be, and they will do so. Even if an entity blusters and acts in a threatening way it cannot hurt you. Just pass it over and make sure it has gone.

Spirit attachments that are found in the body or aura may have human form, look like caricatures, animals, or have nonhuman shapes. I suspect the idea of "demons" came from these. Like other discarnate entities, spirit attachments also come forward to be released, and though they may have been in the body for years or lifetimes, you won't see them until they are ready to go. Again, they are nothing to fear. If you discover them in healing or self-healing, they are on their way out of your energy and moving off of the Earthplane. They can be caused by people who in the process of dying attached themselves to a living person, usually by the living person's unknowing or subconscious agreement. These seem to be human and are indeed human entities. I experienced one in myself that was the dead fetus of a past life baby.

Nonhuman attachments are generally energy forms that create blockage or dis-ease. They may be a manifestation for the working out of a piece of learning or karma, such as a dis-ease or phobia. (Many phobias have past life origins.) Always check tumors for holding spirit attachments. These entities are negative but usually have a reason to be there, and unlike psychic attacks, their source is not someone's attempt to harm you. If you see attachments in a healing or meditation, they are shown to you for the purpose of clearing them. No matter how odd or how awful they may appear, they cannot hurt the healer who is removing them. Though some may resist you, they will leave if you insist.

To clear both human and nonhuman appearing types, shift to the meditative state and call in your spirit guides and angels. It takes a deeper meditative state than for the previous entities. Be very sure to place protection around yourself when handling attachments to prevent them from seeking you as their new host. If they do this, simply pass them over again, removing them from your aura. There is no need to panic if it happens.

Ask to see the entity. If it has human form, ask if it has guides that can take it to the spiritual plane where it needs to be. If it has been a human spirit, its guides or angels will appear to help it. Pass it over as in the last meditation. If it has nonhuman form, it probably doesn't have a human spirit or spirit guides. Your own guides or angels may do the job of removing it and taking it away. Make very sure it is fully gone before taking your concentration from it or ending the meditation.

Some of these attaching entities, particularly the nonhuman looking ones but some human ones as well, may strongly resist leaving. Make the following affirmation or a similar one:

> Go to the light. You will not be punished or
> harmed. You have done your job well and now it
> is time to leave. You can finally go home. The
> Mother is waiting to heal you and comfort you.
> Go to the light. Go to the Goddess in peace.

The entity will go, though you may need to repeat the affirmation a couple of times. Ask your spirit guides' and angels' help. Before ending the meditation, make sure that the attachment is fully gone, and ask if there are any more attachments to remove. There can be several at a session, of the same or different types, and in the same or other places in the aura or chakras. Thank your guides and come back to now.

———— : : ————

Attachments that have come out of my own aura have included three coyotes (tricksters up to no good) from my belly chakra, and a flock of flapping ravens from my solar plexus. One of the first, that came out in an intense psychic healing, was a nonhuman appearing male caricature from inside my head. He was a pain trap, in that the attachment was activated at times when my life was going well, plunging it into pain, hopelessness, and despair every time. It frightened me to find it, as I hadn't seen such things before, and I was very glad for it to leave. I worried for a while afterwards that it might not be completely gone, though I couldn't find more of it and soon forgot it. It surfaced again in another healing over a year later and I released it. When clearing spirit attachments, look for them in the chakras, Hara Line chakras, and on astral, mental, and spiritual levels, but they do not occur beyond. You will not find them in your mental grid, Light Body, or oversoul.

Psychologist and hypnotist Edith Fiore, in her book *The Unquiet Dead* (Ballantine Books, 1987), uses hypnosis to release human spirit attachments, which she calls "spirit possessions." These are cases where a person witnessing a death becomes host to the dead person's unpassed over spirit. It can also happen while the receiving host is vulnerable in a hospital under anesthetics, as these drugs puncture the protecting energy integrity of the aura. The entity that has died nearby, instead of passing over properly to the spiritual plane, becomes trapped in another's living body. No evil is usually involved, the soul is lost, and both entity and hosting person need help and release.

Such human attachments can cause varying degrees of harm to the receiving host. There may even be a complete takeover of the host's personality by the dead entity. They can be the source of body pain, dis-ease, phobias, chronic exhaustion, time loss, memory blanks, addictions, and relationship problems. The possession may occur in childhood and will carry forward into adult life until released. If the host dies with the attachment remaining, both spirits finally pass over, and they are not carried forward to other lifetimes.

Dr. Edith Fiore gives a list of the ten most common signs of such possession. These are possible symptoms of both human and nonhuman spirit attachments in the living body.

- Low energy level

- Character shifts or mood swings

- Inner voices (that are not your guides, subpersonalities, or soul fragments)

- Drug, alcohol, or smoking addictions

- Impulsive behavior that seems out of character

- Memory problems

- Poor concentration

- Sudden onset of anxiety or depression

- Sudden onset of physical problems with no seeming cause

- Emotional and/or physical reactions to reading *The Unquiet Dead* or other descriptions of attachments/possessions.[3]

The process above for releasing discarnate entities and spirit attachments clears these as well. It passes the spirit on to where it needs to go to complete its death and move forward on its soul path. Surrounding yourself with protection in any situation involving death prevents these attachments from occurring. Make the affirmation, "Only what is mine comes to me." If you have been under anesthetic in a hospital where people are dying, or may have died in the operating room nearby, do the attachment release for yourself at home as soon as you feel well enough to do so. After receiving anesthesia, your aura's natural protection is damaged and you are vulnerable for at least a month. Wear a tourmaline pendant of any color, or an amber one, for protection and to repair your energy field.

Psychic attacks are nastier energy, and they cause harm because they are sent to do so. It is no use disbelieving in them, they exist, and I have experienced a number of them. Several years ago, when I first began traveling and teaching, I went to Oregon to lecture there. I did a program in a different place each night for two weeks. It was something I won't repeat. I became very exhausted and got the flu. My aura was weak from stress and illness, and I was not experienced at that time in protecting myself.

Two born-again Christian women followed me from place to place through a large part of the trip, and they disrupted every lecture. While I would not put up with it now, I didn't then know how to stop them from interfering. They were quite obnoxious and somewhat frightening—they informed me that they were praying for my death. They kept asking me in the lectures why, if I could heal myself, did I still need to wear eyeglasses. From that time on I began to experience severe stage fright. By the time the two weeks ended, I also began to have problems with my vision, which resulted in my being unable to read for almost a year.

Fully seven years later in a healing session, my Florida healing friend Jane uncovered their psychic attack in my solar plexus. It looked like a barbed, double-pronged arrow that was working its way deeper and deeper into my aura, with much infection energy surrounding it. The image of these two "good Christians" came immediately to mind, though I hadn't thought about them in years. Jane felt that the attack had been sent with both knowledge and intent and was still being reinforced periodically. I was very sick after its removal for at least two weeks. Once healed, however, my stage fright was suddenly gone and my vision stabilized. Some of the damage seemed permanent and is still being repaired, and I have since found another part of the attack in my vision chakra.

Clearing a psychic attack this deep can be done as self-healing or in a hands on session with another healer. Be sure to place careful protection around all participants. This is so in any healing, as negative energy needing to be released can appear in any session, and more and more of these situations are turning up. The process of uncording and removing chakra hooks is a good preliminary, and many psychic attacks can be cleared through that method. Check any sudden or chronic pain or dis-ease area for spirit attachments, entities, and attacks, especially if other healing has been ineffective. Ask in the session that if any of these are present they will appear and be released.

Dealing with psychic attacks usually requires a deeper trance state than just shifting into meditation. In hands on healing with others, this work begins later in the session. In self-healing, it requires the full meditative state. Done either way, both healer and receiver need energy protection before beginning, and the help of spirit guides and angels. Wishing the greatest protection and healing strength possible, I also ask the Goddess' help with clearing these.

——————— : : ———————

When ready to begin, ask to see any psychic attacks that might be present in your body or aura from this or other lifetimes. You might start with a pendulum, asking chakra by chakra if there is a psychic attack energy present. If "yes," stop at the first instance and ask to see what it is and where it comes from. This is important; you need to know who did it and what made you vulnerable to receiving the negativity. You may not be able to clear it without this information, and in a hands on healing either healer or receiver will be given the source. Psychic attacks from a past life may have been repeated in this one by the same person. There is usually a cord of black energy leading from the attack to its sender; cut it or ask your spirit guides or angels to do so. Make sure you are fully protected first, as the sender may attempt further harm when they know they have been discovered. Ask your guides to shield you if this happens.

With the cord cut, remove the attack itself. It can be in almost any form, but will not look pleasant. I've seen them appear as knives, chrome cylinders, steel snap bolts, barbed arrows, rusty padlocks, black needles, threatening snakes and insects, and black poison powder. Fill the receiver/yourself with light, and keep running light energy throughout the removal. Ask your spirit guides, angels, or the Goddess to take the attack away, to cleanse your body and aura energy of the toxins, and to repair any damage in your past, present, and future. Specify that this be done on all levels, including the physical level, as there may be more damage than you perceive.

Do not put your hands into the receiver's aura to touch this very negative energy. You may instead send light, especially as laser light from your eyes, or from your hands held above the area to help the guides. A method I use is to visu-

alize the area filled with hot, cleansing fire, flames that do not harm other tissues or positive energy. The area may remain open and draining once the attack is removed, as there may still be toxins left to clear. If your spirit guides decline to repair the aura at this point though you asked them to do so, leave the energy to release for three days, then go back and close the opening if it hasn't already been repaired. Some very nasty stuff may take longer than the three days as well.

This drain of negative energy releasing may feel like an oozing infection or like bleeding, and the receiver will probably feel tired or sick. Run energy as often as possible in the next few days to clear and heal it. Use sea salt in the shower until the draining stops, and then go to apple cider vinegar to close and repair the torn chakra or aura. Before ending the healing session where a psychic attack has been released, ask if there is any more evil energy in the chakras or aura and go chakra by chakra to check for it. Clear anything you find as above.

Finish by placing strong and permanent protection around you, including chakra shields. Make sure it offers two-way protection, allowing positive energy in as well as keeping negative energy out. I like the affirmation, "Only positive energy enters here, and anything negative must leave." If you have been or are being attacked psychically, ward (place protection around) your home, car, pets, and workplace. Ask your guides and angels for help; angels are particularly good at protection. Check your aura and chakras at regular intervals to be sure that no more attacks are happening or ready to release. Do regular uncordings. I am sorry to say that I've seen a lot of psychic attacks in the healings I do, and lately it seems that this energy is increasing considerably, both in virulence and frequency.

——————— : : ———————

Space junk seems similar to psychic attack, but is usually more odd than threatening. The attachments are often from past lives and can also be debris from the past in this life. If the energy is negative or harmful it is usually inadvertently so. You may not need to know what the objects are, or why they are there, just remove them. Have your guides or angels carry them away to where they can harm none. You may also put a collection of the items into what I call a "dump bucket," a visualized insulated garbage can with fire inside, and have your spirit helpers carry the whole thing away at once. Never just remove and let go of any negative or possibly negative energy; dispose of it safely so it can't harm someone else or reattach.

The stuff that comes out of people's aura can be strange, amazing, interesting, or just weird. If you died of a knife or arrow in the back in some lifetime, the weapon may still be in your aura. It may cause a pain area at the spot that clears when the artifact is removed. If you were imprisoned in some lifetime, as in the Inquisition, there may be shackles or instruments of torture still there. You may find pieces of rope if being tied up was a trauma in some lifetime.

Some items are not from traumas but from daily life. If you were a spinner or weaver in a past life, you may find spindles or loom heddles in your aura, or horseshoes if you were a blacksmith. There may be necklaces or other jewelry, crystals or ritual tools. You won't want to use these now; it is best to clear them. Most of this junk is in the aura energy layers, rather than in the chakras.

The space junk may not release all in one healing, but reappear in a series of sessions or from time to time. If junk is showing up, it is time to remove it. If it occurs often, you might ask to see the source or to clear the whole lifetime of the objects. The things are usually not frightening or evil, but are leaving for a reason, and I do not consider them positive energy forms. Space junk appears during times when you are clearing, or have recently cleared, the pain energy of past or present lifetimes. They are a part of the clearing and brightening of your aura, and a part of spiritual growth.

In a healing session I once received, some objects looking like plumbing pipe were removed from my aura at the head area. The woman who did the healing said they looked like a frame over my head that rested on my shoulders, and she took it off. Almost a year later, spontaneously in self-healing, I started seeing plumbing pipes again. Pieces cleared nightly for several weeks. During this time I was getting a lot of mind chatter and noise in my head that was very uncomfortable. At worst, it even kept me from contact with my spirit guides, who I talk with almost constantly. Finally, I asked to know what was going on and how to heal it.

The pipes and space junk were coming from a past life. In it, I was male and a political prisoner. The frame on my head and shoulders was a device used to harness psychic ability. I was being used to run what seemed to be mining equipment. An echo device was part of the frame, with an implant in my head to prevent psychic prisoners from using their abilities to escape. It caused psychic thoughts and sending to return, repeat, and echo in the mind. Once I saw it, the guides removed the implanted device. The headaches and chatter stopped, and no more plumbing pipe space junk appeared. The lifetime was not on Earth and was apparently not a good one, and I didn't ask to know more about it.

A lot of space junk, some of it still "live" and harmful, comes from alien implants. I find these to be truly evil and frightening. A human's attack is at least comprehensible, if scary and saddening, but alien attacks can be without any logical reason. Some negative aliens consider humans to be no more than laboratory specimens and they experiment upon us. They have no conception of human emotions or feelings. Some have interest in shutting down and harming those people sufficiently psychic to perceive their activities, people who most often are women.

The war between Orion and the Pleiadian protectors of Earth is still happening. The war began before the fall of Atlantis, and Orion figured heavily in that advanced civilization's destruction. The war then and now is for the freedom of Earth and Earth's peoples. During the Atlantean era and later in the time of the Aztecs in Mexico, Orion placed implants into individuals as a way of controlling and enslaving them. The destruction of the peaceful Mayans by the Aztecs was part of that war. When the Orions left Earth, the implants they placed became dormant but not dead. The implants carried forward from lifetime to lifetime in the auras of those who were implanted.

Orion is now active on and above Earth again. I have psychically witnessed spaceship battles in the Earth energy grid, and I have been harmed trying to fight them while doing Earth healing. The alien attacks filled my aura with a frightening array of wires, electrical boxes, and other junk. Once inserted, the objects increased and multiplied in my aura bodies, where they created fear and stifled my psychic energy. Healing sessions and galactic helpers eventually removed these, since my spirit guides seemed unable to do so. It was a very scary experience.

I learned to connect with the Earth energy grid, and to call the Pleiadian healers and protectors for help. I was eventually taken to a Pleiadian starship. There my energy was cleared and repaired, and the attacks were removed in a process that resembled surgery but was painless. I was given protection and shielding, and told to stop taking part in the battles. A single human is not strong enough to fight in this war, and once the Orions had noticed me I became endangered. I was traumatized enough by that time to obey orders and I was relieved to be out of the war. All this alien activity went on for about a year (1993). It was totally unpleasant, and the battles are still happening, but without me. In doing healing with others, I remove Orion implants frequently, but my own seem finally (and thankfully) to be gone.

These implants appear in the chakras or aura as negative crystals, cylinders or boxes with wires that may lead through the body. An implant near the heart may have electrical wires running into the neck or down through a woman's legs. When the wires are gone, spiders appear in their place. When a receiver in healing has been experiencing much fear, dis-ease, or negativity in her life, usually without seeming cause, or when she gets a new, intense pain area that has no explanation, I look for Orion implants. I have learned to recognize implant energy in an aura by the sense of diffused pain that goes with it. The purpose of these attacks is primarily to create fear and negativity; they actually can cause little other harm. The Orions feed upon this emotion, and it generates the confusion they wish to cause on Earth.

The healers and psychics of today were healers and psychics in the past. They were a threat to the Orions of the past, who placed the implants thousands of years ago to control us. The same healers and psychics are still a threat to them now. When Orion is on or close to Earth the implants activate, shutting down the healers through fear and giving the invaders access to this planet. Orion was also the agent for disconnecting human DNA. By cutting us off from our heritage of information/light, they hope to overcome the Pleiadian protectors and the Earth healers, and take control of Earth and Earth people.

At about the time I stopped trying to heal Earth of this evil single-handed, Barbara Hand Clow's book *Heart of the Cristos* (Bear and Co., 1989) came to me. I was appalled and gratified at once that her writing confirmed what I'd been seeing for a year. She defines the Orion/Pleiadian situation as the source of evil versus good on Earth. When there is violence, separation, war or lack of love, this disruption is caused by Orion. Orion, who can feel only negative emotions, is being given one more chance to learn love. This is the battle between good and evil on Earth from the beginning until now.

Many individuals are realizing that souls on the dark side are drawn to them in order to set up situations in which the dark forces might be given their last chance to choose to cease evil action. Positive energy predominates over negative, but the Men from Orion have charged the karmic memory with much negative experience, which people tend to revert to. It is important to be in the present time . . . for by 1992, every individual with whom you have ever experienced evil in past lives will manifest in your life. Welcome them as your teachers.

The exact moment when the Men in Black (Orion) rejected creation is the only moment in which they can feel! So when you see sexual addiction, love of violence, hatred of self, know that these human poisons are a desperate cry for release by the imprisoned soul which is seeking surrender. Orion first learned to feel while using power and control, not by letting go to a larger force. So, when you find yourself hating another, being enslaved to an addiction or enjoying the bizarre outward expressions of the inner evil of the End Times, then go to the love, to the light exploding within the chakras of your body.[4]

Light as love energy is the primary healing, for Earth and all Be-ings. The Pleiadians and other positive star people are also on Earth to help us. These positive healers and Earth healers can now be called upon to heal and remove negative energy of every kind from people and animals, and from the planet. When dealing with alien or psychic attack energy—which Barbara Hand Clow defines as inherently Orion even if coming from Earth humans—ask these Pleiadian healers into the session. I do this in healing work or meditation by inviting, "Any positive Pleiadian or galactic healers to be here and help." Specify clearly that only positive and healing energy may come in.

Two groups of these positive healers (so you will recognize them) are the blue energy Be-ings and "little blue fairies" I described earlier. They were released from the healing center on Jupiter to help us by the energy shift of the July 1994 comet collision. Another group of these Be-ings appears to me in surgical garb. They have egg-shaped heads with large bulbous foreheads, large black eyes or goggles, and hands with extra fingers. I have been working with what I call the "Jupiter Surgical and Comedy Team" for some time; they are Pleiadians from the Jupiter healing base.

Any of these can work with you to remove Orion implants and negative energy; the surgical team does much more. Other positive nonphysical Be-ings are possible; question the intent of those who appear in a session. Any time I am faced with something I suspect to be negatively alien, or any psychic attack or spirit attachment that proves difficult to remove, I ask for galactic healing assistance.

Invite these beings in along with your spirit guides and angels. They also work miracles of physical healings for Earth Be-ings.

——————— : : ———————

In addition, if despite healing and implant removal you still feel overrun by Orion wires, boxes, and implants, you may *only in that instance* go directly to the Pleiadian starships for help. Do this only as a last resort, after all other helpers have tried and failed. Go into meditation and visualize yourself diving into your pink or green heart chakra like a lake or a deep pool. Dive to the bottom of the pink water. Just above the pool floor, look for a blue-lit hatch or doorway. Don't approach anything that is not blue or glowing. Knock on the door, state what you need, and ask to enter for healing and assistance.

You will be welcomed, placed on a surgical table, and healed without pain. The colors in that place, the sense of advanced healing tools and energy techniques are miraculous. Do this at night at bedtime and let the Pleiadians work on you while you sleep. You may be told to repeat this the next night, or until your energy is fully cleared. Ask the Pleiadians for protection as well. You may feel tired for the next few days and weak, but also very clear, bright and relieved because of the experience.

——————— : : ———————

To remove implants before trying this, do a session similar to the removal of psychic attacks or attachments. Place protection, call in your spirit guides, angels, and the Pleiadian healers, and enter a full meditative state. Ask to see any negative alien implants in the chakras and aura bodies, and be sure to look deeply into the aura through the grid and beyond. Since these implants reincarnate with us, look for them in the etheric template, celestial and ketheric levels, on the mental and spiritual planes, and in the core soul/essence self. They will appear as black cylinders, discs, boxes with extending wires, or any type of electrical circuitry. They may also appear as negative crystals.

When you have located these, bring in your spirit guides, angels, and the Pleiadian healers. Ask them to *gently* remove all negative implants with all their spiders, wires, and extensions, all the way to their source. Ask to clear any toxins from these implants and to repair the damage they have caused in all levels, lifetimes, and in your past, present, and future. It is important to ask for all these things, especially their full repair of the damage. Other world healers think we are self-regenerating as they are, but we are obviously not.

Ask that gentleness be used in this extraction process as these healings can otherwise prove quite rough handling. Alien healers may not have a good concept of Earth energy, or of bodies and their limitations. We are not as strong as they are. The galactic healers will go in and do the work, while your spirit guides will probably step back until they finish. Healing alien damage is beyond our guides' knowledge or job, though they may help you recover and heal afterward. Angels may, however, be able to help you more. Fill yourself repeatedly with light. You may need to send fire to help clear the implants. The Pleiadian and galactic helpers may or may not converse with you during the process.

If you begin to see spiders or black pyramids in your chakras after removing the attachments, you have not cleared the implant source. The Orions seem to know just what we like least and they use this information. These final objects were hard for me to remove. I spent many healing sessions clearing them repeatedly, until I found the mechanism for doing so in a permanent way. The spiders and black pyramids are holograms. However often you remove them, they will return again and again until you remove their root source, the actual implant itself. This implant is a small black electrical box or disc with wires that is basically a movie projector. When the projector is gone, the pictures of spiders, black pyramids, and other nasty things are gone, too. The key is to ask the healers to remove the implant source. The intent of these nasty objects is to scare us and to generate fear. Until I learned the key, it worked on me quite well.

——————— : : ———————

Barbara Hand Clow explains these implants:

> In the last battle, 26,000 years ago, crystals were implanted in the etheric bodies of people by the Orion Atlanteans . . . which were set to be released between August 16, 1987, and August, 1992. These crystals contain programs which trigger beings from all parts of the galaxy into karmic experiences required by the Men

from Orion to offer them one more chance to discover free choice . . . .

> Now the crystals are being removed.[5]

The battle for freedom and free choice on Goddess Earth has been going on since the beginning, and this is what implants, attachments, and psychic attacks are all about. Healing ego separation to accept oneness and love is the only answer, the only way through the Earth changes (Barbara Hand Clow's "End Times"). Negative energies being healed and removed from human auras, and every healing and release, is a win for love, Goddess, and goodness, and for a healed New Age on this planet. Though this talk of aliens and even psychic attacks may seem bizarre, please trust me and take them seriously. There is evil in our world and healers are being called upon to correct it. We now have help, but it has come only recently; I feel it is important to describe what I see and how to deal with it and understand it.

I also feel that it is increasingly important for healers and psychics to protect themselves from negative energy. This does not mean hiding in one's room. It means being aware of and taking care of one's information/light. Run light/energy daily in any of the methods described in this book. This serves to clear your energy, chakras, and aura bodies of anything negative that may have come in, and it brings to the surface anything that shouldn't be there. Remember and use the energy protection methods including chakra shields, making sure that the protection is not a wall but a two-way membrane. Anything negative must leave, and only the positive can come in. If you have been attacked or feel threatened, place shields specifically protecting yourself against psychic attacks, but again allowing positive energy to enter. Some negative energy incarnated with us, and now it can be removed.

Make an effort to clear your aura, searching out and removing any attachments, space junk, psychic attacks, and implants. Check through your Kundalini and Hara Line chakras, all the aura bodies, the template levels, and the planes of existence. Check from your physical toes all the way to your Body of Light.

Your oversoul will not be affected. Every removal of these attachments will make you stronger and your energy more positive; it will increase your ability to bring in Goddess energy and be an effective healer. As a channel for Goddess energy and healing, we can do no less. The result is an ever more numerous group of women able to do high level healing, who will teach healers and help Goddess Earth through the Earth changes. We are here on this planet at this crucial time for this purpose.

The next and last chapter of this book discusses healing, death, and beyond.

Notes

1 Graham Bernard, *The Challenge of Evil: Further Conversations with Richard* (Rochester, VT, Destiny Books, 1988), p. 43.

2 Michael Newton, Ph.D., *Journey of Souls*, pp. 47–48.

3 Dr. Edith Fiore, *The Unquiet Dead: A Psychologist Treats Spirit Possession* (New York, NY, Ballantine Books, 1987), p. 123.

4 Barbara Hand Crow, *Heart of the Cristos: Starseeding From the Pleiades* (Santa Fe, NM, Bear and Co., 1989), pp. 187–188.

5 *Ibid.*, pp. 190–191.

CHAPTER THIRTEEN

Death

There is no getting around it, everyone dies. In these Earth change times, death is everywhere, on the news, on the planet, and in one's own life. The violence of society creates such deaths constantly. The

pollution of the planet manifests in women's bodies as terminal dis-ease. AIDS is epidemic, wiping out whole countries. One in seven women in America contracts breast cancer. The number and scope of deaths in places like Rwanda is appalling. Natural disasters, wars, and dis-ease take lives not singly, but in the thousands and ten thousands. Death surrounds us. We are all immersed in it. It is the death of the old Earth, the painful, toxic place and collective Mind this current Earth has become.

Wicca describes life as a Wheel with no beginning and no end. Death leads to rebirth. We have been in bodies many thousands of times, countless times. Those who remember past lives know they have been here before, but may have no idea of how often. Michael Newton in *Journey of Souls* describes an interview in hypnosis with a very spiritually advanced woman, an old soul:

> I found this woman's span of incarnations staggering, going far back into the distant past of human life on Earth. Touching on her earliest memories, I came to the

conclusion that her first lives occurred at the beginning of the last warm inter-glacial period which lasted from 130,000 to 70,000 years ago, before the last great Ice Age spread over the planet.... Later, some 50,000 years ago, when continental sheets of ice had again changed Earth's climate, she spoke of living in caves and enduring bitter cold.[1]

Lifetimes are mortal, souls are not. We live again and again to experience every form of living, and every form and aspect of moral and spiritual growth. Every culture has known this, but in the present age on Earth the information/light has been withheld. As the planet and people awaken, the light returns. We have been here before and will be here again. There is no beginning and no ending. Death is only a visit home for a while in between our births. The between life state is the paradise most religions promise in some form. The going home is joyful, healing, and loving, but we in bodies have been taught to fear, deny, and dread it. Yet, being born, taking incarnation, is far harder than death and the places we go between lives.

Buddhism's focus on the attainment of Enlightenment means freedom from rebirth after death. Mahayana Buddhism says that everyone can attain Enlightenment in this lifetime or be reborn in a Pure Land (Buddhist paradise) that sets the conditions for Enlightenment to be attained easily. The state of Enlightenment is the bliss beyond the Void, the union with the source of all creation. While Buddhism has no concept of a personified divinity, Wicca calls this Goddess. In further definition, the union is the conscious awareness of the oneness of all life, the dissolution of ego/separation. Embracing oneness is all that is needed to free the soul from further incarnations. Through spiritual practice and awareness of the death process, Enlightenment can also be attained during the stages of death and dying. In Eastern terms, death is not the scary thing the West makes of it.

There are four stages to the death process in Buddhist teaching, called the four bardos. A bardo is simply a period of transition between events. *The Tibetan Book of the Dead* describes four of these interconnected reality states. The first is life (the natural bardo of this life); the second is dying and death (the painful bardo of dying); the third is after death (the luminous bardo of dharmata); and the fourth is rebirth (the karmic bardo of becoming).[2] While the physical body and etheric double dissolve after death, emotion (astral body and celestial template) retreats into mental body (ketheric) which survives and continues. The mental body/mind goes through the bardos, and if it does not attain Enlightenment and Liberation there, proceeds into a new birth. The physical body is impermanent, as are all things on the Earthplane, but mind and consciousness continue. In another way of stating this, lifetimes end, but the essence self/core soul goes on.

The natural bardo of this life is part of the death process, as it is in the body that one accumulates and heals karma. It is also in the body that one chooses growth through spiritual practice. Both of these directly affect what happens at and after death. The second bardo, the painful bardo of dying, is the death itself. It is defined as beginning when you first know you are dying, and ending with the dissolution of first the outer and then the inner senses. The outer senses are the five elements and the five physical senses. The inner senses are thoughts and emotions on the physical plane.

In the dissolution of the outer senses (the second bardo death process), when the Earth element fails, the body loses energy and strength. The person is weak and can no longer care for herself; she feels a heavy weight upon her. Her mind is first anxious and delirious, then drowsy. The failure of the water element involves the loss of feeling and of the control of body fluid functions. In this state, the mind is irritable, nervous, and hazy, and the woman may seem frustrated. When fire dissolved, the person becomes cold, and the cold that begins at the extremities moves toward her heart. The woman can no longer digest food, and her mind alternates between awareness and confusion. Earthplane perception fails. In the dissolution of the element of air, the person finds it harder and harder to breathe. She has visions both blissful and fearful; her intellect dissolves, and with it the woman's contact with the outside world.[3]

Wicca also describes all life existence and Being as comprised of Earth, air, fire, water, and spirit. These form the pentacle, the symbol of the Goddess Craft. In Wiccan terms, the dissolution of the elements and the five physical senses at death means a transference of reality from Earth and the body to the level of spirit. The spiritual level is the source of all creation and this source is, of course, the Goddess. In death one leaves the body and the Earthplane to go to the realms of Goddess. In the Wiccan Wheel of Life, death is another beginning, the ending of the physical lifetime for the start of a new reality. After this next reality also ends, the Wheel turns again to yet another new beginning, a new body, new incarnation, and rebirth. The woman dies but life continues and returns.

The dissolution of the inner senses in the Buddhist second bardo is the shutting down of the chakras and energy channels on both Kundalini and

Hara Lines. The Hara Line and channels cease to function first, and the emotional/astral body fuses with the mental. The Kundalini Line and chakras simply stop, as the outer bodies no longer need to feed energy and support to the physical body plane. The emotions of the physical plane dissolve, and those that have become karmic transfer and are held in the mental body. When physical breathing stops, the person is pronounced dead, but an inner respiration continues for about twenty minutes longer. During that time, a reversal of the energy of conception takes place, a meeting of the Earth and sky.

This meeting is the purpose of the inner dissolution. At conception the male and female (sperm and egg) unite, resulting in the father's essence, a white nucleus, coming to reside in the crown chakra of the new Be-ing. The mother's red essence moves to and resides in the Hara center. These essences or seed atoms are the energy basis for the Kundalini and Hara Line channels. At death, the wisdom winds that flow through and maintain these channels stop, and the essences are no longer held in their places. The father's white essence descends to the heart, and the mother's red essence rises there. Bliss and clear awareness are the resulting states, and all Earthly thoughts of anger and desire end.

As the two essences meet, consciousness is enclosed between them, and Earth and sky are enfolded into total darkness and unconsciousness. The mind is then freed of Earthly ignorance and delusion, shedding the physical plane. As the mind (mental body, ketheric template) becomes conscious again, the Ground Luminosity rises, and the bardo of death and dying progresses into the third bardo, that of the clear light or the luminous bardo of dharmata. The person who has died has now left Earthplane consciousness and life in the body behind. With the regaining of awareness, she has entered the after death state, the place of Pure Mind and all truth.

This third bardo is the Buddha nature/Goddess-within, the mind of the clear light of death, and the place of immortality. This clear glowing mind is who we really are, and its dawning is our greatest opportunity to attain Enlightenment and have a chance to avoid further births. It is absolute truth, the nature of all things that is now unveiled. In this moment of Pure Mind, the soul that attains the oneness of herself with Goddess and all life attains Liberation. This most profound moment, however, is not as easy to make use of as it sounds. Most people are unable to make this final leap of realization into Goddess oneness, unless they have worked at spiritual practice in life.

> Even though the Ground Luminosity
> presents itself naturally to us all, most of
> us are totally unprepared for its sheer
> immensity, the vast and subtle depth of
> its naked simplicity. The majority of us
> will simply have no means of recognizing
> it, because we have not made ourselves
> familiar with ways of recognizing it in life.
> What happens, then, is that we tend to
> react instinctively with all our past fears,
> habits, and conditioning, all our old
> reflexes. . . . Instead of surrendering and
> opening to the luminosity, in our fear and
> ignorance we withdraw and instinctively
> hold onto our grasping.[4]

Ordinary mind is that of the mental body aura in life; the luminous mind of the clear light after death is the mental body, as held at the ketheric template level of the spiritual plane. Meditation and spiritual practice help in transcending the illusions of the ego and ordinary mind, showing it spiritual truth and bringing the person's level of development to the spiritual plane, the Goddess level. Ego, shown the light/information of true reality and working of the universe, is able to make the leap from separation (grasping) to oneness and attain release from karma and rebirth.

This is what we incarnate in bodies to do: to attain spiritual wisdom and union with Goddess and all life. Enlightenment means "shedding light upon" or "making bright and clear." Once that realization of truth (oneness) is achieved, there is no more to be learned by incarnation in bodies. The choice of this realization happens in a moment, and in that moment of the dawning of the Ground Luminosity of dharmata, the soul is either freed or returned to a new body.

This luminous bardo of dharmata, the after death state, has four phases, with the chance for Liberation available at each of them in increasing repetition. I interpret the phases as the essence self's movement through the planes of existence on its way to the spirit world. At the time of the dawning of the Ground Luminosity, the physical plane has been left behind. In this third bardo, the end result is the soul's movement into the Light Body, through and beyond the astral, and into mental and spiritual planes of existence.

The first phase of the bardo of dharmata is "when space dissolves into luminosity."5 This is described as a world of flowing light, sound, and color—the astral plane. The second phase, "luminosity dissolving into union," describes laser lights of extreme and often frightening intensity that manifests into peaceful and wrathful deities. Streams of light join the newly dead person to these deities, heart to heart, and then the lights dissolve. In living spiritual practice, these deities and lights are the subject of many meditations and creations of mind. This phase is movement through the mental plane. Next is "union dissolving into wisdom," the spiritual plane. Light manifests into the five spiritual wisdoms that are the potential for Enlightenment, and the opportunity for Liberation is the greatest at this phase.

The final phase of the luminous bardo of dharmata is called "wisdom dissolving into spontaneous presence." Reality is fully unveiled here: purity, the deities, the pure Buddha/Goddess realms, the six realms of existence. The soul has clairvoyance and knowledge of her Akashic Records, of her past and future lifetimes, until the visions suddenly end. I perceive this ending to be the transition from spiritual plane into the Body of Light, the energy grid of Pure Mind. The incarnation/lifetime has ended, and the soul has reattained her essence self.

If she has achieved Enlightenment, the realization of Goddess oneness, at any point between her dying and this moment, she will not be required to return. She may, however, as a bodhisattva choose to do so in service to all life. Many souls are now on Earth in this role. If she has not attained Liberation, she enters the bardo of becoming after three days of unconsciousness and begins to prepare for a new lifetime.

In the bardo of becoming, the last bardo which ends at a new birth, the soul's karma reawakens and she prepares for incarnation. The soul descends from the Body of Light back to the mental body plane (freedom from which is freedom from illusion, karma, and reincarnation), and into the astral plane. The processes of dissolution reverse: the four elements return, and the red and white essences of a new egg and sperm union create conception and a new physical body. Descriptions of this bardo experience are much like the discarnate entity state. Thought, clairvoyance, and the psychic senses return, and the soul may not know she has died. She may try to return to her previous lifetime's family or home. She goes through a life review of her latest past lifetime, and karmic patterns from that life reassert themselves:

> If our habitual conduct in life was positive, our perception and experience in the bardo will be mixed with bliss and happiness; if our lives were harmful or hurtful to others, our experiences in the bardo will be ones of pain, grief and fear. . . .
>
> The life-review seems to suggest that, after death, we can experience all the suffering for which we were both directly and indirectly responsible.6

Even in this bardo, Enlightenment can be attained by positive thought. This bardo of becoming stage lasts up to forty-nine days, where the luminous bardo of dharmata may last only moments or as long as twenty minutes. At the end of its time, the soul is drawn in to a new body in keeping with its level of spiritual attainment and its karma. The bardo ends with the soul's choice of parents, new conception, and entrance into the womb. The Wheel turns to a new cycle, a new birth.

This ancient Tibetan teaching of the four bardos is reflected in the phenomenon of the near death experience and also in expanded form in hypnotic regressions into the between life state. What becomes amazingly certain is that life and conscious awareness do not end at death, that death is only a transition to another form of consciousness. If the passage to a new lifetime takes forty-nine days for Tibetan Buddhists, it seems much longer between lifetimes, as shown by hypnotic regressions in the West. This is perhaps because the practitioners trained in spirituality revealed in the *Bardo Thodol (Tibetan Book of the Dead)* have evolved beyond requiring the between life phase of rest and learning. Incarnations in the West seem to be happening closer together now than in the past, possibly because the increased population of Earth requires souls for many bodies. The high demand is new to Earth in the last thousand years.

The near death experience is a Western way of learning about death and understanding the death process. In it, people who have gone part way through death and then returned, report an individual but similar experience that is verified again and again by numerous repetitions. The process is as follows. The woman is dying and may hear herself pronounced dead. She hears an unpleasant buzzing or ringing sound and finds herself above and outside of her body, watching it below as attempts are made to resuscitate it. She may be in emotional distress, but has little caring for the body that seems no longer to be herself. There is no loss of consciousness or awareness.

Next she finds herself drawn into a long black tunnel. When she emerges from it into light, she finds she has another sort of body that is mobile, fluid, and healed, an ideal figure of herself in her prime of life. The place she enters is one of beauty, a meadow or a park, green and blooming. Loved ones who have died before her meet her at the end of the tunnel, and her spirit guide comes, a Be-ing of loving light. It is a celebration and reunion.

The spirit guide questions her, and she experiences a review of her current lifetime, an evaluation of her failings and achievements without censure or judgment. She approaches a barrier or border, perhaps a bridge over a stream, or a doorway. Here, she is told either that at this point she must choose life or death, or she is told that she must return to her life. In the near death experience, though she may want to stay in this peaceful place and she resists returning, she finds herself back in her body and her life resumes. Afterwards, she remembers the experience clearly, and it will have profound effects on the woman's life. She no longer has any fear of death from that time on.[7]

Past life regressions into the death process take the descriptions further, when the subject is admitted through the barrier and there is no return to life possible. After conferring with her spirit guides, she is taken to a place of healing and reorientation and then returns to her spirit family, which is comprised of other essence selves. There she begins a course of study and growth based upon the events of her recent and older past lives and her Akashic soul record. She studies with other members of her soul family, whom she has incarnated with again and again, and who are at an equivalent awareness level. The goal here is soul evolution.

The teachers in this after death state are our spirit guides, who are more evolved essence selves. When the soul's learning is completed for that phase of her development, she will begin the process of reincarnation. There is a deliberate and careful series of choices and decisions made with the help of spirit guides and the Lords of Karma. The soul then reenters the physical and begins a new lifetime.

I have had a recurrent dream for as long as I can remember, going back at least to high school or before. In one of its two versions, I am going home but don't know how to get there. I enter an elevator in a busy, tall building, and when it stops I look for a second car to take me higher. When the second elevator goes no further, I know there is a third but cannot find it. Sometimes I walk down a long hall, but don't know my room number, which room or home is mine. In the other version of this dream, I am going to college, but can't find my class. I've lost my notebook with the schedule, or have an old and filled up notebook with last year's classwork in it. I don't know where to go, but know I want to go there and *need* to go there. I have always thought of death as going home or going back to school. Likewise, college in this lifetime was a shelter and a refuge that I didn't want to leave.

Another description of the life and death process, this one by metaphysical teacher Earlyne Chaney, focuses on the silver cord and the vagus nerve. Life in the physical body is directed and regulated by an extension of the silver cord that connects the aura bodies (etheric double, emotional, mental, spiritual, and the planes beyond). This cord enters the etheric body at the crown and becomes the Sushumna, the central Kundalini channel, beginning at the throat. It then descends to the heart where the seed atom of life is located, and where the oversoul is connected to the body through the silver cord.

The dense physical body of this life cord is the vagus nerve, which begins in the brain stem's medulla oblongata (causal body chakra). The vagus nerve divides into two branches, one of which directs the heart rate and the other respiration/ breathing. The nerve then branches further into the abdomen and solar plexus. This vagus nerve extension of the silver cord is the source of the autonomic (nonconscious) nervous system.

The vagus nerve is the bridge between heart and physical brain, and the emotional and mental bodies on the physical plane. Soon after fetal conception, the heartbeat begins, and at death the heart and respiration stop, both by action of this nerve. The physical seed atom is the connection and access of the oversoul to the incarnation, the bridge between body and soul. There are physical, astral, and mental body seed atoms. In the process of death:

> The heart ceases to beat when the physical seed atom departs its home in the pulse-point but life does not entirely cease until it has travelled up the vagus, entered the Sushumna at the throat, ascended through the medulla oblongata and outward through the top of the head. With the

> departure of this physical seed atom, the sutratma or "silver cord" is loosed, and the life principle is completely withdrawn from the physical form. It is indeed "dead."[8]

In Chaney's analysis of what comes next, the seed atoms contain the individual's karmic (Akashic) record. After death, the soul resides on the astral plane for a time, then moves into and through the mental plane, and finally to the Body of Light (which she calls the causal/spiritual plane). In the Body of Light, the karmic seed atoms become inactive and are held in the heart chakra of the Light Body. This causal plane or Light body is the place the soul comes home to, the heaven world. The soul/essence self may remain in this place of bliss until she has finished her time there. Then she must return to Earth for a new lifetime.[9]

The return is initiated by one's life guide or guardian angel in agreement with the core soul/ essence self. The guide or angel has full knowledge of the soul's Akashic Record, its past and future lifetimes, and works in accordance with the Lords of Karma. It is the soul's karmic record that determines its life purpose and conditions for the coming incarnation. Choices are given, a review and analysis of past lives' successes and failures, and a preview of the lifetime to come and its outlined goals. Details of the life are not predetermined, only the learnings the soul agrees to for the incarnation. These learnings and purposes will be imprinted on the Hara Line, but how they are accomplished is left to the essence self, who is free to do the work or refuse it once in body. If she chooses to follow these goals, she will be guided and helped in every way, and to do so heals the karma attached to them.

Once these decisions are made and imprinted, the soul is put into a state of forgetful sleep, from which it is then moved into the newly forming fetus. The soul's guardian angel and oversoul create a new mental body (ketheric level) which becomes the new incarnation's personality. This is described as a sheath around the core soul (essence self/Body of Light) containing the mental seed atom. A new astral body (celestial level) is formed in the same way, becoming a sheath around the core soul and mental bodies, and containing the astral/emotional seed atom.[10]

The ketheric and celestial bodies form the mental and astral planes, the aura bodies, and the etheric template creates the physical aura body. All of these transmit energy and form in decreasing steps into the etheric double, Kundalini and Hara Lines, the chakras, and finally create the dense physical Be-ing. These become the personality/mind, emotions, and body of the new incarnation, descending from its spiritual core soul level in accordance with its agreed to karma and purpose.

Even with this very simplified overview and background, it is obvious that we are highly complex, evolved Be-ings, and that death is only another facet of the whole. Yet Western culture regards death as a final ending, and approaches it with horror, fear, and denial. People dying today may be kept alive with drugs and surgery that only prolong pain, making a harder, more painful end. It may involve "life support" that forces a body to continue functioning after the soul has already left it, or even prevents the soul from freeing itself from a nonfunctioning body.

The medical system considers death its enemy, a medical failure. If the patient is alive, in whatever pain or lack of function, medicine considers the effort a success, though the patient's real choices and needs have been disregarded on every level. Families are bullied into going along with the medical excess. The hospice movement has helped a great deal with these extremes, but there is still a long way to go. The treatment of death is shamefully inhumane in our culture.

Two cases come to mind that are typical examples. In one, Pam had been ill for a long time before she went to the doctor. I believe she knew that she was dying. When she finally went in extreme intestinal pain, she was diagnosed as having an advanced tumor and rushed into surgery. The tumor was removed with part of her intestine, and she was given an ostomy, an artificial bowel opening in her abdomen or side. Within four more days, she was given two more emergency surgeries for peritonitis, infection in the abdominal cavity. She was in a coma and dying. Had she been aware, she would not have permitted these operations, but her family authorized them. They finally placed her on a life support system. At that time, friends called and asked me to do healing. When I looked at Pam physically, I saw the pale yellow outer aura with darkened chakras that means impending death to me. I was able to talk with her psychically. "Help me go," she pleaded. I sent healing energy, telling her to use it as she chose. When I looked at her again psychically a few hours later, her spirit had left her body and was hovering above it, a misty form. "Thanks," she said. Her friends phoned the next morning to say she had died.

In another case, a woman told me about her sister, who though quite young, had gone into a coma twenty years before after a severe heart attack. She was still on life support. The woman wanted to help her sister pass over, because the situation had seemed very wrong to her for these twenty years, but she didn't know what to do. I focused on her sister and saw in her a white apron mixing something in a bowl on a kitchen table. The woman said that her sister loved to bake bread, verifying the image. I asked her sister if she knew where she was. She did, saying she was "between." I then asked if she wanted to move ahead and pass over. "I have to stay while my husband still needs me," she answered.

I asked my friend about my sister's husband. He was holding onto her very tightly, insisting on the life support. The sister couldn't pass over because his need held her on the astral plane. She was no longer alive there but because of his intense desire she could not complete her death process. She needed him to let go. I asked my friend to talk to him and explain what was happening. He understood. Finally, I advised my friend to have him go to his wife in the nursing home and talk to her, knowing she could hear. He had to be the one to tell her that though he loved her, he knew she had to leave. He had to tell her she was free, that she could die when she chose to do so.

The husband finally did this, though it took him some time and inner growth. The woman's sister was pronounced dead a few days later, and my friend said she saw her when she meditated that night, still in her baking apron, smiling and happy. She waved and said, "I'm gone now. Thanks."

Healers will be faced with more and more of these situations. People who are dying are being held here by needs of others and may actually require permission to pass over, though they are terminal and in pain. Those losing a loved one may need as much help as the person who is dying to be able to give this permission. Most Western religions deny reincarnation or life after death, and the medical system denies death itself. People dying or losing a loved one are caught between the two barriers, often in a paralysis of fear. By the time a person is at the point of dying, most have accepted it and no longer fight it, but their family may still hold them back. Remaining technically alive when the body no longer functions and moreover in great pain is not living. Ask the family to tell them they can go and, thereby, mercifully and lovingly set them free.

Pat has worked with hospice for the last four years, and has been helping people to pass over for much longer than that. She wrote the following for this book:

> The first time that I realized a patient
> could hear you, though they were in a
> coma and ready to make their transition,
> was when my brother-in-law was at the
> end stage of his life. I had been called by
> the hospital to come and help my in-laws
> during the death process. . . . I sat down
> and started talking to him, telling him
> that he could go, and everyone was okay.
> His sons were fine, and his wife was
> going back to England. He no longer had
> to be in pain, and there were many angels
> and helpers ready to be there with him.
> He took his last breath and I kissed him
> goodbye. It was so peaceful; I felt like
> he was at peace with everyone. This
> happened in 1969.

For three years, until he died in April 1990, I did Reiki sessions several times a week for a gay man with AIDS. Rudy became a friend I cared about, and his attitude toward illness and dying was a model and inspiration to all who knew him. He was gentle and considerate, and despite his increasing pain and weakness, always put others first. I doubt I ever heard him complain. When he was dying, his lover listed me as his sister, so I could continue the healing sessions in respiratory intensive care as Rudy had requested. He was moved to a hospital room for the end. I was told he could go at any time, but he was still holding on. Rudy had spoken of his dying to me many times; he had wanted to go for a long time and was not afraid.

On the last evening, he was still conscious, but could no longer move or eat and had great difficulty breathing. He said he wanted to go, but was worried about his mother and lover. Another one of his friends was at his side. We told him that his mother and lover knew he was in pain and ready to leave. They loved him too much to hold him back. I told him that watching him suffer was harder for them than his death would be. "Do you think they'll be all right?" Rudy kept asking. I assured him they would. His lover came in. When we told him what was happening, he said, "Rudy, I'll love you and miss you all the days of my life, but go if you want to." He went into a coma that night and died peacefully a few hours later.

The night of his funeral, Rudy came to me while I was meditating. He looked stronger and healthier than I'd ever seen him. "Some funeral, huh?" he said. "You were right. It's nice here. Take care of my lover, will you?" Then he was gone. I've seen him once more when he came in during a psychic reading with the message, "Tell Diane thanks. What she did really helped."

For those of us who love animals, a pet's dying is as hard as losing a person, with the added complication that euthanasia may be involved. There always is confusion and guilt with this—when is the right time, and is it right to do it at all? When Dusty, my Siberian husky dog, was dying of lung cancer, it became clear that she was frightened and in too much pain. I don't believe in unnecessary suffering for pets or people and finally asked her psychically if she wanted to go. She immediately and clearly said, "Yes." I asked her again the next night and got the same answer. I asked her if she wanted to be taken to the vet the next day. She said "yes" again.

As hard as it was, I took her, though I couldn't bear to be there for the death. Debilitated though she was, Dusty dragged me strongly into the vet's office, as strongly as she'd always fought going there before. That night meditating, I saw her running through a meadow of green grass and multi-colored flowers. She was young again, too busy running and playing to pay much attention to me. "I'll be back," she said and then she ran off. I hoped to see her again after that but never did.

Two years to the week later, Pat found in a California animal shelter a red Siberian husky puppy that she said she knew was mine. When the dog came out of her airline box in Florida, I knew immediately and certainly that it was Dusty. When I made psychic contact with the pup and asked her, she said, "Yes, I'm Dusty. I was supposed to find you." She also recognized Copper, whom she calls "Oh, Him." She was convinced that this past life was mine and not hers, and is still confused about this. She seems to have some of Dusty's memories without realizing they are from another lifetime. I named her Kali this time, Pat's name for her, as Kali said she liked it better than Dusty. She also still answers to Dusty, when I occasionally forget and call her that way.

Sometimes a person needs help in the after death process. When death happens normally, the person's guides take charge and the soul is freed from the body to be taken where it needs to go. The normal process generally happens whether the woman dying is old or young, in a hospital or at home, and whether or not she is drugged or on life support. Sometimes the process of passing over is interrupted, however. This usually occurs in a sudden or violent death, where the person is alive and well one minute and dead the next. Car accidents and heart attacks are possible examples, as are the sudden mass deaths of natural and unnatural Earth change disasters.

In some of these cases, the soul may need help to realize she has died. She needs to find her spirit guides and leave the Earthplane. She may be consciously present at her own funeral, wondering why no one sees her or talks to her. Her spirit guides usually find her and help her move on, but the woman who believes she is still alive may refuse them. Whenever I hear of someone having died, I checked psychically to see if they need assistance. You don't have to know the person to help them.

——————— : : ———————

Do this in meditation the same way as you help other discarnate entities to pass over. In the meditative state, ask to see the person who has died, and ask if she is in need. If all is well, you will know, and the woman may tell you so. You may see her spirit guides or loved ones with her, bright colors, or feel a sense of release and peace. If she needs help you will also know, by an emotional feeling of fear or confusion, by seeing the woman alone and lost, or by her insisting that she hasn't died, "Why's everybody acting that way?"

Begin by telling the woman's spirit that she has died. Tell her when and how, if you know. You might psychically show her a picture of the scene. Tell her she needs to go to the spiritual plane for rest and healing now, that she's okay and will be safe and welcomed there. Whether she believes you or not, call in her spirit guides and bring them to the woman's notice. Ask her guides to help her, to take her where she needs to be. That's all you need to do. Be gentle and loving, but do not accept excuses; it's time for her to go. Some people passing over may need to see their version of divinity to believe they have died. For Christians, I call in Mary; she is especially good to call upon when helping children to pass over. Some may need to see a loved one who has gone before them, and that person will come if you ask.

——————— : : ———————

Robert Monroe, in his well-documented journeys out of the body, began discovering souls trapped on the astral plane. He learned to help them complete their deaths. His book *Ultimate Journey* (Doubleday, 1994) is both strange and profound. In it, he describes helping a number of people, including the elderly woman described below:

——————— :: ———————

"But...I'm alive! I'm just the same!"

I told her that being physically dead doesn't change you much at first. You just don't have the pain anymore.... Look around, I said; see for yourself.

She did look around, very slowly. Then she turned back to me.

"It's all black...just deep black."

Except for me, I reminded her. She opened her eyes wider, her body slowly began to straighten out.

"Ernie...? Is that you, Ernie?... Why didn't you come before? I've been calling for you night and day to come and get me."

I said that she had to die first.... We started to move up and out slowly. I asked her about the pain. She looked puzzled.

"The pain? Oh, the pain. It isn't important now, is it?"[11]

——————— :: ———————

Buddhists do the meditative practice of phowa (po-wa) to help the dead leave their bodies and the Earthplane. The word means transfer of consciousness. In it the dying person's soul is directed out her crown and into oneness with the Buddha essence or Mind. Advance Buddhist practitioners are trained to do phowa, and it is said that when the process is completed, the transfer happens and the person will die. When someone has died suddenly, phowa can also be used after the death to help them fully pass over. The following meditation is not the advanced practice, but is a form of it that may be used by or for the dying, as well as for those who are living, as a purification. The meditation is from Sogyal Rinpoche's beautiful *Tibetan Book of Living and Dying.*

——————— :: ———————

Enter the meditative state, with calm, clear mind and full body relaxation. Visualize in front of you an image of your choice of divinity, be it Kwan Yin, the Earth Mother, Mary, or whoever else you wish. She is the embodiment of truth, wis-dom, compassion, and love, and filled with golden light. Focus your mind, emotions and spirit upon Her and ask:

Through your blessing, grace, and guidance, through the power of the light that streams from you:

May all my negative karma, destructive emotions, obscurations, and blockages be purified and removed,

May I know myself forgiven for all the harm I may have thought or done,

May I accomplish this profound practice of phowa, and die a good and peaceful death,

And through the triumph of my death, may I be able to benefit all other beings, living or dead.[12]

Visualize streams of golden light and compassion flowing into you from the Goddess' heart, purifying your karma, healing you, and filling you with radiant light. Your healed body melts and dissolves into this golden loving light. You are now a Body of Light soaring upward to merge with the light of the Goddess Source. Be still in this state of oneness for as long as possible.

——————— :: ———————

This process can be done for oneself or another, and is a way to help someone dying pass over in ease and peace. It is a healing and self-healing meditation for those who are not dying as well. The meditation invokes healing where healing is possible and eases the death process where it is not. After death, it heals the soul who has passed over in every gentle and loving way. During the time someone is dying, do the meditation as often as possible. It heals the karma of the person passing over and the karma of the healer too.

Women who do Earth healing will have much need for the previous meditation or similar ones in times to come. It can be used to help when many people have died at one time, like in Somalia or Rwanda. I have used similar visualizations in these situations, as I am often called upon to pass over frightened people in large groups. During the time of the Somalia famines, a healer friend and I watched single file lines of Somali people moving into a rapidly filling silver spaceship. Those many thousands who died were not of Earth origin, but came here to die so their deaths would awaken the planet. With their sacrifice done, the spirits were free to go home. We helped those who couldn't find their spaceship to locate it.

In his research on out of body travel, Robert Monroe discovered a park or staging area where souls go at death to be met by their spirit guides and taken forward. His Park matches the descriptions that many people give in near death and regression experiences. It resembles the place where I saw Dusty soon after her death. Monroe's park had grass and trees, flowers, benches, birds, and winding paths.

Reaching it out of body, he made the leap of understanding, "The Basic" concept about death and life he had long sought. This discovery is no surprise, as it is the central concept Buddhism has taught for thousands of years: that the Park and all reality are created by mind. Monroe learned that by knowing about the Park as where to go at death, souls reach it and from it move safely and easily to the between life state. He considered this information the key to ultimate freedom (Enlightenment in Buddhist terms), and founded his Monroe Institute to teach others about it while they were still alive and when they were dying. His methods are scientific. It is a wonder to me that science is finally catching up to what ancient healers have always known.

Healers working with the death process and helping those who are dying or who have died become quickly aware of the awesomeness of it. They become fully aware that death is not the end, that consciousness goes on, and that there is far more to living than what happens in the body. I have felt no sense of fear or anything morbid in my experiences with death. I have found instead a wondrous peace, order, beauty, and hope. I have very little fear of my own dying since working with others passing over.

Pat says something similar:

One thing I must state is that I have learned more about myself and the dying process from my patients, and they have been the true heroines for me. My prayer is that I have the consciousness to be aware when my time comes.

Since I have been doing this for several years, I can usually tell on the first visit how long I will have with the patient before they die. If they stay longer, nine times out of ten it has to do with fear.

With awareness of the death process, the fear ends. At death, the soul goes home. I see it as finding the last elevator, the room number, and the classroom to go home to.

Most of those who die will be reborn, either because of unfinished Earthplane karmic learning or the bodhisattva choice of service to humanity. Just as we have had past lives, we also have future ones, though the details may seem harder to comprehend in accessing them. While I have not sought for future information in a concentrated way for myself, I have seen a future life. Others have also done so. Dr. Bruce Goldberg, in his book *Past Lives, Future Lives* (Ballantine, 1982) describes in detail what Earth will be like in the twenty-first through twenty-sixth centuries. The information was gained through dozens of future life progressions done in hypnosis. He commented in 1982 that the future lives field was uncharted ground, and that even psychics didn't write about future lifetimes. This is changing today.

In the twenty-first century, Goldberg's subjects reported a new era of world peace that will last for three hundred years and an end to hunger, greed, and prejudice. He describes "major geographical changes" and advanced scientific progress. The twenty-second century will bring universal use of solar power, and advancements in medicine, psychiatry, and psychology, with an average lifespan increased to ninety years. The twenty-third century on Earth shows more technological advancement, silent and efficient transportation systems, weather control, and universally available higher education. Average lifespans will increase to one hundred and ten years.

The twenty-fourth and twenty-fifth centuries show more problems, including nuclear wars, international crises fueled by politics, and further geographical Earth changes with major population reductions. With the twenty-sixth century come more medical advances and a focus on genetic engineering, sophisticated lasers, underwater cities, and interplanetary travel. There will be no dis-ease or sickness, a democratic government for the whole world, and an average lifespan of over one hundred and twenty five years of age.[13]

Goldberg discovered that in taking people into future lives, a situation brought forward as karma from the present could have many outcomes, a variety of at least five positive, negative, and neutral future scenes. In a process similar to my use of emotional release, the subject can be future programmed to select and choose the most favorable of the possible situations to manifest. These healings of the future can be brought backwards (as age and past life regressions are brought forward) to also heal the present.

———————— : : ————————

Begin by doing some meditation sessions that show your future lives. Ask to be taken to your next lifetime, doing it in the same way as the basic past life meditation of the karma chapter. Become familiar with who you will be in several future centuries. When asking information on a future life, try to get some idea of when and what the scene is. Make sure to invoke your spirit guides for these journeys and full protection. Future life scenes tend to be less coherent than those from the past, and the scenes skip around. You may not recognize the settings and details you are shown, and they may not be on Earth. You will only be shown scenes that do not disturb your required karmic learning beyond this life. Try a few of these to become familiar with the process, but do not yet try changing the lifetimes you see.

———————— : : ————————

Next, do a meditation asking to be taken to a future life that has relevance for a current problem, question, or difficulty. Watch the scene without changing it, then ask to see the other future life possibilities for that scene or problem. Get a sense of your choices. Some will be better than others, some or one may be especially negative or favorable, and some will be mixed. Used the process of emotional repro-

gramming (not karmic release) to choose the most positive possibility and heal the less positive ones. Bring the healing back to now. In a later session, ask to see your choices again for the situation, observing what has changed. We are only permitted to do this with a situation for which the karma has been healed by our choices now; we are not permitted releases for future karma. We will only be shown what we are allowed to change.

———————— : : ————————

My own next lifetime takes place on either a healed Earth or some other positive Earth-like planet. I live, work, and teach at a university of healers, and my soul mate is a teacher there with me. We are both female. We wear loosely draped, ankle-length robes of white and gold-flecked soft material. The robe is held at one shoulder by an insignia or piece of jewelry. It is a woman-dominated culture where healers and healing are highly respected. Our work is supported. The place consists of a white single-story, low square building, almost Grecian looking, very simple, with rooms surrounding a central courtyard of fountains, padded benches, and blooming trees. I'll be ready to go there when an opening becomes available, and the world comes into Be-ing. I'm ready to go there now.

One further comment must be made about the children incarnating on Earth in the present time. While we adults will probably not see the healed planet or three hundred years of peace, these children will both see it and bring it into being. Many of them are ancient souls, and some are helper alien souls, come to bring Earth through the changes. They have the wisdom and abilities we adults cannot yet imagine. These children are here as our teachers; respect and honor them. A woman told me, "I know this is crazy, but I see my two-year-old granddaughter as someone who will save the planet." It is not crazy, it is truth. They know who they are, and what they have come here to do. Help them, but don't hold them back.

This book has been a small beginning of the many methods now available for healing women and the Earth, and healing the past, present, and future.

It is only a beginning, as those who use the methods will use them in their own ways and take them far beyond this writing. I give every blessing for this process, as long as it is used with compassion, love, oneness, and for the good of all Be-ings and the planet. The Goddess is within us, and she watches what we do.

Notes

1 Michael Newton, Ph.D., *Journey of Souls*, pp. 170–171.

2 Sogyal Rinpoche, *The Tibetan Book of Living and Dying*, p. 12. My information on the bardos is primarily from this source.

3 *Ibid.*, pp. 247–253.

4 *Ibid.*, p. 261.

5 *Ibid.*, p. 276.

6 *Ibid.*, p. 291.

7 Raymond Moody, Jr., MD, *Life After Life* (New York, NY, Bantam Books, 1975), pp. 21–23. Similar descriptions come from many sources.

8 Earlyne C. Chaney and Robert G. Chaney, *Astara's Book of Life: The Holy Breath in Man*, Second Degree, Lesson 4 (Upland, CA, Astara, 1966), p. 8.

9 Earlyne C. Chaney and Robert G. Chaney, *Astara's Book of Life: The Science of Rebirth*, First Degree, Lesson 21 (Upland, CA, Astara, 1966), pp. 11–13.

10 *Ibid.*, pp. 13–21.

11 Robert A. Monroe, *Ultimate Journey* (New York, NY, Doubleday, 1994), p. 130.

12 Sogyal Rinpoche, *The Tibetan Book of Living and Dying*, p. 215.

13 Dr. Bruce Goldberg, *Past Lives, Future Lives* (New York, NY, Ballantine Books, 1982), pp. 135–136.

Allow the light to be.
May we be free of a past of pain
    and confusion.
May we let our wombs, our hearts,
    be filled with their own natural light.
May we be whole unto ourselves.
May we be at peace.
May all beings be free from suffering.

Stephen Levine,
Healing Into Life and Death

BIBLIOGRAPHY

Barasch, Marc Ian. *The Healing Path: A Soul Approach to Illness.* New York, NY: Arkana Books, 1993.

Barnard, Graham. *The Challenge of Evil: Further Conversations with Richard.* Rochester, VT: Destiny Books, 1988.

Brennan, Barbara Ann. *Light Emerging: The Journey of Personal Healing.* New York, NY: Bantam Books, 1993.

Brennan, Barbara Ann. *Hands of Light: A Guide to Healing Through the Human Energy Field.* New York, NY: Bantam Books, 1987.

Burtt, E. A. *The Teachings of the Compassionate Buddha.* New York, NY: Mentor Books, 1955.

Chaney, Earlyne and William L. Messick. *Kundalini and the Third Eye.* Upland, CA: Astara, 1980.

Chaney, Earlyne C. and Robert G. Chaney. *Astara's Book of Life: The Holy Breath in Man.* Second Degree, Lesson 4. Upland, CA: Astara, 1966.

Chaney, Earlyne C. and Robert G. Chaney. *Astara's Book of Life: The Science of Rebirth.* First Degree, Lesson 21. Upland, CA: Astara, 1966.

Chang, Dr. Stephen T. *The Tao of Sexology: The Book of Infinite Wisdom.* San Francisco, CA: Tao Publishing, 1986.

Chia, Mantak and Chia Maneewan. *Awaken Healing Light of the Tao.* Huntington, NY: Healing Tao Books, 1993.

Chopra, Deepak, MD. *Quantum Healing: Exploring the Frontiers of Mind/Body Medicine.* New York, NY: Bantam Books, 1989.

"Danburite," In *The Heaven and Earth Network News,* Issue 10, Spring–Summer, 1994, pp. 8–9.

Daniel, Alma, Timothy Wyllie and Andrew Ramer. *Ask Your Angels.* New York, NY: Ballantine Books, 1992.

David-Neel, Alexandra. *Magic and Mystery in Tibet.* New York, NY: Dover Publications, 1932.

Easwaran, Eknath. *Meditation: A Simple Eight-Point Program for Translating Spiritual Ideals into Daily Life.* Tomales, CA: Nilgiri Press, 1991.

Fezler, William, Ph.D. *Imagery for Healing, Knowledge and Power.* New York, NY: Fireside Books, 1990.

Fiore, Dr. Edith. *The Unquiet Dead: A Psychologist Treats Spirit Possession.* New York, NY: Ballantine Books, 1987.

Garfield, Laeh Maggie. *How the Universe Works: Pathways to Enlightenment.* Berkeley, CA: Celestial Arts, 1991.

Garfield, Laeh Maggie and Jack Grant. *Companions in Spirit.* Berkeley, CA: Celestial Arts, 1984.

Gifford, Laura Ellen. "How Do I Know? Learning to Trust in Your Reiki Guides." In *Reiki News,* Winter, 1995, p. 9.

Goldberg, Dr. Bruce. *Past Lives, Future Lives.* New York, NY: Ballantine Books, 1982.

Hansen, V., R. Stewart, and S. Nicholson, Eds. *Karma: Rhythmic Return to Harmony.* Wheaton, IL: Quest Books, 1975, 1981, 1990.

Harding, Elizabeth U. *Kali: The Black Goddess of Dakshines War.* York Beach, ME: Nicholas-Hays, 1993.

Hay, Louise L. *You Can Heal Your Life.* Santa Monica, CA: Hay House, 1984.

Hay, Louise L. *Heal Your Body: The Mental Causes for Physical Illness and the Metaphysical Way to Overcome Them.* Santa Monica, CA: Hay House, 1982.

Huffines, LaUna. *Bridge of Light: Tools of Light for Spiritual Transformation.* New York, NY: Fireside Books, 1989.

Ingerman, Sandra. *Soul Retrieval: Mending the Fragmented Self.* San Francisco, CA: HarperSanFrancisco, 1991.

LeShan, Laurence, Ph.D. *How to Meditate: A Guide to Self-Discovery.* New York, NY: Bantam Books, 1974.

Levine, Stephen. *Healing Into Life and Death.* New York, NY: Anchor Books, 1987.

Marciniak, Barbara. *Earth: Pleiadian Keys to the Living Library.* Santa Fe, NM: Bear and Co., 1995.

Marciniak, Barbara and Tera Thomas, Ed. *Bringers of the Dawn: Teachings from the Pleiadians.* Santa Fe, NM: Bear and Co., 1992.

Meadows, Kenneth. *Shamanic Experience: A Practical Guide to Contemporary Shamanism.* Rockport, MA: Element Books, 1991.

Meek, George W., Ed. *Healers and the Healing Process.* Wheaton, IL: Quest Books, 1977.

Melody. *Love Is In the Earth: A Kaleidoscope of Crystals.* Richland, WA: Earth-Love Publishing House, 1991.

Monroe, Robert A. *Ultimate Journey.* New York, NY: Doubleday, 1994.

Moody, Raymond, Jr., MD. *Life After Life.* New York, NY: Bantam Books, 1975.

Mookerjee, Ajit. *Kundalini: The Arousal of the Inner Energy.* Rochester, VT: Destiny Books, 1982.

Morgan, Marlo. *Mutant Message Down Under.* Lees Summit, MO: MM Company, 1991.

Newton, Michael, Ph.D. *Journey of Souls: Case Studies of Life Between Lives.* St. Paul, MN: Llewellyn Publications, 1993.

Packer, Duane and Sanaya Roman. *Awakening Your Light Body.* Oakland, CA: LuminEssence Productions, 1989. Audiotape Series, Six Volumes.

Pelletier, Kenneth R. *Mind As Healer, Mind As Slayer.* New York, NY: Dell Publishing, 1977.

Raphaell, Katrina. *The Crystalline Transmission: A Synthesis of Light.* Santa Fe, NM: Aurora Press, 1990.

Rinpoche, Sogyal. *The Tibetan Book of Living and Dying.* San Francisco, CA: HarperSanFrancisco, 1993.

Schlemmer, Phyllis V. and Palden Jenkins. *The Only Planet of Choice: Essential Briefings from Deep Space.* Bath, England: Gateway Books, 1993.

Shealy, C. Norman, MD, Ph.D. and Carolyn M. Myss, MA. *The Creation of Health: The Emotional, Psychological and Spiritual Responses That Promote Health and Healing.* Walpole, NH: Stillpoint Publishing, 1988.

Simonton, Stephanie Matthews, O. Carl Simonton, MD and James L. Creighton. *Getting Well Again.* New York, NY: Bantam Books, 1978.

Starhawk. *The Spiral Dance: A Rebirth of the Ancient Religion of the Great Goddess.* San Francisco, CA: Harper and Row Publishers, 1979.

Steadman, Alice. *Who's the Matter With Me?* Washington, DC: ESPress, 1966.

Stein, Diane. *All Women Are Healers: A Comprehensive Guide to Natural Healing.* Berkeley, CA: The Crossing Press, 1990.

Stein, Diane. *Casting the Circle: A Women's Book of Ritiual.* Berkeley, CA: The Crossing Press, 1990.

Stein, Diane. *Essential Energy Balancing.* Berkeley, CA: The Crossing Press, 2000.

Stein, Diane. *Essential Energy Balancing II.* Berkeley, CA: The Crossing Press, 2003.

Stein, Diane. *Essential Reiki: A Complete Guide to an Ancient Healing Art.* Berkeley, CA: The Crossing Press, 1995.

Stein, Diane. *Natural Healing for Dogs and Cats.* Berkeley, CA: The Crossing Press, 1993.

Stein, Diane. *The Natural Remedy Book for Dogs and Cats.* Berkeley, CA: The Crossing Press, 1994.

Stein, Diane. *Prophetic Visions of the Future.* Berkeley, CA: The Crossing Press, 1991.

Stein, Diane. *Reliance on the Light.* Berkeley, CA: The Crossing Press, 2001.

Stein, Diane. *We Are the Angels.* Berkeley, CA: The Crossing Press, 1997.

Strehlow, Dr. Wighard and Gottfried Hertzka, MD. *Hildegard of Bingen's Medicine.* Santa Fe, NM: Bear and Co., 1988.

"Tibetan Tektite Update." In *The Heaven and Earth Network News,* Issue 10, Spring–Summer, 1994, pp. 9–10.

"Tibetan Tektites." In *The Heaven and Earth Network News,* Issue 9, Winter, 1993–1994, pp. 5–6.

Van Straten, Michael, ND, DO. *The Complete Natural Health Consultant.* New York, NY: Prentice-Hall Press, 1987.

Wallace, Amy and Bill Henkin. *The Psychic Healing Book.* Berkeley, CA: The Wingbow Press, 1978.

Weiss, Brian L., MD. *Through Time Into Healing.* New York, NY: Fireside Books, 1992.

Wright, Machaelle Small. *MAP: The Co-Creative White Brotherhood Medical Assistant Program.* Jeffersonton, VA: Perelandra Publications, 1990.

Yoginanda, Paramahansa. *Metaphysical Meditations.* Los Angeles, CA: Self-Realization Fellowship, 1964.

INDEX

Note: illustrations are indicated by *f*

A

abdomen, healing, 85, 85*f*, 87
abdomen position, for healing others,
91, 91*f*
absentee healing, 130
abstraction, 148
Achterberg, Jeanne, 33
acupuncture points, 51
affirmation, 18, 34, 100, 163, 165
after death. *See* bardo of dharmata
(third)
age regression, 31
aggressive imagery, 32, 34
AIDS, 30, 171
Akashic Records, 138, 141, 142, 174, 176
alcohol, 12, 30
alien implants, 166–167, 168–169
alien instruments of interference,
160–161
alpha waves, 15
amber, 103, 119
amethyst crystals, 111
anatomy, 27
The Anatomy Coloring Book, 27
anesthesia, 30, 164
Angel of Healing, 33
angelite, 117
angels, 37, 40, 70–71, 75–76
Angels and Companions in Spirit
(Garfield), 66
animal chakras, 40, 60
animal spirit guides, 71–72, 76
animals, 95, 129, 155
ankles, healing, 86*f*, 87, 91, 91*f*
anorexia, 30
aquamarine, 119
Ariel (spirit guide), 70

arthritis, 30
Asian Hara, 48
Ask Your Angels (Daniel, Wyllie,
Ramer), 75
astral body, 42*f*, 124*f*, 126, 176–177
See also emotional body
astral plane, 124*f*, 146
astral projection, 31, 126
astral twins, 147, 148, 149–150
athleticism and hypnosis, 30
The Aura Body Levels, 124*f*
aura level structures, 125
Aura (spirit guide), 69
auras, 14, 102, 166
auric cocoon, 147
aventurine, 117
Awaken Healing Energy Through the Tao
(Chia), 63
Awaken Healing Light of the Tao (Chia), 63
Awakening Your Light Body (Packer and
Roman), 39, 51, 61, 151
azurite, 117

B

babies and infants, healing, 95, 129
back healing, 87–88, 87*f*, 92–93, 92*f*
back problems, 100
bardo of becoming (fourth), 174
bardo of death (second), 172–173
bardo of dharmata (third), 172, 173–174
bardo of life (first), 172
Bast, 76
behavior modification. *See* biofeedback;
hypnosis; meditation
belly chakra, 44–45, 44*f*, 47*f*, 62*f*, 97,
124*f*
belly chakra gems, 116
beta waves, 15
Bharamus, 67

biofeedback, 29–30, 31
black energy cords, 165
black tourmaline, 116
black velvet tourmaline, 118
bladder infections, 116
Blofeld, John, 23
blood clots, 100
blood pressure, 30, 31
blue aventurine, 117
blue sapphire, 119
blue tourmaline, 119
bodhisattvas, 40, 133, 174
body chakras
kyanite and, 117
See also specific chakras
body levels, 122
Body of Light, 37, 146, 174, 176
body privacy, 88
body temperature, 30
boji stones, 118
Bosnia, 133
brain capacity, 15
brain wave patterns, 15, 30
breast cancer, 100, 171
breath, 17, 19
Brennan, Barbara Ann, 46, 48, 49, 123,
125, 126
Brete. *See* Goddess Brede
Bride. *See* Goddess Brede
Bridge of Light (Huffines), 29, 151
Brigit. See Goddess Brede
brow chakra, 44*f*, 46, 47*f*, 62*f*
See also third eye chakra
Buchenwald concentration camp, 98,
137, 149
Buddha-nature. See Wiccan "Goddess-
Within"
Buddhism
healing and, 79–80

and reincarnation, 135–136, 172
and spirit guides, 77
See also *specific bardos*

C

cancer, 30, 32–33
Casting the Circle: A Women's Book of Ritual (Stein), 19
Causal Body chakra, 49, 50*f*, 51, 62*f*, 176
causal/spiritual plane, 176
Cayce, Edgar, 99
celestial body, 124*f*, 125, 146
celestial quartz, 118
chakras
    above the Crown chakra, 47–48
    clearing, 43
    colors, 60–61
    housecleaning, 101
    locations of, 49
    new series of, 37
    psychic healing and, 128
    scars, 107
    shields, 58
    See also *specific chakras*
champagne topaz, 116
Chaney, Earlyne, 176
channeling, 67
"Charge of the Goddess," 19
chest healing, 83, 84*f*, 90*f*
Ch'i Kung, 48, 61
Chia, Mantak, 63
children, healing, 95
Cho-Ku-Rei, 18, 38, 112, 129
Chopra, Depak, 13, 26
Christianity, and reincarnation, 135
chromosome differences, 37
chronic pain/tiredness, 12, 30, 118
Circuit of Ki in the Body, 62*f*
Clow, Barbara Hand, 167, 169
colds, 100
color healing, 59–61
coma patients, 128
concentration, 12
Conception Vessel, 49, 51–52, 61, 62*f*, 63
confidentiality, 82
consciousness, states of, 14
contemplation method of meditation, 20–21
    See also meditation
cooperation in healing, 81–82
cords. See uncording
cosmic retribution, 54
cravings, 28, 94

creativity and hypnosis, 30
crown chakra, 21, 44*f*, 46–47, 47*f*, 62*f*, 124*f*, 125–126
crystal energy network, 110
Crystalline Transmission (Raphaell), 48
crystals, 109, 110, 111, 114
cystitis, 116

D

Dai-Ko-Myo, 40, 112, 129
Daily, Mary, 19
Dalai Lama, Tenzin Gyatso, 136
danburite, 120
Daniel, Alma, 75
David-Neel, Alexandra, 18
death
    decisionmaking, 12
    four stages of, 171, 172
    medical reaction to, 177
    preventing, 130
    staging area, 181
    sudden, 180
    See also phowa; reincarnation; *specific bardos*
detoxification process, 94
Diana of the Hounds, 76
diaphragm chakra, 50*f*, 51, 62*f*
dimensional movement, 159
dioptase, 116, 117
dis-ease, causes of, 12–13, 24
discarnate entities, 160
dissociation, 31
dissolution, 173
distance healing, 122, 129, 131
    See also visualization
double-stranded helix, 37, 43*f*
Dreaming the Past, Dreaming the Future (Prophetic Visions of the Future) (Stein), 36
driving, 126
drugs, 12, 30

E

earth
    composition of, 109–110
    healing of, 110, 131–133, 180–181
Earth: Pleiadian Keys to the Living Library (Marciniak), 36
Earth chakra, 48, 50*f*, 63, 118
earth crystals, awakening and clearing, 110–111
Earth Star. See Earth chakra

Earthly Ki, 48
eating habits, 12
Einstein, Albert, 13–14
electrical fields, 14, 123
electrocardiogram (EKG), 29–30
electroencephalogram (EEG) patterns, 15
emerald, 119
emotional/astral/Hara energy body, 37
emotional body, 39, 42*f*, 124*f*
emotional health, 25
emotional obstructions exercise, 100–101
emotional stress. See stress
emotions, 97
endorphins, 64
energy, 53, 57–58, 133
    See also thought fields
energy blockages, 28–29, 46, 59, 64, 117
    See also *specific chakras; specific stones*
energy bodies, 37
Energy Body, 147
energy clearing. See uncording
energy cycle in healing others, 95
energy grounding, 58–59
energy pathways, 61
    See also Conception Vessel; Governor Vessel (GV)
Enlightenment, 23, 80, 172, 174
entities, 160–162
epileptic seizures, 30
essence selves, 37, 38*f*, 138, 139*f*
Essential Energy Balancing II (Stein), 145
Essential Energy Balancing (Stein), 145
Essential Reiki (Stein), 83
Etheric Body, 41*f*, 124*f*
etheric double, 13, 37–39
The Etheric Double Chakras/The Kundalini Line, 42*f*, 44*f*
etheric template, 45, 124*f*, 146
ethics of healing, 55–56
evil, 158–159
evolution, on earth, 36–37
extraction, 148
eyes, Reiki I Self-Healing for, 84*f*

F

fairy Goddess Mother visualization, 105
fat, 12
fear, 25
feet healing, 87*f*, 91–92, 91*f*, 93, 93*f*

Fezler, William, 30
fight or flight syndrome, 13
Fiore, Edith, 163
flashbacks, 123
focus in distance healing, 131
forgiveness, 100, 101
    See also uncording
free will, 144
frequency overload, 111
full body healings, 96
full body relaxation exercises, 16–17
future, healing one's, 182

G

galactic access chakra, 47*f*, 48, 120
galactic healers. *See* alien implants
"garbage chakra," 51
Garfield, Laeh Maggie, 66
gemstone layout healing. *See* laying on
    of stones
gemstones
    clearing, 111–112
    color and form of, 114
    and Kundalini chakras/channels,
        115–116
    uses of, 109
    See also *specific gemstones*
genetic engineering, 36
genital area healing, 85*f*
ghosts. *See* entities
Gifford, Laura, 75–76
Goddess, 12–13, 41*f*, 42*f*, 80
Goddess Brede, 68–69, 72
Goddess Craft, 135
Goddess Kali, 33
Goddess Mind, 24
Goddess Oya, 33
Goddess Universal Law, 53, 54
Goddesses, 76
Goldberg, Bruce, 181
Governor Vessel (GV), 51, 61, 62*f*, 63
grace, defined, 40
Grandfather (spirit guide), 67, 72
Great Mother of the Universe, 41
green tourmaline, 119
gridwork, earth stewardship chakra, 47*f*
    See also universal grid
"grief point," 49
Ground Luminosity, 173, 174
grounding and centering, 16, 17
grounding chakras, 50*f*, 51, 62*f*
guided visualization, 30

guides, 68–69, 73, 77

H

"Hail Mary," 20
hands, alternative healing positions
    for, 94, 94*f*
Hands of Light (Brennan), 46
The Hara, 50*f*
Hara Body, 41*f*, 42*f*
Hara chakra, 49, 62*f*, 119
Hara Line, 39, 48, 98, 172–173, 173
    See also Kundalini Line
The Hara Line, 50*f*
Hara Line energy work, 61–65
Hara Line hooks. *See* uncording
Hara Line thymus, 117
Hara Line thymus chakra, 119
Hay, Louise, 56, 100
head healing, 84*f*, 89, 89*f*
headache, 130
Heal Your Body (Hay), 56
healers
    as a conduit for the Goddess, 80
    ethics and, 82
    helping healers, 57
    trusting of, 81–82
    working with, 141–142
    See also crystals
Healers of Karma. *See* karmic release
healing
    in absentia, 130
    charging for, 55–56
    cooperation in, 81–82
    cooperative nature of, 55
    elements of, 12
    environment for, 88
    and ethics, 53–54, 80
    exercises, 104
    modified, 95
    on planes of existence, 146
    programming, 130
    source of, 14–15
    spirit guides and, 66–67
    using Microcosmic Orbit, 65
    visualization and, 28
healing Goddess Void. *See* turiya
Healing Into Life and Death (Levine), 49,
    56, 101, 183
health, 12
heart attacks, 100
heart chakra, 44*f*, 47*f*, 62*f*, 124*f*, 126
Heart of the Cristos (Clow), 167
heat transfer, 30

Heaven and Earth gemstones, 120
Heaven and Earth Network News, 120
Hecate, 76
Helen (spirit guide), 66
Helena (spirit guide), 69–70
Herkimer diamonds, 120
Hidden Self, 147
High Self, 147
Hildegard of Bingen, 19, 99
Hindu rishis, 13–14
holograms, 169
homeopathic opium, 154
Hon-Sha-Ze-Sho-Nen, 39, 104, 105, 112,
    129, 130, 142
hooks, 102–103
    See also uncording
Huffines, LaUna, 29, 150, 151
human attachments, 163
human beings, source of, 36–37, 69
human body, composition of, 36
human DNA, 37–38
human psychics, 132
Human Self, 147
Hurricane Andrew, 133
hypnosis, 30–31, 106, 163

I

I statements, 34
Ida, 42*f*, 117
Ida channel, 40–41
illusion, 23, 24
imagery and images
    choice of, 32–33
    use of in Tantric training, 26
    See also hypnosis; visualization
Imagery for Healing, Knowledge and Power
    (Fezler), 30–31
imaginary playmates, 71
immortality. *See* bardo of dharmata
    (third)
immune system, 13, 30
incarnations, 137–138, 171
    See also reincarnation; *specific bardos*
incest, healing from, 105–106
induction, 30
Ingerman, Sandra, 151
inner child, 104–106, 117
insomnia, 12
irritability, 12
Islam, and reincarnation, 135

J

Joan of Arc, 33
Journey of Souls (Newton), 77, 171
Judaism, and reincarnation, 135
Jupiter (planet), 69
Jupiter spirits, 168. *See also* Aura (spirit guide)

K

karmic consequences, 133
karmic healing, 136–137, 141, 144
karmic release, 142–145
karmic reprogramming, 98–99
karmic seed atoms, 176
Kegel exercises, 63
ketheric aura body. *See* crown chakra
ketheric body, 124f, 146
knees healing, 87, 91, 91f
The Kundalini Channels and the Chakras, 43f
Kundalini energy, 17, 43
    See also Hara Line
Kundalini Line, 39, 40–43, 173
Kundalini Line Central and Auxiliary Channels, 42f
Kundalini root chakra, 118
kunzite, 114, 116–117
Kwan Yin, 33, 40, 76, 155
kyanite, and body chakras, 117

L

labradorite, 120
Large and Small Heavenly Cycle, 52
laying on of stones, 113–114, 115
    See also crystals; gemstones
legal issues, 56
legs, position for healing others, 93, 93f
lesbian culture, 24
letting go, 106–107
Levine, Stephen, 49, 56
ley lines, 110, 111
life force energy, 81
life support, 177–178
lifetimes, 38f, 140
    See also abstraction; extraction
light, 37, 129
Light Body, 39, 41f, 42f, 117, 176
Light Emerging (Brennan), 48
light webs, 152–154
linking crystals and psychic abilities, 111
Lipika, 142, 155

"little blue fairy healers," 69
living beings, composition of, 36
Lords of Karma, 155, 175
    See also karmic release
Love, Medicine and Miracles (Siegel), 32
Love Is In the Earth (Melody), 117
lower abdomen healing, 85f
lower back healing, 87f
lower mental body, 124f
Lucifer, 159
lupus, 30
Lyrans, 36–37

M

Mahayana Buddhism, 14
Maheira, 76
mandalas, use of in meditation, 17–18
mantra/mantram, using for meditation, 19–20
mantras, 34
MAP: The Co-Creative White Brotherhood Medical Assistance Program (Wright), 67–68, 72, 76
Marchiniak, Barbara, 36, 37, 38, 47, 120
Mary (blessed virgin saint), 68, 76
Meadows, Kenneth, 146
medicine, deficits of, 122
meditation, 13
    focus for, 17
    learning how to, 15, 16
    physical changes during, 83
    for self healing, 82–83
    techniques of, 17–22
    and trance, 15
Meditation of the Thousand Petaled Lotus, 21
meditative passages, selecting, 18–19
meditative space, 16
meditative state exercises
    astral twin, 150
    discarnate entities, 151, 162, 163, 179
    during healing, 89, 126–127
    future lives, 182
    life guides, 74
    light protection, 57-59
    Lords of Karma, 142-43
    past life, 138–140
    psychic attacks, 165
    subpersonalities, 152–153
    suddent death, 180
    See also distance healing
Medjugorje (Bosnia), 68

medulla oblongata, 176
Meher Baba , 76
menopausal hot flashes, 42
menstrual cramps, 130
mental body, 39–40, 42f, 176
mental energy body, 37
mental plane, 146, 174
mental seed atoms, 176–177
messages, guided, 129
metabolism, and meditation, 15
Microcosmic Orbit, 52, 61, 63–64
The Microcosmic Orbit Small Heavenly Cycle, 61f
middle back healing, 87f
migraines, 30, 31
mind and brain, 26
miracles, 40
moldavite, 118
Monroe, Robert, 179–181
Monroe Institute, 181
Mother Earth/Mother Nature, 76
movement chakras, 50f, 51, 62f
multiple sclerosis, 30
muscle tension, 30
Myss, Caroline, 17

N

natural citrine, 116
Natural Healing for Dogs and Cats (Stein), 40, 60
Natural Remedies for Dogs and Cats (Stein), 40, 60
nature devas, 76
Navajo people, healing and, 80
near death experience, 175
neck healing, 92, 92f
negative emotions and health, 99–100
negative energy, 158, 159, 160
negative hallucination, 31
negative patterns, 39
negative thoughts, 20, 24
neurolinguistic programming (NLP), 106
Newton, Michael, 77, 171
nirvana, 14
Nonvoid, defined, 14

O

obesity, 30
objects, 17–18
oil spills, 133
"Om Mani Padmi Hum" mantra, 20, 125

oneness, 14, 19
orange Pecos quartz, 116
Orion, 167–168
Orion/Pleiades war, 69, 160–161, 166
Orion star system, 36
overheating, 43
overidentification, 54
Oversouls, 37, 40, 41f, 42f, 72, 138, 139f, 147
Oya, 21

P

Packer, Duane, 39, 51, 61
pain, 25, 30, 163
Paracelsus, 99
Park. *See* death, staging area
passing over, 161
    See also phowa
past life regressions. *See* near death experience
Past Lives, Future Lives (Goldberg), 181–182
past lives recounted, 148–149
Path to Enlightenment, 18, 145
patriarchy, effects of, 79
Pele, 21
pendulum, 109, 111, 112
pentacle symbol, 172
Perelandra Soul Ray flower essences, 154
perfection, separation from, 23
perineum chakra, 50f, 51, 62f, 63, 64, 118–119
permission, asking for, 127, 128, 129
pets, death of, 178–179
phenacite, 120
phobias and fears, 25, 30
phowa, 179–181
Physical Body, 41f, 42f, 124f
physical/etheric double energy body, 37
physical health, 25
physical plane, 146
physics, 14, 136–137
piezoelectric effects, 109
Pingala, 40–41, 42f, 117
pink tourmaline crystals, 111, 119–120
Pleiadian Federation, 36
Pleiadians, 168
pollution, 171
possession indicators, 164
protecting oneself, 169–170
psychic attacks, 160, 164–165

psychic development games, 25
psychic healing, 123, 126–127
    See also distance healing; visualization; *individual chakras*
psychic senses, 27
"psychic vampires," 58
psychotherapy, 98–99
Pure Mind, 173, 174
Purifying Breath exercise, 19
pyramids, 111–112

Q

quartz crystal, 109

R

Raku, 40
Ramer, Andrew, 75
Raphaell, Katrina, 48, 49
reality, 14, 24
rebirth. *See* reincarnation
receivers of healing, 55, 81, 95
red phantom quartz, 116
red spinel, 118
Reiki distance healing techniques, 131
Reiki I Hand Positions—
        Self-Healing, 54
    abdomen, 85, 85f, 87
    ankles, 86f, 87, 91, 91f
    back, 87–88, 87f
    chest, 83, 84f, 85, 90f
    feet, 86f, 87
    Front-Head Positions, 84–87f
    genital area healing, 85f
    head, 83, 84f, 86f
    knees, 86f, 87
    lower abdomen, 85f
    lower back, 87f
    middle back, 87f
    neck, 86f
    stomach, 85f
    throat, 84f
Reiki II, 18
Reiki III, 56
Reiki symbols, 129
Reiki the Hut Yin position, 61
Reiki training, 80–81
reincarnation, 135, 145
    See also bardo of becoming (fourth)
Reincarnations, 139f
reintegration, 143
relaxation, 30
repetition, in meditation, 18–19

reprogramming. *See* inner child
Roman, Sanaya, 39, 51, 61
root chakra, 43, 44f, 47f, 62f, 124f
root lock, 63
rose quartz layout, 114
rubellite, 119–120
"running energy" meditation, 59–60
Russian nuclear power plants, 132
rutile amethyst, 117
Rwanda, 133, 180

S

sacred sites, 110
samadhi. *See* turiya
sciatica, 64
Sea of Ch'i, 49
sea salt, 101, 102, 107, 112, 141, 165
seed atoms, 176
Sei-He-Ki, 39, 104, 105, 112, 129
self-esteem, 25
self-healing, 13, 67–68
    See also Reiki I Hand Positions—
        Self-Healing
self-love, 100
self-protection techniques, 54
sensory dissolution. *See* bardo of death (second)
sensory pictures, 123
sexual abuse, 31, 98
sexual disinterest, 12
sexual response, 30, 31
Shakti, 41–42
Shamanic Experience (Meadows), 146–147
Shamanistic totem animals, 71
Shealy, Dr. Norm, 17
Shiva, 41
sickness, root causes of, 148
Siddhasana yoga posture, 63
Siegel, Bernie, 32
silver vision chakras, 120
Simonton, Carl, 32
Simonton, Stephanie, 32
Sirius star system, 36
Small and Large Heavenly Cycle, 61
Small Heavenly Cycle, 63
smoking, 30
smoky quartz crystals, 111
The Society of Illuminated Minds. *See* MAP: The Co-Creative White Brotherhood Medical Assistance
Sogyal, Rinpoche, 77, 180

solar plexus, 44f, 45, 47f, 102, 124f
solar plexus chakra, 62f
solar system access chakra, 47–48, 47f
Somalia, 180
soul, structure of, 37
soul damage, 148
soul integration, 152–153
soul loss, 147
soul retrieval, 146, 152–154, 154–156
    See also astral twins
Soul Retrieval: Mending the Fragmented Self
    (Ingerman), 151
Soul Seat, 48
Soul Star, 48
Soul Structure I, 38f
Soul Structure II, 41f
Soul Structure III, 42f
space junk, 160, 165–166
spiders, 167, 169
spirit attachments, 159–160, 162, 163
spirit guide healing teams, 67–68
spirit guides, 26, 38f, 66, 175
    effect on animals, 67, 69, 70–71, 76
    healing abilities of, 69
    meeting, 74–75
    pendulums and, 111
    working with, 73–74, 77
    See also Goddess; spirit guide
        healing teams; specific spirit
        guides; specific types of spirit
        guides
spiritual body, 42f, 124f
spiritual energy, channeling, 111
spiritual energy body, 37, 40
spiritual plane, 146, 174
spiritual rebalancing, 13
spiritual separation, 12–13
spirituality, place of, 125
St. Francis, 76
stage fright, 30
Steadman, Alice, 99–100
Steinhice, Laurel, 36
stomach aches, 100
stomach healing, 85f
stress, 12–13, 30, 31
strokes, 100
subpersonalities, 150–151
suffering, reason for, 159
sugar, consumption of, 12
sugilite, 117–118
surrogates, use of, 131
Sushumna channel, 40, 42f, 117, 176

T
Tachyon energy bead, 120–121
Tantric Buddhism, 17, 26
Tara, 40
technological mind, 122–123
tektite, 116
telepathy, 46
terminology, New Age metaphysics
    usage, 36
Theresa of Avila, 19, 72, 76
Theresa (spirit guide), 66–67
theta waves, 16
third eye chakra, 117, 124f
thought fields, 25–26
thoughts, effect on auras, 25
Thousand Petaled Lotus method, 29
throat chakra, 44f, 45–46, 47f, 62f, 123,
    124, 124f
throat healing, 83, 84f
Through Time Into Healing (Weiss), 138
thymus chakra, 13, 39, 48–49, 50f, 62f,
    119
The Tibetan Book of Living and Dying
    (Sogyal), 77, 180
The Tibetan Book of the Dead, 172, 175
time distortion, 31
Tinker Woman healing, 128
tiredness, 12
torso position, for healing others,
    90–91, 90f
transpersonal point, 48, 50f
(transpersonal point)/invisible realms
    chakra, 47f
trauma, 80–81, 100, 104, 147–148
Tree of Life, 47
    See also Wiccan Tree of Life
        meditation
tumors, 100, 162
turiya, 14, 17
Twelve Strand DNA—The Twelve
    Chakras of Barbara
    Marciniak, 47f

U
ulcers, 30, 100
Ultimate Journey (Monroe), 179–181
uncording, 101–102, 103–104
unfinished emotions, 99
"unified field theory," 14
universal grid, 110, 111
Universal Mind/Goddess, 39
universe chakra, 47f, 48

The Unquiet Dead (Fiore), 163
uterine tumors, 100

V
vagus nerve, 13, 176
vinegar rinse, 101, 102, 107, 141, 165
violet tourmaline, 117, 118
vision chakras, 50f, 51, 62f
visualization
    benefits of, 25
    cancer, 32–34
    as directing medium, 123
    exercises, 26–27, 28–29
    healing example of, 33–34
    during inner child therapy, 104
    meditation and, 17
    Trantic Buddhism and, 25
    See also distance healing; hypnosis
vitamins, 12
Void, defined, 14
"vomit chakra," 51

W
water, 12
We Are the Angels (Stein), 145
Weiss, Brian, 138
Wheel of Incarnation, 42
white blood cell levels, 30
Who's the Matter With Me (Steadman), 99
Wicca, and Buddhism, 80
Wiccan "Goddess-Within," 14, 123
Wiccan mantras, 20
Wiccan Tree of Life meditation, 17
Wind Position, 63
women, healing from abuse, 98–99
words, consequences of, 20
Wright, Machaelle Small, 67
Wyllie, Timothy, 75

Y
Yidam meditation, 18
You Can Heal Your Life or Heal Your Body
    (Hay), 56, 100

Z
Zimmerman, Robyn, 69

Printed in the United States
by Baker & Taylor Publisher Services